Higher and Faster

Higher and Faster

Memoir of a Pioneering Air Force Test Pilot

ROBERT M. WHITE
and JACK L. SUMMERS

Foreword by Neil A. Armstrong

McFarland & Company, Inc., Publishers
Jefferson, North Carolina, and London

Publisher's note: General White died on March 17, 2010, after completing the manuscript for this book.

All photographs come from the collection of Robert M. White unless otherwise noted

LIBRARY OF CONGRESS ONLINE CATALOG DATA

White, Robert M. (Robert Michael), 1924–2010.
    Higher and faster : memoir of a pioneering Air Force test
pilot / Robert M. White and Jack L. Summers ; foreword by
Neil A. Armstrong.
      p.   cm.
    Includes index.

    ISBN 978-0-7864-4989-7
    softcover : 50# alkaline paper ∞

    1. White, Robert M. (Robert Michael), 1924–2010.
    2. Test pilots—United States—Biography.
    3. United States. Air Force—Officers—Biography.
    I. Summers, Jack L., 1939–   II. Title.
    TL540.W445A3   2010
    358.40092—dc22   2010034529
    [B]

British Library cataloguing data are available

On the cover: Return from Mach 6 (1983, Michael J.
Machat); inset: detail of Robert White in the cockpit
of his 345th Fighter Squadron North American P-51D
Mustang (courtesy of the author)

Manufactured in the United States of America

McFarland & Company, Inc., Publishers
  Box 611, Jefferson, North Carolina 28640
   www.mcfarlandpub.com

Acknowledgments

R.M.W.: One cannot write a book that involves historic events and not have a number of people to thank. I wish to do that. Unfortunately the thanks come a little late for some, who have already joined the heavenly squadron in which one day all pilots reluctantly participate.

A special thanks to my old friend and fellow X-15 test pilot Neil Armstrong, who went on to greater glory by becoming the first man to set foot on the moon. Thanks, Neil, for reading the manuscript and for your kind words of encouragement in the foreword.

Al Hallonquist, noted aerospace historian and dear friend, deserves thanks. Thanks not only for your support of my nomination to the Florida and National Aerospace Halls of Fame, but for your support of this project and all you did to help it come to fruition.

Another friend, World War II triple ace and author C.E. "Bud" Anderson kindly reviewed the manuscript and wrote some helpful comments. Thanks, "Bud."

To Fitzhew Fulton, whose B-52 took the X-15 aloft, thank you for your words of encouragement after you read the manuscript.

I have four great kids, each unique in their own right. Greg, Pam, Maureen and Dennis: Thanks for your love over the years and the support you have given me for this project.

I would be remiss not to thank one whose knowledge and experience in writing a book and without whose persistence this project would never have gotten airborne. Whether it is a success or a failure, without Jack Summers, it would never have seen the light of day.

And, last but certainly not least, I thank the countless men and women of the United States Air Force, without whom the things I did would not have been possible.

MAJOR GENERAL ROBERT M. WHITE,
USAF RETIRED

J.L.S.: It has been my great pleasure to come to know my golfing buddy, Bob White; a great deal better after the hours we spent in his den while he told me about his historic life. Thanks, Bob, for allowing me to be your scribe. And, since I am a fiction writer, not a biographer, not a pilot, and a Navy man, rather than an Air Force one, I needed lots of help in getting this manuscript ready for press.

To Suzanne and Carl Metoff, for encouraging Chris White to nudge Bob into finally telling his story to someone. If you hadn't pushed, we'd still be waiting.

To Al Hallonquist, a great aerospace historian, who was a rock of support and a constant cheerleader for me from the beginning. Thanks, Al.

George Marrett, aviation writer and military pilot, thanks for your invaluable guidance and support.

No matter how many times you look at a page you have written, sometimes it is impossible to see your own mistakes. For that you need a good editor. I have three. Thanks first to my wife of forty-five years, Pat, without whom nothing is possible.

Next there is my friend Dawn Nassise who has edited my fiction work for me. A busy mom, divinity student, working flight attendant and wife of a successful fiction author Mike Nassise, she still found time to do the copyedit on this one, too. Thanks, Dawn.

And last, but certainly not least, Mike Machat, renowned aerospace artist, pilot and historian who did the technical edit and helped me to get the manuscript ready for press. And, who kindly gave us his famous painting of the X-15 for the book cover.

JACK L. SUMMERS

Table of Contents

Foreword

by Neil A. Armstrong

In October 1901, in Chicago, the Western Society of Engineers gathered to listen to a lecture on the nascent field of aeronautics. The speaker said, "The inability to balance and steer confronts the students of the flying problem. When this one feature has been worked out, the age of flying machines will have arrived, for all other difficulties are of minor importance."

The speaker was Wilbur Wright, explaining his, and his brother's, experiences in three years of designing, building and flying man-carrying gliders. Two years later, Wilbur and his brother, Orville, made the first successful flight of a heavier-than-air, powered aircraft. The brothers achieved that success because they recognized the problem of balance and steering, and they solved it. Balance and steering or, in contemporary language, stability and control, have continued to bedevil aircraft designers and flyers throughout the history of aviation.

Many readers of this book will know well the history of the research airplanes. The research aircraft is one that has no commercial, military, or other operational role. Its sole purpose is to investigate the problems and unknowns of flight.

It's an old idea. The 1903 Wright Flyer was just such a research aircraft. Over the years a number of other flying machines were built just to find out whether or not some idea would work, but those machines were generally built by independent entrepreneurs.

Active government interest in research aircraft arose immediately after World War II at the Army Air Force's Wright Field, the Navy Bureau of Aeronautics and the NACA, the National Advisory Committee for Aeronautics. That led to contracts to build a research airplane designed to break the sound barrier, the XS-1, and a number of other such craft to investigate swept wings, flying wings, delta wings, variable *sweep wings* and vertical takeoff and landing.

1

A proposed research airplane, the X-15, was envisaged to be the first manned hypersonic aircraft to fly at more than five times the speed of sound. In 1954, when bids were first solicited for its design and construction, the fastest any aircraft had flown was Mach 2.44. At that speed the aircraft, the Bell X-1A, diverged out of control and the pilot was very fortunate to recover from the resultant spin to save the aircraft. In flight testing, increases in maximum Mach number were typically accomplished in small increments and with substantial difficulty and danger.

So stability and controllability were a principle concern for very high speed flight. The other major concern was the increasingly high structural temperatures encountered. Aluminum was a satisfactory material only to a bit over twice the speed of sound. The Bell X-2, a swept wing design, was designed to be able to fly to Mach 3.5 and was constructed of K-Monet and stainless steel. It reached a speed of a bit over Mach 3 in 1956, but, unfortunately, it too diverged at that speed and the aircraft and the pilot were lost.

At that time, research results were rapidly being incorporated into prototype and production military aircraft. The century series of fighters were becoming operational. Several were capable of the Mach 2 region. With the loss of the X-2, there were no test vehicles available to probe the flight regimes substantially above the production aircraft. Fortunately, the proposed X-15 was becoming a reality. The project was approved in late 1954. It would be a joint Air Force, NACA, and Navy program. North American Aviation was selected to construct the aircraft.

The highest temperature metals which might be suitable for an aircraft structure were the nickel alloys, Inconel and Inconel-X. They were capable of withstanding working temperatures of 1200 degrees F. The X-15, therefore, would be constructed of such materials and would explore flight up to those temperatures, corresponding to a Mach number of approximately 7. Any aircraft with that much velocity would have enough kinetic energy, if converted to potential energy, to zoom to well over 100 miles in altitude. This opened up a completely new field of potential research, i.e., flying outside the atmosphere, atmospheric entry, and atmospheric science. Based on all high speed flight experience up to that time, Mach 7 was audacious by any standard— stability, control, aerodynamic heating, hypersonic flow fields, and flight outside the atmosphere. It seemed an enormous jump from all previous flight experience.

In *Higher and Faster,* Major General Robert White tells the fascinating story of this remarkable aircraft and of his vital role in its development. As a senior project pilot he flew critical performance envelope expansion flights, confirming the aircraft's flight worthiness and setting a number of speed and altitude records in the process. Equally importantly, he recalls the experiences leading up to his selection for, and involvement in, the X-15 project and his consequent achievements as he rose through a succession of ever increasing responsibilities in the United States Air Force.

Those who enjoy aviation history and military history will find *Higher and Faster* to be a rare insight into the challenges of flying on the edge. Bob White writes candidly and accurately of a fascinating period in the world of flight. I think you will enjoy it as I have.

Neil A. Armstrong is a former astronaut and test pilot. He was the first person to walk on the moon.

Preface

by Jack L. Summers

One day while sitting on the porch of our clubhouse, one of my golfing partners, Carl Metoff, asked me how my book was coming. I had just finished a biography of a friend of mine who had been an anorexic for forty-two years and now had her life in order.

When I answered his question, Carl then asked, "Why don't you do Bob's life story?" I knew Bob White. He was a long-standing member of the golf group I had just joined, and I'd played with him several times. But I had no idea what he had done in his other life ... before retirement.

"Why should I?" I asked naively.

Over the course of the next year, I not only found out why, but marveled that it had not been written already. Major General Robert M. White had been asked before, by professional writers, to do his biography, but he had politely declined. The reason was simple. This great American hero is an unassuming man who feels that his historic achievements are nothing more than a man doing his job.

But when I asked him if I could do it, I had an edge. Carl's wife Suzanne, and Bob's wife Chris doubled up on him. He soon asked to read the biography I had just written, and in a few days agreed to let me help tell his life story.

Since Bob's story begins in the days of the Great Depression, and covers three conflicts and the development of flight to the exploration of space, the decision was made to simply march through Bob's life and tell the story as it unfolded. And since I had no experience with aviation or its history, I had a lot of work to do.

Before we began a series of personal interviews, I read everything I could find about Bob on the internet, and in a number of books about the X-15. Al Hallonquist, a friend of Bob's, contacted me early in the project and was of enormous help in pointing me in the right direction.

About this time, Bob was inducted into the National Aerospace Hall of Fame. My wife Pat and I, along with a number of his friends from Sun City Center, Florida, accompanied Bob to the ceremony. There, I had an opportunity to listen and talk to a number of legends in the aerospace program about Bob and his accomplishments.

When I realized all that Bob had done, the enormity of my task became apparent. He flew 52 combat missions in World War II and was shot down on the 53rd mission. Captured by the Germans, he escaped, was recaptured then liberated at war's end.

As pilot of the X-15 he set a speed record at Mach 3.5, then went on to become the first man to fly four, five and six times the speed of sound. He also was the first person to fly over 100,000, 200,000 and 300,000 feet. He still holds the altitude record for a fixed-wing aircraft at 60 miles, straight up. For that one, he became the fifth man and the first fixed-wing pilot to earn a set of astronaut wings.

When Vietnam came along, Bob volunteered to go and flew 72 combat missions over North Vietnam. For destroying a bridge in North Vietnam that had been a target since the conflict's inception, he was awarded the Air Force Cross, the nation's second highest award for valor in combat. If that wasn't enough, Bob led the team that developed the F-15 fighter plane that became the standard of fighters worldwide for the next two decades.

Over the next year, I sat with Bob in his den and listened as he took me on a fascinating journey through the history of flight from World War II to the Cold War. The hardest part of the project was getting enough details from Bob to make the story come alive. Bob just didn't think the things he did were so extraordinary. He was simply a pilot, doing his job. When there was a problem, you didn't panic, you just worked it out.

Thanks to Mike Machat, recommended to me by Al Hallonquist, I was able to sort out the technical data and keep it all straight. The end result is the life story of a quiet, soft-spoken American hero who by simply "doing his job" pushed the envelope of flight from the propeller toward the moon.

But Mike may have said it better when he wrote, "What is unique about this book is that it's more the story of a young boy from the scrappy streets of Manhattan during the Great Depression who saw promise in the sky, and whose fortitude, persistence, and ability to excel under pressure led him to a career that propelled him into the history books. Bob White's aeronautical achievements have inspired generations of future pilots and will never be equaled. This book, therefore, is more than just another story of a test pilot during the "golden age" of America's aviation supremacy. It is a success story that celebrates the realization of the American dream. Moreover, it is the compelling story of a great person, a great pilot, and a great American."

Prologue

The date was February 23, 1945. It was a beautiful day and adrenaline fueled my good mood as we flew southward towards Germany in a sky so bright and clear that I could see all the way to the Alps in the south. The stunning view only added to my exhilaration, for today marked my fifty-third combat mission in the North American P-51 Mustang. I'd served my penance over the last six months in the 354th Fighter Squadron as wing man, element leader, and flight leader where I was part of a tight-knit four-plane fighting force. Today, for the first time at the ripe old age of twenty, which was not an unusual age for a World War II fighter pilot, I was the squadron leader taking four flights of four aircraft each into battle.

With a great sense of pride, I looked around at those sixteen deadly fighting machines spread across the sky giving each of them better visibility to search for their quarry on the ground. I was pleased to be their leader, which had been my goal from the beginning. Today's task was not our usual day's work of escorting bombers on their way to targets deep inside Germany. Today, we had no responsibility for any bombers. We were a lethal band of predators out on our own hunting for targets of opportunity.

Then I saw it! The enemy airfield lay ahead below and to my right, just loaded with prime ground targets. There were German fighters all over the place, and every one of those babies we could take out would be one less threat that would be going after our bombers or strafing our troops on the ground. I signaled the rest of my squadron that we would attack multiple times. I had attacked airfields before and it was dangerous business. Flying below four thousand feet exposed me and my squadron to lethal gunfire from the ground, but the more cumbersome bombers had no choice but to fly directly over those guns and the resultant losses were staggering. My boys in their P-51s were all courageous, but I think the men in those bombers were exceptionally brave.

Passing to the north of the German airfield, I glanced first at my watch and then at my airspeed indicator and noted my time and speed as I continued to fly straight ahead. At that instant my radio crackled to life and almost simultaneously, two other planes in the pack reported spotting the target.

"Squadron leader to all aircraft, maintain radio silence!" I ordered, and the airways abruptly fell silent. I felt certain that the spotters at the airfield had seen us, and were frantically reporting our presence, but I didn't want to give them any help by way of radio chatter because I had a plan.

Early in my tour, I devised my own airfield attack plan that began by flying past the target without attacking it. It was a simple triangulation problem that involved several turns in different directions. With each turn I decreased altitude until I was at tree-top level and approaching the airfield from an entirely different direction than the one the spotters had noted on our decoy flyby. Surprise was the key element that would cut our losses, and by coming in at tree-top level we would be out of sight until the last possible moment when we would suddenly burst into the enemy's view from seemingly out of nowhere. I had spread the formation out so that each pilot could get in, pick his target, and get out in one pass. I looked at my watch. We'd passed the target five minutes ago so I gave the signal to begin initiating the turns. It had worked well in the past and I felt confident as I set my plan in motion.

Turning on course for the final attack, the exhilaration of speed caused by seeing the tops of the trees hurtling past mere feet below my wingtip, and the thought of suddenly bursting into sight over the airfield was interrupted when I spotted something moving on the autobahn running adjacent to the airfield. A German staff car raced down the highway as if the Devil himself was chasing it. Staff cars are prime targets, as you never knew who might be riding in one of them. I decided to assume the role of the Devil.

Breaking radio silence I passed attack control to my deputy leader and broke right after the car while the rest of the P-51s hit the airfield. Bringing the staff car to bear, I fixed it in my gun sights and fired a solid burst from my six Browning machine guns, blasting the car off the road and leaving it engulfed in flames by the side of the autobahn. Pulling up over the burning automobile, I found myself at the edge of the airfield. I adjusted my heading, trained my sights on an Me-109 parked on the ground, and fired, satisfied that my .50-caliber rounds were pounding the German aircraft.

Then whump! My P-51 jolted as if it were a car that had just hit a log in the road. I had taken a direct hit from anti-aircraft fire, and my head flew forward cracking into the gun sight I had just been riveted to. The instrument needles on my panel were spinning drunkenly around their dials and I realized engine failure was imminent. When I looked up, I couldn't see a thing as oil from my wounded engine washed over my canopy, coating the windscreen with a thick black curtain. As in other times in my flying career when catastrophe seemed just outside my cockpit, I began to formulate a plan that would get me out of the predicament. Was I feeling anxiety? Sure, but I was so busy concentrating on survival that I didn't have time to be afraid.

I rolled the canopy open so I could see out the sides and to vent the thick acrid smoke that was now pouring into the cockpit and choking me. I could see that I was now flying over a thick forest when the Mustang's engine gave a mortal shudder. Its end was near, as the only reason for the canopy to be covered with that much oil was that I'd experienced a direct hit on the engine. The words of my old flight instructor drifted back to me: "Get up there. Give yourself room to recover from a mistake."

My engine power was failing rapidly. The faithful Packard-built Rolls-Royce Merlin was a great engine, but no engine can run long without oil, and mine was now leaving its oil in a wide swath over a German wood. Coaxing every ounce of power that was left in the engine, I disconnected my radio and oxygen lines, glanced over the side of the aircraft and figured I had about as much altitude as I was going to get. It was time to leave her. This presented another dilemma, for I'd never jumped out of an airplane before! Our flight instructor had walked into the room one day and passed out manuals that described the appropriate way to exit a P-51 that had sustained a lethal hit.

"This manual tells you how to parachute from your aircraft. You probably won't need it, but I'd advise you to read it ... just in case," he said with a sardonic smile.

It may sound like a crass way to treat young pilots, but the fact is with the war on, and the expedience of getting new pilots to the front, there just wasn't time for any real parachute training or facilities either, for that matter. Besides, they were being used to train combat paratroopers. Unlike the paratroopers who amassed many dozens of jumps, when airmen bailed out of their stricken aircraft, it was usually their first time.

Fortunately, I'd done my homework. Unbuckling my harness, I crouched in the seat as the manual suggested. With my heart pounding so hard I could hear my pulse in my ears, I took a deep breath and dove out of the right side of the cockpit with my target being the right wing of the aircraft. The manual said the wing would be gone when I got there. Thank God the book was right.

Due to the forward motion of the airplane, the prop wash carried me over the wing and under the aircraft's horizontal stabilizer which barely missed bashing my brains in. Had the manual told me about that part, I'd probably have looked up to see where the tail was, and the outcome would have been decidedly different. I immediately pulled the ripcord and felt the welcoming jolt of the chute opening. "So far, so good," I thought to myself.

No sooner had the open chute jerked me slightly upward breaking my fall than I hit the tops of the trees. Crashing through branches, I came to a jolting stop hung-up in a tree high above the ground. Amazingly, I was still in one piece and didn't have a tree branch stuck in any embarrassing parts of my anatomy. Aside from a few scratches and bruises and a cut on my knee, I was okay.

I looked down at the ground below and remained perfectly still. It was deathly quiet. Perhaps not the best analogy to use, but it's the one that came to mind. My world had gone from the high speed roar of my engine, the chatter of machine guns, the impact of a direct hit and the frantic exit from a dying aircraft with no room to spare, to sudden silence and a total lack of movement, save for the mild swing of my trapped parachute.

And what about my P-51? It couldn't possibly have gone much farther. When the engine died, it would have spun wildly out of control and crashed in a spectacular fireball. It couldn't have come down too far from where I bailed out. Didn't anyone take notice? Was a squad of German soldiers hastily making their way to this very tree?

Waiting there in the silence I had the opportunity to think about how close I had come to not making it. The shell that destroyed the engine of my plane had only missed me by three or four feet. At the speed my plane was flying, a millisecond faster and the shell would have ripped squarely through my lap! I'd bailed out with barely enough height to open the chute. I thought about all those things, but I must have been in a state of shock because at the time it didn't register. It was only upon much later reflection that the gravity of the situation I had just experienced really sank in.

I did think the boys back at the squadron would probably be saying, "Too bad for Bob! It looks like he bought it this time. It was the end for him." Then, I realized another truth. It was not the end. For me, it was a new beginning. Despite my circumstances, I was right where I was destined to be.

Former Secretary of State and Army Chief of Staff General Colin Powell once said of the military, "I have found a home."

I felt the same way that day hanging from a tree in Germany. The military was my home. I was part of an elite fighting force, doing an important task that would affect the history of the world for decades to come, and I had to get on with the next phase of it—just as soon as I got down out of this tree! However, a lot of unexpected things were about to happen to me before I was safely on the ground once again.

Chapter 1

The Formative Years

Two days after July 4, 1924, I was born in the Lying In Hospital on Third Avenue and 16th Street in New York City, the first son of Michael and Helen White. That year, Calvin Coolidge was reelected president and a bottom-of-the-line Ford, without a self-starter, could be purchased for $299, the lowest new car price in history. Buster Keaton filled the flickering screen in movie theaters in the *Navigator* and *Sherlock Jr.*, while Douglas Fairbanks, Sr., made the ladies swoon in *The Thief of Baghdad*. New York City homicides would climb to an alarming two hundred sixty-five that year. Each year the city was becoming more dangerous, yet it was still a very safe place to raise a family in 1924.

Mine was a working-class family that lived on the Upper West Side of Manhattan near Amsterdam and Broadway near Westside Drive. My father was a baker for the National Biscuit Company, a fortuitous circumstance for the White family when the stock market crashed in October of 1929. Although his hours were cut back to two or occasionally three days a week, he was never completely without a job. Like everyone else in the Depression, things were tight, but we got along.

We lived in a multinational neighborhood, not uncommon for the melting pot that was America in the 1920s. There were Protestants, Catholics, Jews, and atheists of Irish, Greek, German, Polish, Hungarian and mixed ancestry in our corner of the world. Since some were more recent émigrés than others, a plethora of accents and European languages filled the air of my neighborhood. Still, English was the language of choice because in those days everyone wanted to fit in and become part of the American dream. The first order of business for a new arrival in the neighborhood was to learn English as quickly as possible while reserving their native tongue for private conversations at home. Many of us, though our parents spoke another language, were not encouraged to become proficient in the mother tongue.

Although my parents were born in New York City, my father's mother immigrated to the United States from Ireland, but I am not sure from where or at what age. The White side of my ancestry was definitely as green as the hills of the Emerald Isle since Grandma White married a fine Irish gentleman in the States.

Mom, on the other hand, was born in the Austrian area of the old Austria-Hungarian Empire and spoke German while growing up. Grandfather Butz was a firsthand witness to the horror that was "The Great War," and sage enough to foresee that the armistice signed in a French railroad car in 1919 was not the end of war but the prelude to greater human tragedy. It compelled him to make a monumental decision.

Mom's older sister, Elizabeth, was sent to the United States and settled in Milwaukee. It was the first step in ensuring that his daughters would be safe and shielded from the terrors of another war. As a young teenager in 1913, my mother was packed off to Milwaukee to live with her sister. At that time, her name was Karoline. How she picked up the name Helen, I'll never know. In 1916 she came to New York City to work where she met and married my father in 1921.

I have only one sibling, my brother Al who came along six years after me, in 1930. Due to the discrepancy in our ages, we were never battling Irish Brothers, but were still close. Too young to fight in World War II, he went to the City College of New York where he obtained a degree in engineering and still lives in Westchester County.

If I had to choose a single word to characterize my childhood, that word would be "happy." Blessed with a genetically rugged constitution, aside from the occasional sniffles and childhood illnesses, I was amazingly healthy.

Since my parents were Catholic, I was raised in that faith, and at the age of seven was confirmed and attended my first communion at the Ascension Catholic Church between Broadway and Amsterdam. Religion has always been important to me, even at a young age. Not long after that religious experience, an event occurred that would shape my future life. I've never shared this story with anyone before, but decided to share it here. Perhaps it will provide insight into the man I was to become.

For those old enough to remember such a place, I was in a five-and-dime store. Today, such an establishment might be classified somewhere between a small department store and a dollar store. They carried everything imaginable. As I wandered aimlessly among the aisles heaped with display cases filled with wonderful things, my seven-year-old eyes fell on a treasure.

On the counter directly in front of me, in a box with several others of various colors, was a beautiful, red, pencil sharpener. It was not one of the drum-shaped varieties with the side crank that was so familiar to every school child. This one was different. This small bit of red plastic with a cantilevered razor blade in its side neatly fit the head of a pencil. Since electric pencil sharpeners hadn't been invented yet, a twist of the wrist shaped any pencil into stiletto-tipped perfection. I had to have it.

Unfortunately, I had not yet begun to receive the weekly stipend of ten cents that would be mine to spend on such frivolities if I so desired, so I had no money. But the temptation was beyond my control. My eyes darted up and down the aisles. No one was watching. Rubbing my sweating hands on the sides of my pants, I took one last furtive glance and with the speed of a striking cobra, I snatched the prize and slipped it into my pocket. Standing still as a statue and panting as though I had just run a race, I was overwhelmed by my action and paralyzed by the fear of discovery that I felt certain was imminent. It didn't come. When I looked around no one was watching.

I'm still not sure how I was able to casually walk up to the front of the store and outside onto the crowded sidewalk without running. Maybe I didn't. Maybe I ran. I can't be sure. In any event, nobody paid any attention to me.

As soon as I could break through the crowd, I began to run. I was half a mile from home, and for the first few blocks I was propelled by the euphoria and adrenaline rush of my daring escapade. Then, as it wore off, and I considered the enormity of what I had done, it began to sink in. I slowed to a walk.

I was a thief! Just like Clyde Barrow and Bonnie Parker whom I read about in the newspaper. They were just beginning to make a name for themselves shooting up banks in the Midwest. It's a longstanding joke that Catholics have the market on guilt cornered. I'll have to vote for that. But, this time, I had earned the guilt. The guilt so overwhelmed me that I could barely put one foot in front of the other. I wasn't sure if I could even make it home. I knew that I had done something terribly wrong. What should I do? My seven-year-old brain could only think of one solution. Turning on my heel, I dashed back in the direction I had come like an Olympic sprinter out of the starting blocks.

When I got back to the scene of the crime, I was red-faced and drenched with perspiration. It took a few minutes before I was composed enough to push open the big glass doors and step inside. Later in life, I would do many things other people considered courageous, but believe me, the simple act of opening that door took as much of that scarce commodity as I could muster.

I slithered down the aisle as if I were a reptile skulking through a field of tall grass. After what seemed like a millennium, I arrived at the counter with the pencil sharpener. Repeating my earlier reconnaissance, I assured myself that no one was looking. Reluctantly, I returned my treasure to the bin with its mates. Much to my relief, no one saw me do it. It was as if the world, which I had been holding on my shoulders, had been taken back by Atlas so he could continue his eternal punishment. With the humility of a repentant sinner, I retraced my steps to the street so I could start my half-mile trip back home for the second time. To my knowledge, that was the only purposefully illegal or dishonest act I have ever done.

I learned one of life's most important lessons that day: Guilt was an unpleasant feeling, and I could not live with it.

As I mentioned, my neighborhood was a working class one, and although we were a smorgasbord of religious and ethnic backgrounds there was virtually no class distinction. In my eleventh year, I learned two more valuable lessons that would remain with me for life and shape my relations with others.

A girl from my school had a birthday party and invited eight of us to celebrate with her. She lived close to the public school we all attended, so I put on my Sunday best and walked the several blocks to the party. Immediately on arrival, I suffered my first embarrassment of the day. Since birthday parties were not regular social events in my neighborhood, I didn't realize I was obliged to bring a birthday present. Everyone else did. One boy, who lived in the affluent section of the neighborhood, even brought her a dozen red roses! Needless to say I was mortified. Another lesson: Always know the territory and the local rules.

Social graces were an important part of life and social affairs had a protocol that needed to be followed. I vowed to make certain I would be better prepared in the future. Later, in my life in the military, that proved to be a useful vow. Unfortunately that vow provided me with little solace for the rest of the afternoon, and I squirmed my way through the remainder of the party. I felt a profound sense of relief when the party finally ended, and I started home.

Betty Cicero and Rose Wilson, two of the other revelers at the party, walked with me. Remember, it was 1935, and youngsters then were free to roam the streets of midtown Manhattan without adult supervision. We walked from Columbus to 110th street where Rose would part company with us.

Rose was not from our neighborhood. She lived in a fancy high-rise, complete with an elevator and a doorman. I have no idea what her family did for a living, but I supposed her father made more money than mine did, since we didn't live that way. However, I hadn't even considered that until this day.

As she turned to leave, Rose said to me, "Bob, since you are poor, I know you didn't know that you were supposed to bring a present to the party." With a pleasant smile and a wave, she skipped away down the street.

I stood there flabbergasted with my mouth open and my jaw slack. Confused and flushed with embarrassment, I looked down at my shoes, shined to a mirror for the supposedly joyous celebration.

Was I poor? What did that mean? I didn't feel poor. I had everything anyone could ever want. I had a home, family, plenty to eat, a warm place to sleep and pals to hang out with. No, I didn't live in a house with a doorman or an elevator, but did that make me poor? No way! But was I wrong about that? The nagging doubt I couldn't shake drained some of the redness from my face, as my embarrassment turned to sadness. Atlas was threatening to give me that world back. Then Betty came to my rescue.

Wrapping her thin little arms around me, she hugged me as a mother hugs an injured child and said, "It's okay, Bob. You're just fine."

At home, I told the story to my mother. I could see the sympathy for my pain in her eyes as she listened. Then, she reiterated nearly the same thing Betty had said to me. I was all right after all.

The episode made me keenly aware of class distinctions. I realized that day that on the other side of Broadway, there was another world, and I wasn't part of it. A sage once remarked, "God must have loved poor people, because he made so many of them." I was happy. I lacked nothing that I really needed. So what if I was poor by someone else's standard. I was happy with my lot, and that was all that mattered. And I knew it didn't matter, as long as there were people like Betty Cicero in this world who thought I was fine anyway!

Life's third lesson: Be happy with your lot, as long as you are comfortable with who and what you are, not who and what someone else thinks you are. From my father, I learned the work ethic that made America great and whose principles have allowed me to accomplish so much in my life. And, I learned it watching a card game.

One of my father's favorite pastimes was playing cards with his cronies once a week. During the hard years of the Depression, the conversation around the table invariably turned to economics. Like my father, most of the men were scraping along, but things were difficult for all of them.

A common topic of conversation was the newly established welfare system. Not everyone was as fortunate as we were, and through no fault of there own, many American families found themselves at the bitter end of their financial resources. To alleviate the hunger and hardships these families endured, the federal government established a system to provide enough resources to barely keep these people alive. It was a noble program, and a needed one. Still, to those men around the table, and to the large majority of men who signed up for relief, it was still charity as far as they were concerned.

I can remember my father's forceful exclamation to his confederates, "I don't want any relief!" From the tone of his voice as he said it, I could tell he considered relief a loathsome thing. The comment was greeted by emphatic nods from around the table. From the sets of their jaws and the fire in their eyes, I could tell they would rather assault the gates of hell than accept relief.

To underscore their resolve, when a winter game was in session and it started to snow, they abandoned the game at once. Leaving the cards on the table, they donned hats, coats, boots and mufflers. Shovels in hand, they moved to the more affluent neighborhoods and went door-to-door asking people if they could shovel their steps and sidewalks for whatever people were able to pay.

Dad was fortunate enough to be able to work enough hours to stay off relief. As I reflect on it now, I am sure if he had needed to go on welfare, it would have broken his spirit, as it did so many other hard-working Americans during that tragic period in our nation's history. Although it has not completely died out in America, I fear some of the pride, some of that stubborn resistance to handouts may be disappearing. If so, it's a reason to take pause.

Young Bob White learned life's lesson number four: Work, no matter how menial, was something to be embraced. In the end, it would be its own reward.

Perhaps the most life-altering experience of my childhood took place on 108th Street on Manhattan Avenue at a building owned by the New York Telephone Company. The main entrance was a big glass door on 108th, but off to the side was a smaller door used for deliveries to this central switching building. In front of this little door were two stone steps. Since the door was infrequently used, the steps became a meeting place for me and my pals. When we needed to meet to solve the problems of the world, to negotiate a pick up game of basketball, or just to hang out, the admonition was always, "meet you at the two steps!"

One perfect summer afternoon, I sat on the two steps waiting for my gang to assemble, daydreaming, when a sound interrupted my reverie. It was the drone of a low-flying aircraft making its final approach to LaGuardia Airport. For reasons I still can't explain, I was mesmerized by the sight. I wondered what it would be like to be up there! What would it be like to soar in the sky high above the concrete canyons of the city as free as a bird? Sitting there on the two steps, I made a vow to myself. If I were ever given the opportunity, I would do everything within my power to find out.

Movies in those days fit very nicely into a budget of ten-cents-per-week, and I was later enthralled with the movie, *The Flying Tigers*. I was so enthralled that I saw it four times. Little did I know that in a very short time, I would be flying my first fighter plane, the Curtiss P-40 Warhawk, just like my celluloid heroes.

We had a gang when I was a kid, but it was the "Our Gang" variety with Alfalfa and Ring Eye, and bore no resemblance to the mayhem, drugs and bloodshed associated with criminal gangs today. To underscore how tame we were, I was only involved in one fight in my entire childhood. Steve Repach was the closest thing we had in our gang to a street fighter. To this day, I can't remember what my momentous grievance was, but one day, I called him out ("challenged him," in today's vernacular), despite the fact that he was five years older, and bigger and tougher than I was. I fought fiercely, but was more than halfway through a sound thrashing, when Mrs. McGourty, God bless her, waded into the fray and rescued me. While berating us for being Hooligans she boxed our ears and sent us on our way.

Lesson number five learned: Fighting may not solve anything, but sometimes a man must fight regardless of the odds. A corollary to the lesson was if Mrs. McGourty wasn't going to be around, I'd better go into the fray with superior firepower.

Most of the time, we were a peaceful hodgepodge of ethnicity who wiled away our leisure time playing stickball or basketball. It was our good fortune to live one-and-one-half blocks from the home of the Police Athletic League (PAL), and its magnificent recreational facility, a field house once owned by the Catholic Church and donated to the League. Considering most of us lived between 108th and 109th streets, it was convenient for the whole gang.

Since I have already described my pugilistic skills, needless to say the boxing rings were not my usual destination. Instead, the gang had a team in the PAL basketball league. We called ourselves "The Hawks" but unfortunately, we seldom soared over the opposition. More frequently, the Hawks were grounded. But we had fun, win or lose. That was great because most of the time, we lost.

Although I grew up with kids of nearly every ethnic background, I had little experience with blacks or Hispanics. Although Harlem and Spanish Harlem started at 110th Street, we simply had little contact with each other since schools were segregated and racial tension was years in the future.

Like most active boys, I spent a great deal of time on the streets with my gang. But in quiet times at home, I liked to build radios. Using sources at school or the public library, I found wiring diagrams. Starting with a relatively simple crystal set, I progressed gradually to more complex designs. As my hobby grew, the cost of parts and tubes in particular required that I develop a practical sense of money, balancing the cost of my hobby against other things I wanted to do. It also helped me learn to construct, organize and complete a project while allowing me to develop some facility with working with my hands.

My public education until ninth grade was unremarkable, and I was a decent student when it came time for me to matriculate to high school. Then, unlike now, many students chose not to go to a traditional high school, but rather to vocational education schools, or trade schools as they were called. Along with very basic bookwork, one was taught the elements of a useful trade such as carpentry or auto mechanics.

Most of my teachers voiced the opinion that I should follow the academic path, which would provide me the prerequisites for college, if that was in the cards for the future. However, college was not as much a destination then as it is now. A high school diploma opened a plethora of opportunities that might now require a bachelor's degree from some college or university. It was the Great Depression, and my Germanic mother had ideas of her own about my future.

"No regular school! If a man has a trade, a man can always find work," she said, in a tone of voice that precluded debate. Besides that, there was a practical side. I really couldn't afford to go to college. Of course, I acquiesced. Each morning, I rolled out of bed in time to complete my morning ablutions, gobble down a quick breakfast and catch the subway for the ride to the Bronx and Samuel Gompers High School, named for the founder and perpetual president of the American Federation of Labor. Since I loved building radios, I studied "Electricity," as it was called.

The book work was not demanding, but I learned a lot of practical things that any self-respecting electrician would need to know. It also allowed me to become comfortable with a variety of hand tools. Those skills were honed over the years, and only recently I used those skills to work on projects in the bathroom of my current home.

You will note a dearth of information about the girls in my life to this point. Aside from a puppy love and an occasional junior high crush, I had limited opportunities to interact with the opposite sex. Samuel Gompers was an all-male school. When I ponder the problems facing educators today, it makes me wonder if things might not be little easier for today's students if they returned to some of these gender-segregated schools. Despite the practical climate of no-nonsense education at Samuel Gompers, one particular teacher felt there should be more to it than that. Most of my life, I have had the good fortune to be in the right place at the right time. This was one of those times.

Proficiency tests are nothing new. In my days they were called Regent's Tests. If one had aspirations toward higher education, a passing mark on these tests was mandatory. Those of us from vocational high schools were sorely handicapped when it came to passing the exams because some of the subjects we needed were not part of our curriculum. Mr. Newman, one of our English teachers, made an offer to anyone in school who wanted to take the exams. He would tutor us to make up the deficiencies in the curriculum so we could sit for the exams with reasonable expectation of passing them. I jumped at the opportunity and was surprised when only a small percentage of the student population joined me.

After several weeks of additional work covering a variety of subjects, Mr. Newman pronounced us ready for the exam. To my delight, I was able to pass all parts of the exams. Although it would be many years before I finally was able to enroll in college, when I did, I was only one subject short, trigonometry, which wasn't on the test when I originally took it. I can't thank Mr. Newman enough for going that extra mile for us. Another lesson learned: When life presents you with an opportunity, *carpe diem*, seize the day! Even if the opportunity is lemons, don't just make lemonade, make some lemon curd and save a little of the peel for your martini, too.

True to my father's example and like many boys my age, I worked a number of odd jobs. But, in high school, I landed a real job. Each Saturday and Sunday I donned the uniform of a Western Union bike messenger. Leaping onto my trusty Schwinn, I pedaled to the main office at Madison and 86th to get my first assignment of the day.

The territory I usually rode was between 5th Avenue to the east end and between 79th and 89th streets. For my services I was paid the princely sum of thirty cents an hour! For two weekend shifts of eight hours each, I netted a whopping four dollars and eighty cents, a far cry from the ten cents a week of my childhood. Although tips were ostensibly part of our payment, since many telegrams were delivered to apartment buildings, the doorman took them with a nod and an occasional thank you, but seldom if ever a nickel or dime tip followed.

Working as a cycling messenger was good exercise and kept me fit. At times, though, it was difficult. When I got a message that needed to be delivered to the far reaches of the east end, and then came back to dispatch to find one waiting for delivery at the other end of the territory, my legs sometimes felt as if they would fall off. I also remember the uphill pull toward Madison Avenue that was a frequent route.

We also worked in all kinds of weather. Sunny and hot days were interspersed with showers and at times thunderstorms. I really hated the official raincoats we were issued. Pedaling toward the east end on a humid August day in a downpour turned the inside of those waterproof shrouds into a classic Swedish sauna.

Traffic at times was heavy, but nothing like the New York traffic of today. For one thing, motorists were less likely to take a bead on a hapless bike rider, or purposely drench you by driving at high speed through a puddle on a rainy day. The road we used most often to cross Central Park was only two lanes, and at times the traffic was quite heavy there, but I don't remember a single close call or angry fist wave from a motorist. Remarkably, Central Park was safe to ride through then, or play in, or walk through.

My one major brush with an auto came along 5th Avenue. Slightly behind schedule and peddling furiously, I huffed and puffed my way along the famous thoroughfare. I was passing a row of limousines when a chauffeur opened the driver's door on the street side directly into my path! Slamming on the brakes as hard as I could, I almost, but not quite, avoided impact. Although I slowed down enough to avoid serious damage to me or machine, I still hit the door. To this day I still chuckle when I think about it. Here I was, a red-faced, sweating teenager on a bicycle, tongue lashing a liveried chauffeur in full dress regalia. I chastised him in no uncertain terms for his carelessness and for not paying attention. My honor satisfied and my dignity restored, I mounted my trusty steed and sped off down the avenue leaving the poor man standing in the street with a perplexed look on his face.

As previously mentioned, tips were not a usual part of the job, but one delivery stands out. I was working the evening shift on Christmas Eve delivering between 5th and Madison avenues. Stopping my bike in front of an imposing single family brownstone, I hurried up the sidewalk and rang the doorbell.

An elegantly barbered man wearing a white long-sleeved shirt answered on the second ring. I handed him the telegram and the clipboard for him to sign his name. Scribbling his signature, he handed me the clipboard, and I turned to leave.

"Just a minute, young fellow," he said, and turned back into the house. In a few moments, he returned with a crisp one-dollar bill. Handing me the money he said, "Thank you and Merry Christmas."

Muttering a profound and startled thank you, I pocketed the money as if I were afraid he might change his mind. Starting down the walk towards my bike, I took out the bill and looked at it again. Three hours! Three hours, I thought to myself. It takes me three hours to earn this much money. I had a hard time grasping the concept of that kind of wealth. That man has enough money that he could just blithely give away the equivalent of three hours work, just for receiving a telegram. My father was correct. Hard work has its rewards.

I was also working for Western Union on a day that would change not only my life, but the lives of many young men not only in America but all over the world. It was a pleasant December Sunday. Message traffic was slow and the sun was shining. Several of the bike messengers sat in the dispatch room in the main office at Madison and 85th bantering with Mrs. Sassic, the office manager.

The radio was crooning a tune promoting the upcoming Christmas holidays when the broadcast was interrupted for a special message from the president of the United States. After a brief introduction, President Franklin Delano Roosevelt's distinctive voice filled the tiny office. He announced that the United States Navy had been attacked by the Japanese Navy at Pearl Harbor. It was a brief announcement. The famous "Day of Infamy" December 7th speech would not actually be given until December 8th before a joint session of Congress. When the announcement was over, everyone was contemplative for a moment until Mrs. Sassic looked up at us and said, "Well, boys, I guess you'll all be trading in your Western Union uniforms for different ones."

With a nod of agreement, we validated her prophecy.

I was seventeen years old then, with my eighteenth birthday looming on the horizon. At eighteen, I would be required to register for the draft. I knew I would have to go. And, if I had to go, I wanted to be "up there." Here was my chance to learn to fly. I had already learned about the Aviation Cadet program, that I felt sure I wanted to join, even before the Japanese attacked Pearl Harbor. It required a high school diploma and screening tests, both mental and physical. If one was sound in mind and body, they next tested aptitude to further stratify the candidate into pilot, bombardier or navigator training. This was the thing for me. I was sure of it.

Because of an experiment in lower education, I had been part of an accelerated program in which I completed the seventh grade in only half a year, and then started on the eighth grade material. After that, they abandoned the program, but as a result, I graduated high school at age seventeen. To enter the Aviation Cadet program, I would need parental approval. So, I asked my mother.

"No!" she said emphatically, and that was the end of the discussion.

Johnnie Madden (not the coach) and I were the only two of the old gang left who hadn't enlisted or been drafted in the five months between Pearl Harbor and my now impending July birthday. We were both itching to get at it. One afternoon, after Johnnie had been drafted and was gone, I reflected on my plight and screwed up the courage to beard the lion in his den, or her den as the case was here.

That evening after dinner, I saw an opening and said to my parents, "You know, I'll be eighteen real soon, and it will be my duty to register for the draft. Since I'm so healthy, chances are a hundred percent that I'll get drafted. Johnnie Madden's gone and I'm the only one left."

My mother began to fidget, and my father looked up from his evening newspaper.

"Since I'm not in the Aviation Cadet program, chances are I'll either be in an infantry rifle company or in the Marines. I understand a lot of the guys are going to the Marines," I said. From the looks on their faces, I knew my folks didn't like where this conversation was headed.

"I just want you to know that despite the hardships and dangers of life as an infantry rifleman, I'll be the very best soldier I can possibly be, regardless of which branch of service I'm in. I will make you both proud of me."

As was his custom, my father said nothing, but as I panned his face in search of a glimmer of hope that signaled my plan was working, I saw a twinkle in his eye. I had seen that twinkle before, and it meant that if this is what I really wanted, he was one hundred percent behind me. When he had to, Dad could put his foot down, but the majority of the time he tacitly went along with whatever pleased my mother. Like many husbands, he always was allowed to have an opinion, but not always a vote.

"Do you still have those Aviation Cadet program papers?" my mother asked as her brimming eyes overflowed and tears tracked down her cheeks.

"Yes, I do," I replied, my heart in my throat.

"Then get them, and I'll sign them," she said reluctantly as the tears came in earnest. I was elated. Although it had taken every ounce of courage I could muster to force the issue with my mother, I was one step closer to my goal. If I were lucky enough, I'd be "up there" at the controls of one of those graceful, magnificent machines. The thought that one of them could be my coffin never occurred to me. Aren't almost all eighteen-year-olds immortal?

Chapter 2

Up in the Air, Junior Birdman

So it was I found myself on a train headed for Atlantic City for basic training. With the mobilization for the war in full swing, the government had commandeered the resort hotels for barracks. In typical government fashion, they had stripped the rooms bare of any social amenities that might remind us of civilian life. Besides, after the war, it would provide jobs for legions of laborers who would restore the resort to more civil conditions.

One of those missing amenities was elevator service, and my room was on the eighteenth floor of the hotel! It made me thankful for my days as a Western Union messenger. The muscles in my legs had been hardened by the miles of pedaling, and the stairs were manageable but laborious. Still, I planned my days to minimize trips to and from the room.

As any soldier will tell you, basic training is not the most memorable part of a military career. It is something to be endured, and I decided to make the best of it. It was simply a means to an end. In my heart, I knew my war would be fought in the sky, so basic training was a necessary evil to get me where I really wanted to go. They taught us to dress properly, salute in an acceptable military fashion and march in what passed for straight lines while endlessly singing rhyming, mindless little ditties that occasionally pushed the limits of decorum and good taste.

We also learned to fire weapons. Since all the modern ones were in use in Europe and the Far East, we used leftover World War I carbines. The weapons weren't the same as our brothers had in the trenches, but the mechanics of shooting are universal. I took to it reasonably well, considering I had little experience with guns at home.

As basic was winding down, we received the news that there was a backlog of cadets waiting to get into the Aviation Cadet program. The frantic mobilization had taxed the training facilities beyond their limits. While we waited, we would be assigned to a College Training Detachment. We would be sent to colleges or universities around the country to take classes until a spot opened up in the ACP.

One hundred twenty of us graduated basic training. We were placed in the care of a two-striper nicknamed Tennessee, after his native state. Tennessee was very impressed with being in charge and had a flare for the dramatic. I believe he already thought that third stripe was on his arm as he did a passable imitation of a Marine Gunny trying to whip a gang of raw recruits into potential killers.

Marching to the train station, we boarded our coaches. Tennessee treated the whole operation as if we were Roger's Rangers headed off to a clandestine mission behind enemy lines. Everything was on a need-to-know basis, and as aviation cadets we didn't need to know anything, let alone where we were going. He refused to tell us! Despite our best wheedling and cajoling, he was as mum as a mime.

Hunkering down in my seat by the window, I watched the shore line of New Jersey slip quietly into the nondescript, rolling farmland of the eastern United States. My mates and I passed the time reading, sleeping, telling jokes or speculating about our final destination. There were even a few wagers about where our new home would be. An impromptu game of poker broke out in the next car and some of the fellows drifted over there.

Time has mercifully blurred the length of the journey, but we were on the train part of a day and overnight. Once we stopped for coal, and someone said that he was sure we were somewhere in Pennsylvania. From the looks of the terrain around us, I considered that a reasonable guess.

In a few hours, the rumor proved to be true as the train eased into a rural station. The sign over the entrance to the waiting area read, BEAVER FALLS, PENNSYLVANIA. This was the town that would later become famous as the cradle of National Football League quarterbacks. But Joe Willy Nameth was not waiting to greet us. This was only a wide place in the road to us, the intrepid band of adventurers on the troop train. None of us had a clue as to where it was on the map.

The reason we had been brought here stood on top of the hill above the town. A central three-story bell-tower with flanking third-story dormers gave the Gothic stone building a sinister, brooding appearance as it gazed down on the sleepy town. One could envision a mob of angry farmers, pitch-forks in hand, storming up the hill to confront the mad scientist and his monster. The truth of the building was far from sinister. It was founded in 1848 and built on land donated by the Harmony Religious Society. This was Geneva College, and it was to be home to our College Training Detachment. Imagine that, a college that was over ninety years old and none of us had ever heard of it.

It was six in the morning as we stumbled from the coaches and fell into formation for our march up the hill to the dormitory. I prayed I would have a room lower than the eighteenth floor. Seeing nothing on the horizon that approached that dizzying height, I felt sure God was listening. Breaking into song, we stepped off and marched up the hill. With the racket we made, I'm certain we woke up the few remaining citizens who weren't already up peering through their curtains at this invading army of teenaged boys trying to act like soldiers.

In front of the dorms, we were introduced to Second Lieutenant Rosakus, our commanding officer. After a short welcoming address, he informed us we would be confined to quarters for the first two weeks while we began our classroom work. He said he had no idea how long we would be there, but assured us that the moment an opening for air cadet training opened up, we would be shipped out. The thought of long, tedious days in the mountains of Pennsylvania, while the war raged on without me, filled me with dread.

Then his expression turned serious. He warned us that there were no other military bases in the area and that we were the sole representatives of the United States Army in this part of Pennsylvania. Strict rules concerning behavior were enumerated, along with a description of the punishment to be meted out to offenders. He pointed out that our behavior had to remain beyond reproach, particularly when in full view of the public. Fraternization with the local female population wasn't forbidden, but from the tone of his comments, the Army would take a dim view of any unseemly liaisons. "After all, you are officer candidates. Act like it!" were his final words.

The subsequent two weeks were a whirl of settling into a new place with new routines, registering and finding our way into the classrooms. The classes, mostly math and science, were taught by the college faculty. In my case, I think perhaps the Emeritus faculty, because my professor was ancient, at least to my eighteen-year-old eyes. He was an "oldie," but still a "goodie." As I reflect on it now, there had to be a shortage of teachers then, since most able-bodied men were off to war.

At the end of the two weeks quarantine, our Commanding Officer Lt. Rosakus, himself a Fordham graduate, called us together again. He complimented us on our deportment for the first two weeks and launched into a detailed review emphasizing the fraternization policies and punishments. That accomplished, he informed us that the next afternoon, we would be marching to the local Elks Club for a reception and dance hosted by the people of Beaver Falls. Even though we were in formation, a buzz of excitement rippled through the ranks.

The next afternoon, shoes shined to mirrors, trouser creases honed to razor edges, we lined up in formation. With anticipation in our song, we started for town. To an eighteen-year-old who had been in the military two months, the sight was overwhelming. An observer might have thought we had just returned from Guadalcanal.

Streets teemed with men, women and children. I think everyone in Beaver Falls was out on the street. Little girls in starched dresses waved tiny American flags. Aging World War I veterans stood at attention, campaign ribbons pinned to their suit jackets. They saluted smartly as we passed by. Fathers, mothers and grandparents shouted words of encouragement and applauded enthusiastically all along the route. It was a march I shall never forget.

After being cooped up for two weeks with the same old faces, it was wonderful to see new people, particularly the pretty young women lining the dance floor, each eager to dance and talk with us. Despite the temptation, the whole detachment behaved as gentlemen and the afternoon passed in a delightful whirl of sandwiches and punch, high heels and handshakes. All too soon, it was time to march back up the hill at the end of a day I will always cherish.

That experience was not unique while we were in Beaver Falls. One Sunday another cadet and I stopped into a local diner for breakfast after mass at the local parish. When we were finished, I asked for the check.

With a smile that would have melted butter, the pretty waitress said, "It's already been taken care of by the couple over there by the window."

Following her gesture, we turned to see a beaming middle-aged couple sitting in a booth. The smile on their faces and the warm wave they gave us said, "thank you," when it was us who should be thanking them. We did thank them for our breakfast, but their warmth and words of encouragement returned to us more thanks than we gave to them.

It was like that everywhere we went. You couldn't buy a beer in any of the taverns. At times, the hospitality was almost embarrassing. But we loved it, and on Army pay, I don't think anyone turned it down.

That attitude extended far beyond the boundaries of this friendly Pennsylvania town. Everywhere I went, that attitude permeated the entire country. I have never seen such a sense of unity, purpose or pride in our country before or since. There was a single-mindedness involving nearly everyone on the home front that I believe is unparalleled in our history. An enemy was out there that had to be defeated, and there was a pride and confidence in the armed forces that would lead the way toward final victory. Unfortunately, America has not always treated its warriors with that kind of love and respect.

The most marvelous aspect of being here was the flight experience. Each Cadet got ten hours of flight time in the little workhorse of civilian aviation, a Piper Cub. Of course the instructor was always with us, and we were carefully supervised, but even these few hours at the controls cemented my decision to fly as the proper one for me.

I will always remember sitting at the end of that grass runway, my heart pounding so loud I could hear it above the thrumming of the Piper's engine. I had never even been in an airplane before, and here I was getting ready to take off! I could barely contain myself.

We started to move. Faster and faster the grass flashed beneath our wheels. Then, after what seemed like an eternity to me, we lifted into the air. Remaining nonchalant on the outside, so as not to embarrass myself, I whooped for joy like a ten-year-old on the inside! After years of dreaming, I was "up there." Watching the tree tops fall away and the hanger morph into a matchbox below us, I knew that I was home. This was where I belonged.

During our tenth week at Geneva College the orders came through to report for classification in the ACP. Although the atmosphere, the people and the college had been delightful, we all felt we were marking time. When we got the orders, I couldn't pack fast enough. Not all of us would be leaving at the same time. I'm not sure how they decided who would go first. It certainly wasn't alphabetically. White always goes last. The first group consisted of forty cadets, and I was thrilled to be included in that group.

Nashville, Tennessee, was the next station on my odyssey. Cadets converged on the classification center from all points of the compass. There were big-city kids, solid Midwesterners, Texas cowboys, and Southern crackers mixed together for ARMA, which translated means Adaptability Rating for Military Aeronautics. The military is truly fond of acronyms.

Our first stop was at the doctor's office for a stringent physical examination. They tested our eyes and ears, poked, prodded and thumped. The old joke that said if you can see lightning and hear thunder you passed might have been true for the infantry, but it did not apply here.

From medical we moved to the paperwork and comprehensive testing that included math and a ton of reasoning problems. Oddly enough, there was no hand-eye coordination test included. The program as a whole was designed to determine where the army should place us for training; single engine (fighters, spotters), multi-engine (bomber, P-38, transports), navigator, or bombardier classification. All but the first classification, though the others were critical jobs needed to win the war, were low on my list. My dream was to become a fighter pilot.

We went straight from college to Nashville, Tennessee, where they divided us into twelve-men platoons for the final battery of tests. Bob Wilson, who had been with me in basic in Atlantic City, was in my platoon. One day I happened across Wilson and a southerner named Whitehead coming out of the doctor's office. Unlike the physical exams, this was the psychiatric portion of the tests. They were discussing the unusual questions posed by the doctor.

Whitehead, who was from Bessemer, Alabama, and had a southern drawl that sounded as if he had a mouth full of mush, asked, "Did that doctor ask you if you ever had sex before?"

"Yeah, he did," Wilson answered.

"What did you tell him?" Whitehead queried.

"I told him no," Wilson said.

Stopping, Whitehead planted his hands on his hips and with an incredulous look on his face asked, "You mean you lied to that doctor?"

I thought if Whitehead asked me the same question, I would answer as Wilson did, which would have been the truth. Whitehead would probably think I was lying, too, but the morality of the forties, and my Catholic background, made it the truth for me.

After a few days, word flashed through the camp that they were posting classification. The anxiety was palpable as everyone crowded around the board. I wanted to look, but I was afraid, too. What would I do if I didn't get fighter training? It's the only thing I ever wanted to do. I had to get it! I just had to!

I said a silent prayer, "Please God, please let me make it!" Crossing my fingers for good measure, I scanned the list. When I saw my name there, I thanked God for an answered prayer and, in a rare display of public emotion for me, let out a shout of joy as I joined the jubilant celebration the other pilot candidates had started.

Looking around at the others, my celebration was tempered with a bit of pathos. By the drooping shoulders, the painful smiles, the suppressed tears and frowns of dejection, the bitter disappointment of the navigator/bombardier groups was evident. Nearly everyone came here to be a pilot, and now half of us had our dreams shattered. But, as an excited teenager whose dream had just come true, I couldn't linger long on the negative. With a prayer that God would comfort them, I enthusiastically joined in the celebration.

After classification, we were no longer privates, but were given the official rank of Aviation Cadet, a special war-time rating. It was off to Maxwell Field for the first phase of our training, a two month program called Preflight. During the first month, we were called underclassmen.

There was daily marching, calisthenics and lots of running. All the activities were tailored to promote discipline and cohesiveness. Ground school was held every day. It included the basic skills we would need as pilots such as navigation, map reading, meteorology, and Morse code.

New recruits joined the program each month. When we completed the first month, as we began the second month, we would became the upperclassmen as the recruits that had been there for two months graduated. Hazing of the underclassmen by the upperclassmen was routine.

By today's standards, hazing was pretty tame. It was mild, silly stuff. For example, we were required to balance on one foot on the iron rail at the bottom of the bunks. Without falling, we had to flap our arms in chicken-fashion and crow like a rooster.

My favorite hazing experience involved a water fountain. On the ground around each building and across the campus sidewalks was a yellow line. Underclassmen were required to move double-time wherever we went, and to toe the line. One sweltering day, while I jogged across campus, I stopped at a water fountain for a drink of water.

"What's wrong with you, mister?" snarled a surly upperclassmen's voice from behind me.

Snapping to attention as we were required to do I said, "Sir?"

"Don't you know enough to salute the General?" he demanded.

"What General?" I asked, frantically looking around for someone with stars on their shoulder boards.

"There!" he retorted, pointing to the name plate on the front of the water cooler bearing the manufacturer's name, General Electric. "So salute!" he commanded.

I did as commanded. From then on, every time I passed the General, I stopped and saluted.

On our last day as underclassmen, we had a chance for revenge. The P.T. instructor for morning calisthenics proposed a relay race between the upper and lower classes. The winning side would be allowed to direct the push-up phase of the days' exercise while mercilessly hazing the losing side. Without delay, the underclassmen picked up the gauntlet.

I was on the relay team, but unfortunately our performance didn't live up to our bravado, and we lost the race. When the race was over, I was at the opposite end of the field from the formation, so I double-timed back to the formation to join my mates for the hazing.

As I began my push-ups, a scrawny, pimple-faced upperclassman got in my face and screamed, "Stop dogging it and get with the program!"

Hot, a bit winded from the run and frustrated from losing the race, I was in no mood for this little maggot to be screaming at me with his garlic breath. I lost my composure. "Get down here and match me push-up for push-up and you'll drop dead before I get my second wind," I growled at him.

The outburst made me feel good, but I paid for it. Marching the Quad was standard punishment for infractions in this phase of training. Any miscreant was obliged to get his rifle and report to the assembly grounds after hours. The severity of the offense dictated the time spent marching dully around the quadrangle. My outburst was worth one hour of marching. I resented the marching, but I'd do it again in a heartbeat.

Maxwell Field is situated near Montgomery, Alabama, and the Fourth of July was brutally hot that year. To honor the country, we had a drill and parade, and were then required to stand at attention for a long period of time to listen to patriotic addresses.

As most military people know, standing at rigid attention with the knees locked is a prelude to disaster. Locking the knees alters the circulation, and if held too long can result in fainting. Add the heat of an Alabama July, and the conditions were optimal for a heat stroke or heat-related swoon. A number of my college associates ended their day face down on the parade ground.

Our squadron commander was a first lieutenant, but our group commander was a captain. After the ceremony, we were told to assemble behind the barracks to meet with the captain. For a moment, I thought I was in the Royal Air Force instead of the Army Air Corps. The captain arrived dressed in khaki shorts with a pith helmet squarely atop his head. I don't actually remember a swagger stick, but I can easily imagine one tucked tightly beneath his arm.

Livid, red-faced and screaming, the captain dressed us down in no uncertain terms. He was particularly critical of our physical condition and lack of military decorum.

"If you can't stand at attention while the National Anthem is played, then when you fall down, you will bloody well lay there at attention!" he shouted as if he were an escapee from an asylum.

From this experience came my conclusion that life in the military is not significantly different than life on the streets of New York City. It is impossible to please everybody, no matter how hard you try. And, they may have captain's bars or general's stars on their shoulders, but there are unreasonable people everywhere.

Shortly before graduation to Primary Flight Training, the next phase of training on our journey to the sky, my group excitedly assembled at the airfield. After anxious minutes of scanning the sky, someone pointed to a tiny speck on the horizon. "There! There it is!" he shouted.

The distinct outline of a fighter plane gradually took shape. Coming closer, it circled the field and landed. As the P-51 taxied toward us, we were in heaven. It came to a stop and the canopy opened. Removing his helmet and goggles, the pilot stepped out and joined us on the ground by the plane. We crowded around him as if he were Zeus freshly returned from Olympus.

Relishing the attention and understanding our excitement, he told us about the plane and answered our questions with the aplomb of a rock star. And, I knew in my heart that some day soon I would be there with him.

Ground school was over. I had learned enough meteorology to stay out of major storms and enough navigation skills to keep from getting lost. It was important material that I knew I would use. Still, I was itching to fly. With buoyant spirits and the prospect of a new affluence, I headed for the Mississippi Institute of Aeronautics outside Jackson, Mississippi, for my six months of flight training. We would get two months each of Primary PT-17, Basic PT-13 and Advanced AT-6 training.

Once we completed classification, I was officially elevated to Aviation Cadet and the pay grade raise that accompanied it. My pay jumped from the stately sum of thirty dollars a month of a private to the princely sum of seventy-five dollars, the same as a three-striper, or sergeant.

The institute in Mississippi was a civilian facility with civilian instructors. It was housed at a small, rural airport with a grass runway. Here, we would be given sixty-five to seventy hours of flying time.

Our aircraft was a Boeing Stearman, an open cockpit, bi-winged plane with the student seat in the rear and the instructor seat in the front. The plane was made famous after the war when many of them were converted to crop dusters.

The dependable old craft contained a fixed, narrow landing gear. When landing on the bumpy, sometimes damp and slippery grass field, it required furious rudder pedal work to keep the plane from tipping over to one side or the other. If we could land on grass and control the aircraft with its narrow landing gear, nearly anything they threw at us in the future would be a piece of cake.

The unenviable tipping of the plane was known as a ground loop and usually concluded by ripping off the tip of the wing or worse. The upside of the Stearman's narrow gear was that it was very similar to the narrow gear of the P-40. "Handle this baby, and the P-40 will be a piece of cake," our instructors told us.

We were issued the classic World War II leather flying helmet and a set of goggles to use in flight. But until we were able to solo, we had to wear our goggles on the back of our flight helmets when we were on the ground. No one could solo in less than eight hours, and we were mandated to solo before twelve hours of training. If a cadet didn't solo by then, he would be subject to a check ride.

On the check ride, the instructor took the student up for one last flight. If they were unable to solo, they were washed out. They weren't through with the Aviation Cadet Program; they were reclassified to bombardier or navigator training. Of the six students in my group, three were washed out.

Each day, as my group came into the flight room, more and more of our mates had their glasses on the front of their foreheads. I was approaching eleven hours in the air, and I still hadn't made my solo flight. I was beginning to sweat. Hadn't I been doing as well as the others? I thought I had. Why wouldn't my instructor let me solo?

We were in the air shooting landings at different outlying airstrips. They were nothing more than a grassy farmer's field with a wind sock, but they sufficed for the purpose of training us in landings and takeoffs. Each time we made a landing, I silently shouted, *Get out! Get out!*

After two or three iterations of the drill, my instructor called to me through the Gossport. The Gossport, a British invention, was a tube that ran from the instructor's seat to the student's seat. In this perfect setting from the teacher's perspective, the teacher could talk to the student, but the student couldn't talk back.

"I've had enough. I need a little rest. Land so I can get out and rest in the shade while you practice some more," he said with a lightness in his voice.

Making a perfect landing, I taxied to a stop, and he got out. Revving the engine, I taxied to the end of the field and turned into the wind. As I hurtled across the grass and pointed the nose of the Stearman skyward, I felt as if I were the king of the universe.

Our civilian instructor was a particularly kind man. As graduation approached, he took the three of us who had flown solo out behind the hanger to explain to us why our three comrades had washed out. He also told us as we walked, that he could have soloed us in eight or nine hours, but an extra few hours would make us safer and better pilots. I really couldn't find fault with his logic.

"Two of the boys just needed more time. They weren't quite as quick to pick up things as the three of you. If they had another few hours they could have made it. But, the war's on and there's just not enough time," he said, spreading his hands in a gesture of helplessness.

"The other boy was different," he continued. "You see, he's a bobsledder. On the bobsled, the rudder controls and the hand controls work exactly backwards from the airplane. He just couldn't make the transition. I doubt he could have done it in another fifty hours."

"Now, let me give you a graduation present in the form of a piece of advice," he said, turning serious. "Flying low, howling over the treetops is a lot of fun because you get a real feeling of speed. But when you're doing something up there," he said, pointing skyward, "get some air underneath you. If you make a mistake, you got time to recover. If you make a mistake while you're down on the deck, you have no margin for error."

I don't think I ever received a better piece of advice. I kept it in mind whether I was on a training flight, in combat, testing a new aircraft or sitting in the X-15. That advice saved my bacon more than once.

After graduation it was back to Montgomery, Alabama. However, this time, it was to Gunter Field for Basic Flight Training. We arrived at Gunter at night, and the flashing beacon was a welcome sight. With it came ominous overtones. To this point all our flying had been in the daytime. Here, we would learn to fly at night and get a taste of advanced maneuvers.

In Montgomery, we were introduced to the Vultee BT-13, a low-winged, closed-canopy monoplane with wide landing gear. When its powerful engine coughed to life, the entire plane vibrated with the horsepower. In no time it earned the irreverent nickname of "The Vultee Vibrator!"

This time, all our instructors were military, and mine was Lieutenant Bone. He was a good one. Years after the war, I received a message that he was retiring, and I was invited to the celebration to give an address in his honor. As part of that delightful chore, I reminded him of an incident he had forgotten.

We had learned to handle spins with an instructor in previous training, and the Stearman was a forgiving aircraft. The BT-13 was less forgiving and did not possess ideal spin characteristics. At times, it could be balky to straighten up. One afternoon, Lieutenant Bone proceeded to demonstrate to me just how you did it.

Dropping into a right hand spin, Bone followed classic procedure. Moving the rudder to the left in opposition to the spin, he waited until the spin hesitated then neutralized the rudder. Pushing the stick forward to the instrument panel, he expected the machine to recover from the spin and pick up air speed. We continued to spin!

Without a word, he began the recovery sequence a second time, with one slight variation. When it came time to push the stick firmly forward, he slammed it forward with enough force to crack the covers on the instrument panel. The instrument covers survived, the spin broke, and the aircraft leveled out. Bone smiled and said nothing.

After we proved to Bone that we could break a BT-13 spin, Bone still suggested none of us should do it on solo flights. I learned two important lessons from the lieutenant. First, when something goes wrong, a good pilot never loses his head. He remains calm and follows procedure. Second, if following procedure fails, repeat the procedure, and whack it with a bigger hammer!

Even though we were not yet instrument rated, we learned to fly at night. These were simple flights with fixed way points over lighted terrain. Still, it was always a sense of relief to see the lights of the beacon at the end of the runway when I came home.

Each phase of training had its tension. This was the last phase in which all pilots would be together. At the end of this session, we would be divided into single-engine and multi-engine pilots. Although we had already been asked to declare a preference, and I had chosen single engine, I still had no idea which group I would be in.

One morning near the end of the phase, we were told to assemble in the flight operations room right after breakfast. In a few minutes, the captain came in. I snapped to attention and whipped a salute. When we were told to take a seat, I moved to the back row and got behind some taller pilots. I always liked to be inconspicuous.

"We have a quota for both single-engine and multiple-engine trainees," the Captain said without preamble. "As of now, we need two people to volunteer to change from single-engine to multi-engines."

As his eyes swept the room like twin lasers, the words of Bob Wilson on the train from Atlantic City swept across my mind like a tidal wave.

"Do I have any volunteers?" the Captain asked again.

The room remained as silent as Pharaoh's tomb.

"If I don't get any volunteers, I'll pick the volunteers," he said.

To this day, I'm not absolutely certain if the captain got any volunteers or not. I was on a bench at the back. Directly in front of me was a large table. Ducking down, I dived under the table as if the back row had suddenly caught fire. It was ignominious, but I didn't care. I didn't want those laser beam eyes to fall on me. I didn't want to cross the captain's mind. In the process I skinned my knee and ripped my trousers. That didn't matter. In the end, either that, or the constant stream of prayers on my lips must have worked. The foxhole isn't the only place where there are no atheists. At graduation, I left with the single-engine boys.

The next stop was Craig Field, in Alabama near the little town of Selma. Little did I know that the bridge I crossed numerous times in this sleepy Southern town would one day go down in civil rights history.

This time the aircraft was the North American AT-6, a larger low-wing trainer with a big radial engine. It was an airplane that truly separated the men from the boys in pilot training, although washouts at this stage were becoming exceedingly rare. The next two months would finish things, and I'd be ready for combat duty. The last skills to be learned were cross-country night flying, and instrument flying. To this point, the night flights had been short jaunts. These would be a lot longer.

They were not night flights on instruments as we do today. There was just a clipboard with coordinates and a compass. Since the compass was magnetic, it had a tendency to gyrate wildly at times, an unsettling characteristic to an insecure airman.

Once the night flight began, there were check points to be made to be sure I didn't stray too far off course. These were big things, like Mobile, a city with lights from houses and businesses and street lights that could be seen miles away. Leaving one check point to go to the next was another matter. The check point lights faded out behind leaving me in total darkness. An occasional light from a farmhouse or gas station was the only sign of civilization.

Alone with my thoughts and a spinning compass made for anxious moments for a young pilot. There was no way to tell where the wind was, or where you might encounter bumpy air. The main focus was keeping the plane level and on course. The sight of the beacon flashing at the end of the runway after a successful flight was an even more welcome sight than it was in the last phase.

Along with the night flights, we learned advanced aerobatics, navigation and instrument flying. The night flights were all done with visual cues, so that was not really instrument flying. Since there was no better way to learn, we went up with the instructor, and he covered the canopy with a hood so we couldn't see. It was primitive, but effective. In a few weeks we were all flying easily on instruments.

I went to Eglin Air Force Base in Florida for gunnery practice. There was an air-to-air gunnery range where we fired at a target towed by another aircraft. In other exercises, we strafed moving and fixed targets on the ground.

These planes had synchronized machine guns that fired through the rotating propeller. On one run, as I fired my weapon I heard a distinctive ping sound. When I landed, the mechanics checked the propellers. There was a nice thirty caliber hole in the prop blade. It was not an unusual occurrence because the mechanics knew exactly what to do.

First, they cleaned the bullet hole with a file by sanding until it was a neat, circular hole. Then, they drilled a neat, circular hole of exactly the same size in the diametrically opposite propeller blade. You could always tell when a prop had been shot by the distinctive whining sound it made when the props were turning. I asked how many holes there had to be before they changed propellers, but got only an incredulous look from the chief mechanic.

Graduation was near and the topic of conversation among the students concerned our rank. Upon graduation, we would no longer be aviation cadets. We would either be flight officers, similar to army warrant officers, or second lieutenants. I had no idea which title I should have printed on my graduation cards.

We were notified the day before our graduation which rank we would hold. At six o'clock the next morning, we assembled in the base theater. When the commander entered the call, "Cadets Attention," we all rose and repeated the oath that swore us in as officers and gentlemen. When were finished, the command was, "Officers be seated." The vast majority of us were second lieutenants, with relatively few flight officers.

After graduation, we stayed on for P-40 training before going on to our duty squadron. The Curtiss P-40 had a long, heavy nose that accommodated an inline engine. To practice for the new plane, I was required to land the AT-6 trainer from the instructor's back seat, simulating the extra length of the P-40's nose.

One afternoon, a group of us were studying the mockup cockpit of the P-40 in the hanger when the commanding officer came in.

"White, do your check out," he commanded.

Turning to a subordinate instructor who was getting ready to go home for the day, he told him to take me up. The lieutenant, who had other plans, was furious. He tried his best to get out of it, but the captain was insistent. Grabbing his gear, he stormed outside.

As we walked toward the plane, he said, "This is a done deal!"

He flunked me! I thought I did an adequate job with the flight, but he flunked me. I still think it was because he was angry, and not because of the job I did. That thought was vindicated on the next check-out flight.

This time, I had a different instructor. We took off and were flying a designated course that would eventually lead us back for the landing check.

"Do an Immelman," my instructor said.

The Immelman aerobatic maneuver is a classic of aerobatic flying. It involves a standard half loop. As the aircraft inverts at the top of the loop, the maneuver is concluded by a roll back to level flight while keeping the nose on point. At the top of my loop, I did a half roll out instead.

"Why did you do that?" the instructor asked me.

"It allows for a better airspeed, and when I'm in a dogfight, I want all the airspeed I can get," I replied.

"Good. I like that, White. Let's do it again," my instructor said.

I repeated the modified Immelman, and we started for home. Back at the airfield, I made several good landings.

"I have no idea why you failed your last flight. You did everything just right. You pass," he said with a smile and a handshake.

I didn't answer his question about my failure or try to make an excuse by blaming his impatient fellow instructor. That would be like talking back to an upperclassman, and I'd already done one punishment parade. I didn't need another one. Besides, now I could fly the P-40 solo. After ten hours in it, I felt like John Wayne in *The Flying Tigers*.

On one of my last flights before assignment, I was in the air with a fellow student who was acknowledged as the best pilot among us. We engaged in a mock dogfight, and I outmaneuvered him and put my P-40 on his tail. He looped, rolled, dived, and barrel rolled, but I stayed right with him. He even blasted over Craig Field at three thousand feet, which was definitely against the rules, and he still couldn't shake me! And, if he couldn't shake me, I was ready for combat.

Now, we were truly finished. Our assignment orders would be coming any day. Once again my anxiety level went up. After all this, I still might not get a combat billet. My instructor, who was a first lieutenant, was always grousing about being here and not in combat. I could be assigned as a flight instructor, or as the commanding officer of a college detachment. I could be assigned to ferry fighters from depot to combat unit. There were a dozen jobs I could get that would never involve combat. Fortunately, I did not chew my fingernails, or I would have had none left.

Much to my relief, I was assigned to one of the two squadrons at Pinellas Army Airfield, St. Petersburg, Florida. The old strip is now the St. Petersburg International Airport near the pier. Here we were to train with sixty to eighty more hours of flight time, and then we would be sent overseas. I had about thirteen hours in my P-40 when word came that one of the St. Petersburg squadrons would be receiving the new P-51. There were not enough for both of us, so one squadron would continue in the P-40.

My squadron was elated to find we were the chosen ones. Once again, I was in the right place at the right time. Later, I asked my commanding officer how we were lucky enough to get the new planes. How had they decided which squadron it would be?

"It was luck, White," he said. "I got together with the other squadron commander, and we flipped a coin. I called heads, it came up heads."

When I recall all the times during training, and later on, in which my career could have gone in another direction, I have to believe that being in the right place at the right time was predicated by the fact that Someone way, way up there was watching over me.

The day the P-51s arrived, my squadron lined the airstrip as if we were a gang of five-year-olds waiting for Santa to come in the Thanksgiving Day parade. My plane landed and taxied toward the flight line, and I ran toward it to greet the ferry pilot and to thank him for bringing me the plane.

Rolling to a stop, the pilot cut the engine, slid back the canopy and removed the flight helmet. Long, flaming red hair tumbled down over distinctively feminine shoulders! An absolutely stunning young woman, a Woman's Auxiliary Service pilot, emerged from the cockpit as I stood there with my mouth open in surprise.

We flew the wings off the new planes in the next few weeks. There was gunnery practice at air and ground targets, strafing, bombing and aerial combat. And there were extra hours just to fly and familiarize ourselves with the aircraft.

When I was up there alone, I did a lot of maneuvers I felt might be useful in combat. Combat was always on my mind. It was going to be my job, and there was no room in it for failure. I always felt luck and practice went hand in hand, and the more I practiced, the luckier I would be.

The P-51 had great spin characteristics, and I was easily able to break the spin when I practiced it. I mentioned it to some of the other pilots who were surprised that I was doing those kinds of things while flying alone. But they soon got on the bandwagon and were trying all sorts of things in the air.

One day, as we talked about spins, one of the other men asked, "Have any of you done a loop yet?"

Most of us replied in the negative. It was a truly elemental maneuver, and we just hadn't thought about it.

"Well, when you do, be sure to fly it all the way around the loop. If you don't, you can get into trouble," he said authoritatively.

The next time I was in the air, I decided to do a loop. Following the advice of the ready-room sage, I flew the plane through the loop and was almost to the top of the loop when near disaster struck!

I started the loop and was slightly past vertical going straight up when my speed began falling off rapidly and the aircraft stalled. When it did, the nose went forward like a shot. In an instant I was looking straight down at the earth, and in the next straight up at the sky as the aircraft began to tumble end over end! Despite my mild disorientation, I knew I had to act immediately, or I could lose the airplane.

Recalling the event now, I realize I must have been frightened, but I cannot recall that emotion. All I can remember is thinking that if I could just regain airspeed, I could regain control of the situation. I quickly outlined a plan of action in my mind.

First, I cut the engine's power to idle. Next, I got control of the control stick, which had been wrenched out of my grasp and was rattling wildly back and forth in the cockpit from the conflicting pressures and tumbling motion of the aircraft. Now, I was ready.

My view at that moment was the sky. I waited for what seemed like an eternity, but was in reality only seconds, for the horizon to come into view. When it did, I applied full power, with a force that would have caused Lieutenant Bone to smile, and the nose of the airplane kept coming down until I was in almost a vertical dive! As the airspeed increased, I slowly reduced the power and eased out of the dive into level flight.

Once again, the graduation present from my civilian flight instructor had paid life-saving dividends. I was high enough when I started the loop that I had the clearance to take a tumble and then a power dive and still not hit the ground.

Then, I breathed for the first time since the aircraft began to tumble and flew around for several minutes until my heartrate returned to normal. Analyzing what had just happened led me to the conclusion that I was the dummy. It was my fault that the stall occurred and reminded me that you cannot be too casual about anything you do "up there."

It was by far the scariest moment in my flying career to date. But it gave me a confidence I couldn't have achieved any other way. It taught me that I could handle the unexpected if I kept my wits about me.

For the most part, this period of my training was enjoyable. I was doing what I loved, surrounded by good men of like persuasion. Life was good.

One of the activities that proved to be both recreation and training was skeet shooting. I had limited experience with firearms, and I relished the opportunity to get more. Practically, it taught us about leading a target, a useful skill in a dogfight, and I got to be a pretty fair skeet shooter.

One afternoon, I had just finished reloading my shotgun and was waiting for the soldier in the skeet shack to get ready to send up the next round of targets when a real bird flew into the air. In a reflex action, I swung up the shotgun, led the bird perfectly and blew him out of the sky.

Immediately, I was filled with remorse. Why had I done it? What possessed me? I walked over to the shattered carcass and picked it up. Holding the dead bird in my hands, I was filled with disgust. After that experience, I never developed much of a taste for hunting. In the sky over Germany, any bird I shot would be trying to shoot me. That would be different. To me, killing the defenseless bird was a senseless act of cruelty.

In those days, downtown St. Petersburg was only a fraction of what it is today. It was a sleepy little village some distance from the airfield. Now, the airfield is engulfed by the modern city. Liberty was tame in St. Pete, but I enjoyed it just the same.

One night, near the end of training, it was my turn to be Aerodrome Officer. When on duty, you were in charge of the airfield and its operation from the end of the work day until the next morning. We all took turns doing it. The job included checking the control tower and handling any problems the night crew might encounter. A jeep went along with the job because we were also required to check the runway landing lights, and to periodically drive the length of the runway to be certain it was free from obstruction.

This particular night, the duty jeep was in the motor pool for repairs, and I was issued a dump truck. I can still see the looks on the faces of the gang in the mess hall when I wheeled in and parked the huge hulk in the duty officer's space.

Later that night, June 5, 1944, I was asleep on the duty officer's cot when there was a pounding on my door.

"Yes, come in," I called out.

An enlisted man stuck his head in the door and in an excited tone said, "Sir! Sir! It's happened! They've invaded Europe!"

I thanked him for the news, and he left. Instead of the elation I should have felt, I felt cheated and a little angry that I wasn't there to be part of such an historic day.

"Damn it!" I said out loud to the empty room. "They didn't wait for me. I've got to get there before it's over!"

Finished with this segment of training, I was transferred to Fort Dix, New Jersey, to await orders to go overseas. The transfer was accompanied by a two-week pass, so I went home to New York to see my parents.

My folks were happy to see me, and overall it was an enjoyable visit, but the atmosphere was tense. War news was everywhere. They knew the danger I would be in, and that concern was etched in their faces. I knew that danger was real, too, and I did my best to remain cheerful. I admit, it was a relief to go back to duty.

At Fort Dix, we learned shipboard manners, how to climb ladders and landing nets. We were issued a Colt .45 pistol, and had time to practice with it. I got quite proficient at the strip, clean, grease and reassemble routine.

In time, we were assigned to our troop transport, *The Empress of India*, a British liner that was part of a troop convoy headed for England. I had never been aboard a ship any larger than the Staten Island ferry, and I didn't know quite what to expect.

I was fortunate enough to be assigned a stateroom with two other young officers. We had free reign to explore the ship, and when I saw how the enlisted men lived in the lower decks, like sardines in a can, I was grateful for my accommodations. We spent a lot of free time in the officer's wardroom where there was scuttlebutt, a continuous card game, and an occasional movie.

There were no rough seas and the cruise was uneventful. With the exception of a few submarine drills (fortunately we never encountered any), the week-long voyage was tedious, the boat being able to move only as fast as the slowest vessel in the convoy. At this stage of the war, German U-boat activities had been crippled and convoys were much safer than they had been earlier in the war.

We landed at the Firth of Clyde in Scotland and disembarked. Next, we boarded a train for the trip to Stone, England. When the train made a stop near some workmen, an interesting exchange took place.

"What are you chaps doing here? Don't you know the war's all but over," they said derisively.

The words stung me and made me angry. But they proved far from prophetic. World War II was anything but over.

Stone was a replacement depot, where pilots were sequestered until a replacement was needed in a squadron. Fortunately, I was only there for five days. It was an awful place! The quarters were squalid and the climate less than hospitable. To top it off, on my first trip to the mess hall, my hat was stolen!

At last the orders came, and I boarded the train for the town of Steeple Morden, in East Anglia. There, I joined one of the three squadrons of the 355th Fighter Group. Mine was the 354th Squadron.

As I settled in, I realized that I was a brand new second lieutenant in the Army Air Corps. My horizon was no longer short. It was as limitless as the sky I flew in every day. I had realized the dream every parent has for their child. My lot in life could be better than theirs. All I had to do was make the most of that opportunity. And that opportunity was here. Training was over. It was time to go to war.

Chapter 3

My First War

After settling into our Steeple Morden quarters, the first order of business was check-out flights in the squadron's P-51s. New men did not have their own plane at first, so I was assigned to planes that were not scheduled for combat duty that particular day. It was good to be back in the air. I thought that I might be a little nervous the first few times up, but on the contrary, I felt no nerves at all. I was ready to get at it. It's great to be twenty and immortal!

They always started us newbies on a milk run to get our feet wet. Mine was escorting bombers to some U-boat pens in the south of France. It was a short flight with no deep penetration into hostile territory. The Luftwaffe wasn't really a threat, and we went along more as a precaution.

Despite the ease of the mission, I was thrilled to be in the air with those bombers. It was an impressive sight as they flew along in formation. Watching them drop their bomb loads gave me a sense of accomplishment. This is what I came for, to do my part to help end the war. We never broke formation the entire mission, and the round trip was without incident.

Back in the flight room, my brashness, which retrospectively was quite embarrassing, came to the fore when I said, "I thought there would be some flak. I heard all this talk about flak, and there wasn't any at all."

"Just wait. When you go deeper into enemy territory, you will be sufficiently entertained," one old hand said with a rueful smile.

In truth, my combat experience was tame compared to the battles that had already been fought. Earlier in the war, the German fighters had come up *en masse* to attack the bombers that were pounding Germany's heartland. Our guys did well, so the Luftwaffe I faced was a shell of the proud German air force that started the war.

On missions, there were sixteen planes in our squadron, divided into four groups of four planes each called flights. The flight leader flew in the center with his wingman on his right. Next to him was the deputy-flight leader with his wingman on his left. I started as a wingman, as all new pilots did. It was the wingman's job to be the eyes and ears of the leader. Our job was to protect the leader's blind spots while he attacked the primary target. When a combat situation occurred, the flight frequently broke into two groups of two. Each group of two, the leader and his wing man, was called an element.

While I was still very new, and flying other people's planes, I was assigned to the plane belonging to the squadron's ace pilot. Each time a pilot downed or destroyed an enemy plane, a swastika was painted on the side of his plane. This plane was loaded with the twisted crosses.

One day, I drew that plane for a routine escort mission. While flying at about twenty to twenty-five thousand feet, I had my first and only opportunity for an aerial dogfight. As we flew along, the alert was sounded, and I looked up. Above us was a group of Focke-Wulf Fw-190 German fighters. I was mesmerized by the Maltese crosses on their wings. The planes rolled over and dived toward the bombers. I turned to look at my leader. My Maltese cross hypnosis had lasted too long. To my horror, my flight leader was gone!

I had often wondered what it would be like to meet the enemy in the sky for the first time. Once I thought, *Well Bob, I hope the first time you meet the enemy you won't be running into a great Luftwaffe ace.*

But I was determined to be the aggressor. The sight of the enemy had

A group photograph of some pilots from the 354th Fighter Squadron during World War II.

pumped me so full of adrenaline that my senses were working in overdrive. I jammed the throttle to full power and literally jumped on the first German aircraft I could find.

Recovering my senses, I frantically looked around for my element leader, but couldn't find him so I joined the fray and locked onto a target. My target dove for the deck and I stayed hot on his tail. Maximum designed flight speed in the P-51 was five hundred five miles per hour, and my air speed indicator pegged during the dive.

As we headed down, I tried to figure out the new gun sight that was in this plane. It was a brand new one that I had never seen before. I had been briefed, so I knew how it was supposed to work, but figuring it out during a combat dive proved to be a challenge.

The new sight was a circle. By twisting the throttle grip, the circle expanded or contracted. The object was to center the target aircraft in the center of the circle and close it down until the enemy aircraft's wingtips touched the edges of the circle. When that happened, the six fifty-caliber machine guns on the P-51 would be centered on the target and reduced the importance of leading the target. It seemed good, in theory.

At tree-top levels we blasted along at four hundred miles an hour, my 1,650-horsepower Rolls Royce/Packard Merlin engine burning fuel at a prodigious rate. I thought I had the sight figured out and opened fire. Either I miscalculated, or didn't use the sight properly because I could see my rounds stitching a nice pattern on the ground behind the Fw-190. Cursing my ineptness, I tried to draw another bead on the fleeing German.

Alerted by my gunfire, my adversary did the expected thing. He pulled suddenly up, and banked hard in a turn right back at me. I had no shot, and we passed dangerously close to each other.

By the time I mastered my surprise and turned my plane around, the German was roaring away at four hundred miles per hour in the opposite direction. I knew that I'd never catch him. Besides, the mad dash across the treetops had taken me dangerously close to the outskirts of Berlin. Fuel consumption was a problem. I needed enough gas to get home. Going back was the better part of valor. Disappointed, I climbed off the deck and started to look for the rest of my flight. Where were they?

As I climbed I realized I had just learned important lessons about aerial combat. At four hundred plus miles an hour, things happen quickly. In the blink of an eye, my flight leader was gone, and I could never find him. And with a dozen or so airplanes buzzing around the sky as if they were angry hornets and all shooting at each other, it gets real confusing. To stay locked on a single objective too long could lead to burning too much fuel, getting too deep into enemy territory, getting lost or have someone sneak up behind me. But by far the most important lesson, one I already knew, was to be prepared. I hadn't been prepared with the gun sight and it cost me an opportunity to down a German fighter.

When I was a little higher, through the broken clouds I saw a number of scattered parachutes floating toward the ground. I wasn't sure if all of them were ours, but at least some of them were. I prayed, for his sake and mine, that none of them belonged to my element leader. Those poor devils were on their way to an unpleasant reception on the ground, and I added another prayer for their safety.

Looking anxiously around, I spotted the distinctive blue noses of two P-51s to my right. When I got close, I realized they were not from my group, but I felt it would be better to fly back with them in case of trouble. Plus they were flying slower, which would allow me to conserve fuel, since blasting around the tree tops at full speed had sucked a considerable amount of petrol from my tank.

I signaled to them that I wanted to join up. They agreed, and I tried to fall in behind them. To my surprise, they slowed down and signaled I should take the flight leader's position. I wasn't sure why they were doing it, but I slid into the flight leader's spot as they suggested.

Flying along in the now peaceful skies, I analyzed their unusual behavior. Then it struck me like a thunderbolt. It wasn't me! It was the airplane. With all those kills painted along the fuselage, they thought they were flying with a real ace instead of a raw rookie who was still so wet behind the ears that I couldn't figure out how my gun sight worked, and had no idea where the man I was supposed to be supporting had gone. I tried contacting them on the radio to no avail.

When we reached the Dutch coast, the two good Samaritans waggled their wings and turned away towards their home base. My flight across Holland and the Channel gave me time to plan my apologies. Not only did I have to apologize to my element leader for losing him, I also had to take the humiliation of losing my German target. I discovered that eating crow took more courage than chasing Fw-190s!

Fortunately, or unfortunately, depending on one's point of view, that was my only aerial combat with a German fighter in the fifty-two combat missions I flew over Europe. It was disappointing to me in one sense, but it gave me an opportunity to do some real damage to a number of ground targets.

My commanding officer was Major Gordon Graham, later to become Lieutenant General Graham. He was a solid commander and a great guy as well. And he had his hands full with the Whites. In a squadron that had a total of twenty pilots, three of us were named White. Besides me there were Dick and Al White. Fortunately, we all survived the war.

Al White later became a test pilot at Edwards Air Force Base. He left there just before I arrived to join the test pilot group. After that he worked for North American Aviation Company and flew backup to Scott Crossfield on the X-15 project.

After the war, as a major, I was invited to the Air Force Academy to give a lecture. When I was finished, a man from the back of the room came down and stuck out his hand.

"Hi Bob," he said with a familiar grin.

It was Dick White! After the war he had obtained an engineering degree and worked for a company involved in the production of missile systems. It was really great to see him and reminisce about the old days. It also allowed us to trade information concerning the whereabouts of some of the other men in the squadron.

My squadron was part of the mighty Eighth Air Force. After the war, my fighter group would stay in contact with each other more than most, and in Savannah, Georgia, at the Eighth Air Force Museum, there is a replica of the memorial the British established for us in Steeple Morden. As many of us as health and finances allow still gather there for reunions. Sadly, each year there are fewer of us. Time has proved more lethal an enemy than a German fighter plane.

The majority of our combat experience involved the attack of ground targets. Trucks, trains, airfields, particularly those with planes on the ground, were all appealing targets. These were in some ways more difficult and hazardous than attacking aerial targets.

In a dogfight, the targets are visible, and it is easier to assess where the threats will come from. Occasionally an enemy plane might sneak up from behind, but a good wing man would come to your rescue, if he wasn't daydreaming when the fight started like I did that first time.

With ground attacks, you could never be sure what kind of defense the target had. Trucks were usually safe, but occasionally, one would be harboring hidden fifty-caliber machine guns or anti-aircraft weapons under their canvas shells. The same was true for trains.

In a train attack, the element leader and his wingman attacked the engine. The hiss of steam from an exploding engine made great newsreel footage. But the real damage was done by the other two planes in the element that began at the rear car of the train and raked its entire length with deadly fifty-caliber fire. When a train carried a flak or anti-aircraft battery or batteries on flatcars, it exponentially increased the risk to the pilots who were flying straight down the line of cars toward the enemy guns.

Airfields were routinely ringed with anti-aircraft weapons and machine guns. They were often skillfully camouflaged and could do a lot of damage.

In my flights, I was able to destroy four German planes on the ground as well as a number of trucks and other vehicles. Locomotives and train cars were also on my hit list. They didn't paint locomotive engines or trucks on the side of the plane like they did for aerial combat so I don't really know my final score. Besides, getting credit for a kill was not totally up to the pilot. I usually got the appropriate credit for creating a spectacular newsreel segment, but a stray kill here and there still went unreported.

Damage from ground fire was not uncommon, and aside from the stray bullet holes in my planes that were a common occurrence, two events stand out. The first time I destroyed an airplane on the ground, I came back with major damage to a wing spar. It deformed the main spar so badly that the wing had to be replaced. At the time I was hit, I didn't even realize it.

I was still the new guy when the policy was introduced that after we dropped off from bomber escort we were allowed to go hunting. My leader, Lt. Schultz from Pennsylvania, spotted an Me-109 at low altitude. Schultz roared down, got on his tail and blasted him with gunfire. The German pilot pulled up and bailed out. Flying in the proper supporting position for my leader, I was startled when the German's parachute opened directly in front of my plane. Turning abruptly, I barely missed the hapless fellow. As I passed perilously close to him, I'm not sure whose eyes were bigger, his or mine.

From my vantage point above and behind Schultz, I had also spotted a small grass field on which an Fw-190 and an Me-109 were sitting. I told Schultz about it.

"Take the lead," he said to me.

On my first attack, I set the Fw-190 on fire, and Schultz and I peppered the Me-109 with fifty caliber rounds. Focused totally on the targets, something that I had already learned was unwise, neither of us saw the lone gunner on the ground. We both took hits; me to the wing and Schultz to his cooling system.

Monitoring the plane's instruments provided the best clues to a serious hit. Engine temperature increases meant the cooling system had been damaged. We knew Schultz had a major problem when his engine temperature started up. My instruments told me my hit hadn't done anything major to my aircraft.

Praying the leak in Schultz's cooling system was a small one, we headed for home. While leaving an area after an attack, it was common for the leader and his wing man to fly around each other and inspect the partner's plane for damage. On a fly around, I couldn't see coolant flowing from his engine. If he lost too much coolant, the engine would overheat and seize, and the plane would have to be abandoned. It was an agonizingly long flight home, and we both breathed a sigh of relief when Steeple Morden came into view. We both landed safely, and headed straight for the local pub to celebrate.

As the Allies moved deeper into Europe, our bombers were tasked to bomb targets in western Poland. Since neither the bombers nor their fighter escorts had enough fuel for the return trip to England from these shuttle runs, as the missions were called, the planes flew on to land in eastern Russia. We got assigned to fly support for a shuttle run that was dropping supplies to Polish partisans in the Warsaw area where a major uprising was in progress.

These shuttle runs were also milk runs because there were no enemy contacts other than a little ground fire. We landed in a little village called Poltava in the Ukraine, while the bombers flew to another landing strip. It was a rural farming village with a grass airfield covered with pierced steel planking. I remember the distinctive sound it made when we landed on it.

The Soviets treated us like conquering heroes. Any Allied pilot who had a small Swastika kill marking painted on the side of his fuselage was lifted from the plane to the ground, toasted and clapped on the back amid smiles and handshakes. It was really great. Unfortunately we only stayed there overnight, so there wasn't much of an opportunity to visit. It didn't matter much because most of our hosts spoke little to no English, and I certainly spoke no Russian.

We slept on the ground in sleeping bags inside tents. It was not my most comfortable quarters of the war but adequate. After a hearty peasant breakfast, we climbed into our planes to rendezvous with the bombers for the second leg of the shuttle.

After linking up with the bombers, we flew over Zolnoch, Hungary, and they unloaded their bombs on a railroad marshalling yard. We flew on to Southern Italy and landed near the town of Foggia. This time, we stayed a little longer and were able to sample Italian hospitality for five days.

We slept in tents again, although this time we had cots. My flight mates were billeted in the tents along a wire fence that marked the perimeter of the compound and separated it from a public street. Just outside our tents were our showers, in full view of the passing pedestrians! I never did get used to standing there buck naked while amused Italians walked by saying things I couldn't understand. You can never convince me they weren't talking about equipment that wasn't Government Issue.

The trip home turned out to be quite interesting. We were to pick up the bombers near Rome and escort them back across France. When we arrived at the rendezvous point the sky was empty. After forty-five minutes of cruising and waiting, the sky was still empty. Finally, we were released to fly to England. The bombers would likely be safe, since we now controlled the skies over France.

During World War II, meteorology was still an emerging science. Our major source of weather information came from weather flights. A flight of four would take off and fly the proposed route of the attack and radio back the weather to the rest of us. It doesn't sound like exciting work, but these were some special pilots. They flew out, on their own, exposing themselves not only to ground fire but also to attack by the Luftwaffe in the days when control of the sky was still an issue over Europe. They gave us all the information they could, but later, when the attack force actually arrived over the target, the weather could have changed drastically from the time they reported it. What we wouldn't have given for Doppler radar.

There was no weather flight in front of us on the way to Steeple Morden, and the closer we got to the English Channel, the worse the weather got. Hitting the coast at wave top level, we flew across the channel thorough pea soup fog, wind and rain. To top it all off, my canopy kept threatening to steam up.

None of that really bothered me. I had flown in bad weather before and had always been up to the challenge. What did bother me were the fuel gauges. They were clanking on empty, and Steeple Morden was still out there somewhere in the driving rain.

My group rated missions by their "pucker factor." That is, the amount of pucker a particular situation placed on one's anal sphincter. The more dangerous the situation became, the higher the factor. This flight had suddenly become a pucker factor four out of four. I kept waiting for the telltale sputter of the engine that would be the prelude to an impromptu swim in the raging English Channel. Even on a good day, that wasn't a lot of fun, and thoughts of it now were enough to send chills up my spine.

My gauges stopped fluttering and settled on empty. That was a bad sign. The propeller could stop turning at any moment. Trying not to think about that, I furiously wiped the condensation from my windshield. Suddenly, through the gloom, I saw the air strip and dropped onto the runway on fumes. I was never so happy to be home in my life. That may have been the most hair-raising flight of my combat tour.

There were two common jokes about the Eighth Air Force. We were in England while the British Eighth Army was in Africa. The first joke was, the Eighth Air Force had better get out of town before the Eighth Army gets back. I can't imagine where that one came from. Didn't the British know that all of us had been thoroughly indoctrinated in the fraternization policy when we were Aviation Cadets?

With wartime production peaking and losses down, planes were streaming into England from the United States. That second joke was, if they send many more planes over here, this island is going to sink.

I was overwhelmed by the might of the Eighth Air Force one spotlessly clear day as we formed up over Holland. By this time, I was a flight leader, and as we settled into formation, the condensation trails of a thousand bombers heading west filled the sky.

"Look," I shouted excitedly to my wing man. "It's the road to Berlin!"

That sight made a lasting impression on me. At twenty years old, I was involved in an historic event as part of a mighty armada embarked on a noble cause. I was as proud of my country and my fellow pilots in that moment as I could ever be. The thrill must have paralleled that of a medieval young knight as the Crusaders started for the Holy Land. But, instead of a horse, my steel steed possessed the wings of the legendary Pegasus.

From element leader I gradually progressed to flight commander. At this stage of the conflict, there was little danger to the bombers except from flak. If there was no enemy interdiction along the way, the fighters were usually released to go hunting. Each of the squadrons' four flights set out as individual hunting parties looking for targets of opportunity. We found lots of them, and I think we did our part to shorten the war.

Things weren't all work in Steeple Morden. About six weeks before he was lost, the famous band leader Glenn Miller brought his band to the base for a concert. He was a really good guy. While his band belted out hit tunes, Glenn rolled dice backstage with the boys.

Glenn Miller's disappearance has sparked everything from the ridiculous to the sublime in the way of explanation. Some of the more popular are: that Miller had survived a plane crash and later died in a bordello; that he died of medical conditions in a hospital; that his plane was downed by friendly fire; and that he crashed due to bad weather. Theories abound but following facts are known.

Glenn Miller had remained in England while his band had gone on to prepare for a Christmas concert for the Supreme Allied Command and its troops at Versailles near newly liberated Paris. A chance encounter with a Lt. Col. Norman Baessell at the Milton East officer's mess on December 14th changed his plans. Baessell said he was flying to Paris the next day and offered Miller a ride. Miller accepted and the two spent the evening at the club indulging in Miller's favorite pastime, playing poker.

It was bitterly cold and densely foggy outside the morning of December 15, 1944, when Lt. Col Norman Baessell contacted pilot John Morgan, who confirmed that he would soon be arriving at the RAF field at Twinwood Farm near Northampton. Miller, who had been waiting in a car with a man named Don Haynes, quipped that Morgan would fail to locate the field as it was 24 degrees F and "even the birds were grounded"; he was forced to eat his words minutes later when an aircraft appeared through the dense fog and landed on the airstrip.

When the car reached the plane, a Noorduyn Norseman C-64, where

Morgan was waiting, Miller must have had some last minute doubts about flying into the fog in the single-engine plane when he muttered: "Where the hell are the parachutes?" In a twist of irony Baessell replied: "What's a matter with you, Miller, do you want to live forever?" Charles Lindbergh had made it across the whole Atlantic on one engine; their C-64 would only be going as far as Paris. Miller made no further comment. Don Haynes watched as the Norseman took off down the fog shrouded runway. He was the last person to see them alive.

I have my own feelings about what happened to Glenn Miller. Several military flights were cancelled that day because of the inclement weather. After my pucker factor four flight across the Channel in pea soup fog and driving rain, I feel certain that they suffered the fate of many overly optimistic pilots who try to fly through impossible weather. This is a common mistake many civilian pilots make today, with disastrous results. And remember, in those days, there were very few if any navigational aids to rely on.

On a brighter note, three small towns ringed Steeple Morden, Baldock, Hitchens and Letchworth. Liberty was commonly spent in one of the three villages. A common announcement over the loudspeaker in the mess hall was, "Bus now leaving for Baldock, Hitchens and Letchworth."

Once a month the tables were turned. Two trucks from our base would make the rounds of each of the three towns. A team of two would drive to one of the towns, park on a side street and open the tailgate. Returning to the truck cab, they would smoke a cigarette or two and then close the tailgate and return to the base. At the officer's club, they'd open the tailgate, and the wonderful English ladies would disembark for the monthly dance.

The girls loved it, and so did we. Rationing was rampant because of the war, but here, there was plenty of food and drink and dancing. Around midnight, the tailgates opened, the ladies disappeared into the trucks and they were gone until the next month.

We lived in Quonset huts on base, approximately twelve pilots to a hut. Occasionally, we had foreign exchange pilots with us. One of these was a British pilot who came to us after a considerable number of combat hours in a Spitfire.

The British Spitfire was a marvelous little fighter, but it lacked the range of the P-51 or the German planes it engaged in combat. When things got heavy, the Germans simply moved out of range of the Spitfires. So, this British pilot had no aerial kills to his credit. On one of his missions while flying our P-51, he shot down an Me-109 over Germany. To celebrate, and perhaps rub it in a little, he went back to visit his old unit, and they hoisted a few in honor of the occasion.

A few days later, he downed a second German plane, and went back to

Me as a first lieutenant in the cockpit of my 354th Fighter Squadron North American P-51D Mustang.

his old squadron again. This time, he bragged so vociferously about the kill and the performance of his P-51, that national pride surfaced, and he met some resentment from the British pilots.

"You get in your plane, and I'll get in mine and we'll meet at 10,000 feet. Then we'll see who's got the best airplane," an irritated British pilot said to him.

After a moment of reflection, the British pilot from our squadron said, "I'll meet you over the airfield at 10,000 feet if you'll meet me at 10,000 feet over Berlin."

That was the point. As fine a fighting machine as it was, the Spitfire could not match the nearly one-thousand-mile range of the P-51.

On September 17th, 1944, I was peripherally involved in the biggest single airborne assault in history. We were tasked to fly over Holland and search for any German air activity and to eliminate it while the 20th Fighter Group was tasked to take out the ground targets. There were no German planes to be found and as the fuel gauge pushed toward empty, we broke off and headed back across the Channel.

When we got to the Channel, I felt as if I were in Times Square going the wrong way on a one-way street. The sky was filled with bombers and transports, many with gliders in tow. It was indeed impressive. Later on, we found out that this was the beginning of Operation Market Garden, later popularized in the film *A Bridge Too Far*.

British General Montgomery had convinced the Allied High Command that airborne units could seize a series of bridges across the Rhine, with the linchpin being the bridge at Arnham. This would open a short route into the heart of Germany. That was Operation Market. The Garden portion involved a desperate eighty-mile run by tanks to support the paratroopers who would secure the bridges. The plan did not succeed because Allied intelligence failed to locate seasoned German tank units hiding in the area.

The 20th didn't fare as well as we did. They ran into heavy resistance and withering ground fire. In the after action report, their commander stated, "If the 20th Fighter Squadron is assigned any more flak busting duty, the 20th Fighter Squadron will cease to exist."

The Battle of the Bulge was the last of the German attacks that began on December 16, 1944, and lasted until January 28, 1945. It was the largest land battle of World War II. More than a million men participated in this battle; 600,000 Germans, 500,000 Americans and 55,000 British troops were fighting. And I was peripherally and disappointingly involved in that one, too.

Hitler built up large armies with newly built tanks, artillery and airplanes. The plan was to march 85 miles from southern Belgium to Luxembourg and launch a surprise attack on the Allies. He would attack during the Christmas season in the Ardennes Forest, in an invasion designed to split the American and British armies in half.

When the attack began, we were staged in Belgium to provide close air support for the reinforcements being rushed in to repel the Germans. Unfortunately, the winter weather was so severe that we were grounded, and after a few days orders came though telling us to return to our base in England, ensuring that we would miss one of the great battles of the war.

At this stage of the conflict, a fighter pilot's tour of duty was measured in combat flight hours. Three hundred and fifty hours of combat ended the tour and you rotated home for leave and then reassignment. I had completed my fifty-second mission and was a seasoned first lieutenant. For a twenty-year-old, the world was my oyster.

On February 22, 1945, I was called into the commanding officer's office. "Bob, you've been a good pilot here, and I want you to come back for a second tour with us," he said without preamble. "I also want you to know that I've put in the papers for your promotion to captain. I don't expect you to give me an answer right now. You think about it. But I do want you to lead the squadron on tomorrow's mission," he concluded.

If a pilot requested to return to his unit, and the unit commander made a similar request, the pilot would return to the unit after a thirty-day leave at home without going to the reassignment pool. It was truly an honor for me to be asked to return. A promotion and chance to lead the sixteen aircraft in the squadron were added bonuses, and I was nearly overwhelmed. This time I could fly in the lead position and would actually belong there. I was so excited; I could hardly sleep that night.

The following morning dawned bright and clear, and I led the flight over France into Germany. There, I unleashed my hounds for the hunt. Anything was fair game, and I led my squadron into southern Germany.

This is the ill-fated mission that began my story. Now you are completely up to date on the events that transpired to get me into this tree, but I still had to get down!

Chapter 4

A Guest of the Enemy

Now it was time to get out of that tree I told you about earlier. Swaying gently in the tree, I assessed my physical damage. A cut on the knee that wasn't bleeding badly, and a few bumps, bruises and abrasions were all I could find. Then, a chill ran up my spine. Was I already in the sight of some German sharpshooter's rifle? At the very least they would be scouring the countryside for me. I listened intently, but heard nothing out of the ordinary. Hope always springs eternal. Maybe, since my chute opened so close to the ground, I had gotten lucky, and they didn't see me jump. Either way, it was time to move.

As carefully and quietly as I could, I slipped out of my parachute harness and found a branch sturdy enough to support my weight. Since I had grown up in New York City, my tree climbing skills were severely limited. Despite that, I managed to make it to the ground with only a few more minor scrapes.

On the ground, I dropped to my uncut knee and listened intently. The only sound was the rustle of the wind in the trees. Still a bit shaken by my experience, I waited until my breathing normalized, and my pulse was no longer pounding. Unanswered questions flashed though my mind in a dizzying torrent. *What next? Which way should I go? Where are the Germans?*

Wait a minute, I chided myself. *Treat this just like you would if you were in a spin in your airplane. This is only a problem. Treat it like you do all the problems you face. Follow what you have been taught and handle one thing at a time*, I told myself.

Getting slowly to my feet, another realization dawned on me. This was not a movie, and I was not Errol Flynn. I might still be an immortal twenty-year-old kid, but I was still a nervous twenty-year-old kid who was down in enemy territory. I quickly decided there would be no, "Gun Fight at the O.K. Corral." My forty-five against a couple of German rifles would be the equivalent of bringing a knife to a gun fight. Since the weapon was pretty much useless, if I were captured, would I be better off without it?

Pondering my dilemma, I moved cautiously through the woods for the next few minutes in what I determined was an easterly direction until I came upon an obvious path or trail. Stopping to reconnoiter, I had a short debate with myself and decided the weapon should go. That may seem like an ill-advised decision, but I arrived at it rationally. First, if I was discovered by even a pimple-faced teenage German soldier with a rifle I would be out-gunned. So, a shoot out was out of the question. Second, since the Germans were part of the Geneva Convention, I would most likely be treated a little more humanely if I wasn't armed when they captured me, which was a real possibility.

Moving cautiously down the trail, I called on my hours of practice while in training and began to field strip this weapon for the last time. I deposited each piece of the pistol in a different place. One part went into a thicket, the next behind a tree and so on until all the pieces were scattered over a significant portion of real estate. If anyone found one of the pieces, it was highly unlikely they would ever find all of them.

I had barely finished disposing of the forty-five when I heard a noise. Someone was coming down the path. My pulse quickened as I desperately searched for a hiding place. Spying a likely thicket, I slipped into it as sound-lessly as I could, held my breath and waited.

An old, two-wheeled donkey cart rounded the bend. It was filled with German soldiers! Without moving a muscle, I watched as they moved past. They were mostly bored looking older men, which made sense to me. With the war turning against the Reich, both here and on the Eastern Front, the younger, able-bodied men would be at the front.

With the brashness of a youth who still didn't fully comprehend the peril of my situation, I thought, *I bet those guys would be scared to death if they knew I was hiding here where I could easily ambush them!* Then, I rationally thought, *What with?*

Reflecting on this period of my life, I realize now that this cocky attitude that I sustained all during my captivity could have proven disastrous for me. If I said I was never afraid or anxious, that wouldn't be the truth. But death was still an abstraction to me. It happened to old people. It happened to other people, but it wouldn't happen to me. In that respect, fighter pilots were much like race car drivers. We understood what we did was dangerous, and other people got hurt or killed, but it wouldn't happen to us.

Since in its infinite wisdom, the Army Air Corps never trained us to bail out of a crippled aircraft, it was not surprising that escape, resistance and evasion training had been equally avoided. That training would come years later in conjunction with another war. Still, I had sense enough to real-ize that I should keep moving. I needed to get away from the tell-tale para-chute that hung like a beacon from the tree in which I landed.

After what seemed like an eternity, but in fact was only an hour or so, I came to the edge of the woods. Before me stretched the green, open fields of Bavaria. Realizing that I would be a sitting duck out there, but also understanding I had no choice, I moved out across the field.

Walking for a number of anxious moments while constantly looking over my shoulder for the enemy, I came to a shallow depression. Plopping down in it, I knew I needed a plan. I think during the war, nearly everyone smoked. Pulling a pack of cigarettes from my flight jacket, I put one in my mouth but didn't light it. I wasn't sure if the flare of the match or the smoke would attract attention.

Which way to go? I was headed east, and that seemed reasonable. It would be suicide or certain capture to move toward the western front. The number of German patrols would increase geometrically in that direction. No, go east or southwest to Switzerland or France. Switzerland would mean internment, because they were a "neutral" country. I decided to just keep moving and see where it led me. At this point, I'd settle for either destination.

For the first time I felt the icy fingers of depression caress my spirit. My chances of walking across Germany to France undetected were astronomical. What would I eat? What would I drink? Were would I hide out for the night? Perhaps I should look for a German patrol and surrender to them. No, my American spirit and my Irish heritage wouldn't allow that. If I had to walk, then I'd walk. I was determined to get out of Germany.

Then I remembered that there was an escape kit in my flight jacket pocket. They were issued to all members of the flight crews of all Allied aircraft. I had no clue what was inside, but I figured this was as good a time as any to find out. Opening it, I found a number of things inside. There was a map of Germany, some money, a compass, fishing line, matches, cigarettes, all potentially useful items.

One of the items was particularly puzzling. It was a cardboard strip that had been covered with wax. Turning it over in my hand, I examined it carefully. When I was finished I still had no idea what it was or what it was for. I slipped it into my jacket pocket and opened the map. Before I figured out where to go, I had to figure out where I was! Time was wasting, and I needed to get moving.

"Achtung!" said a no-nonsense male voice from behind me, accompanied by the ratchet clatter or a rifle being cocked.

A German soldier stood staring down at me, the very large rifle in his hands pointed at the center of my chest. He was an older man, and his uniform bore the patch of Rommel's Africa Corps. I felt a tinge of relief that I had been captured by a combat tested veteran and not a trigger-happy teenager. A second younger man joined him.

"Pistola?" the older man asked me.

"Nein," I replied, exhausting all the German I knew at that point in my life.

He motioned for me to get to my feet. I moved carefully, so I would give him no reason to pull the trigger of his rifle, which remained sighted on my chest.

"March," he commanded, and gestured toward a small village visible in the distance.

We began to walk, and he periodically prodded me in the back with the muzzle of his weapon for emphasis. The walking was difficult and he made sure we moved along at a rapid pace. For the first time, the thought that I might actually die crossed my mind. Why it chose that instant to surface, I wasn't sure. A number of my problems had already been solved. I wouldn't need to worry about which way to go, what I would eat or where I would sleep.

I finally came to the conclusion, *He's going to shoot me in the back!* With that in mind, I whispered the first of many prayers I would utter over the ensuing months.

"Please God, if he is going to shoot me, let me face him. I don't want to be shot in the back in a Bavarian field like some coward who was running away," I whispered.

He didn't shoot me. Instead, he marched me into a small farming village whose name I never did learn. As we passed the civilians on the street, some of them stopped to glare at me while their curious neighbors peered at me from the windows and doorways of their homes. Stopping in front of a two-story structure that served as their headquarters, he motioned me inside.

Most of the soldiers were on the second floor. Two local policemen were in the downstairs office. I was ordered to sit on the floor with my back to the wall. I complied.

To my surprise, no one asked me any questions at all either initially or the whole time I was here. My guards gave me a cursory search. They found the items from my escape kit, including the strange cardboard strip. The Africa Corp veteran took it from me and snapped it between his powerful fingers. A piece of hacksaw blade fell out! I was surprised. He wasn't. But the incriminating blade treated me to a thorough strip search. I can only imagine what it might have been if I still had my pistol.

In a while, a car drove up and stopped outside. The younger of my original captors stood on the sidewalk surrounded by a pack of curious young boys. My guard ushered me unceremoniously out the door and toward the nondescript black sedan. As I passed the children, I winked at one of the boys who smiled back at me.

Our exchange prompted a venomous scowl from my captor at both me and the smiling child, and then he slammed the car door shut. He continued to glare at me through the window. His action got my Irish up and my brashness surfaced. *Go ahead and glare, you S.O.B. I'll get you later,* I thought. Exactly how I was going to carry out that threat had yet to be considered.

A little over an hour later, the car arrived at a prison for Royal Air Force prisoners. Here, I received my first real interrogation.

The camp commandant was an army major who bore a striking resemblance to the German actor Eric von Stroheim. I was ushered into his office where he sat behind a small desk. Other camp officers, who were seated behind him in a row of straight backed wooden chairs, stared at me as if I were a prized aquarium specimen. Again, these officers were all older men. From the way they studied me, I got the impression that they did not see many Americans. That was probably the case because this was a prison for British flyers.

"Who are you?" the commandant questioned, through another officer who interpreted in perfect English, tinged with the lilt of a British accent.

I responded with my name, rank and serial number, as I would for every question I was asked. It was my standard answer. He asked me a number of other questions, but I responded only with my standard answer. I wasn't about to tell him anything.

"All right then," he said with a disgusted snort as he shoved a sheet of paper toward me. "Sign your name, rank and serial number on this."

"I will not," I responded indignantly. "If I do, you'll fill in the rest of the page with a bunch of things you'll claim I told you. No, I won't do that."

Where did I find that kind of gall? This wasn't the streets of New York, and this wasn't a liveried chauffer who had just wrecked my bicycle. This man wore the uniform of a German officer and had the power of life and death over me. When I look at the way I behaved throughout my captivity, maybe I *was* immortal at twenty. Later in my life, I certainly knew I wasn't.

His face scarlet with frustration, the major gave me an index card sized piece of paper and said, "Write it on this then."

I signed the card.

"We have treated you well," the major said. "We didn't have to. There was an attack on a train by your aircraft and many civilians were killed or injured. Sentiment in the village is much against you."

Eyeing him coldly, I replied in an even tone of voice, "I'm truly sorry that civilians were among the casualties. But, you know, I was in England when your V-2 rockets were raining down from the skies. Seldom did they hit anything of military value. Usually, it was only civilians who died in those explosions."

The major looked at me for a long moment, but didn't respond to my challenge. Instead, he nodded to one of the enlisted men in the room who marched me off to solitary confinement.

Had this been a Japanese prison camp, I wouldn't have gotten off so easily. They were far less hospitable to downed fliers than were the Germans. My insolence with a Japanese officer would have likely gotten me beheaded, or worse.

After a cold night in a squalid cell, I was rousted the next morning by two older German soldiers who spoke absolutely no English. They took me to the village railroad station, and we boarded a train that I ascertained would take us to Munich.

I still had no clue as to exactly where I was, and the train station carried no identifying signs. Later I would learn it was in the area of Ingolstadt. Then, I only knew that I was somewhere in the area of southern Bavaria.

My minders were friendly enough, and when we were seated on the train, they opened the briefcases they were carrying. Inside were their lunches, consisting of wurst, bread and cheese. They shared them with me, and I really appreciated it. They also tried to converse with me.

"Sprechen sie Deutsch?" one of them asked me.

"Nein," I said, falling back on my extensive German repertoire.

"Ya, nein," he replied with a grimace.

I was tempted to ask, "Sprechen sie English," but since they had shared their lunch with me I chose respectful silence. And, after all, it was their country.

That didn't deter them in their attempts to communicate. We continued to converse in a combination of grunts and pigeon English. It helped to pass the time.

For example, one of them looked at his wedding ring and nodded to me with a questioning look on his face. I shook my head and repeated my one-word German vocabulary.

The train ride was monotonous, and I was tired. I fell asleep. I awoke as the train approached the outskirts of a large city. There was bomb damage everywhere, and the closer we got to the centrally located train station, the worse the devastation. This time, the railway station was marked. I was in the battered city of Munich.

At the station, my friendly guards transferred my custody to a no-nonsense German in full uniform. He asked me in German if I spoke his language, and when I responded in the negative, he told me in reasonable English to sit on the floor. I was beginning to wonder if I would ever be asked to sit in one of the empty chairs.

Following a short wait, I was taken to an interrogation center near the railway station. It was not far, and I relished the opportunity to stretch my legs.

It really wasn't much of an interrogation, and I again responded to all their questions with my standard answer. Realizing he wasn't going to get a lot more out of me, he glanced through my papers given to him by the older men who brought me here. Then he ordered me back to the train station.

As I walked back toward the station, I noticed a work detail along the side of the road. Coming closer to them, I realized that they were Americans. I waved and shouted.

"Hi guys. Keep your chin up. It'll be over soon," I told them confidently to the scowl of my minders who didn't understand what I had said. Later that evening, I was back on another train.

We got off the coach in the middle of the night in the city of Augsburg. There was a Red Cross center at the station, and we went in. I had no watch, but as best I could calculate it was near midnight.

"Soup ... bread?" my captor asked me in German, and I understood well enough to answer in the affirmative. When my guard went to order our rations, I noticed another German man asleep with his head on the table. It was one of the two minders who brought me to Munich. What a coincidence. I woke him up. He seemed glad to see me, and when my new guard came back, he was surprised to see us talking to each other in our pigeon German.

"Where are we going?" I asked.

They exchanged a few words in German and my new guard said, "Frankfurt."

"Frankfurt on the Oder or Frankfurt on the Main?" I asked them.

I had studied enough maps of Germany to know there were two German towns with the same name situated along different German rivers, the Oder and the Main.

Startled looks crossed both of their faces. They were surprised that I knew that.

"Frankfurt on Main," my guard said.

With this information, I was certain of my final destination. It was Oberussel, Germany, where American pilots were taken for classic interrogation. We had been briefed on the town and the prison compound. Oberussel was also the home of the Leika camera, one of the best cameras of its time. After some time, another train arrived, and I said goodbye to my old guard and boarded the train with my Munich guard. Since there was no place to go, my guard left me standing in the rear of the train in the aisle outside the compartments.

An older soldier caught my eye and came over to me. He spoke to me

Dulag-Luft. Kriegsgefangenenkartei.	Gefangenen-Erkennungsmarke Nr. 0430	Dulag-Luft Eingeliefert am: 27.2.45 L

NAME: W H I T E

Vornamen: Robert M.

Dienstgrad: 1/lt. Funktion: Pilot

Matrikel-No.: 0-823 186

Geburtstag: verweigert Aussage

Geburtsort:

Religion: kath.

Zivilberuf:

Staatsangehörigkeit: USA

Vorname des Vaters:

Familienname der Mutter:

Verheiratet mit:

Anzahl der Kinder:

Heimatanschrift:

verweigert Aussage

Abschuß am: bei: Flugzeugtyp:

Gefangennahme am: 22.2.45   bei: S-Deutschld.

Nähere Personalbeschreibung

Figur: mittel

Größe: 1,78

Schädelform: lang

Haare: d-braun

Gewicht: kg 68

Gesichtsform: lang

Gesichtsfarbe: gesund

Augen: blau

Nase: gerade

Bart:

Gebiß: gut

Besondere Kennzeichen:

Rechter Zeigefinger:

PRISONER of WAR 1945

0-823186   0-823186

Front   Profil

My official German prisoner of war record.

in very good English and told me he had lived in the United States and worked in Chicago. As we talked, my radar antenna went up. Was he a plant? Would he pump me for information? Could he be SS or Gestapo, posing as a friendly soldier? I decided to be very careful about what I said to him.

After a few minutes of small talk, the man looked furtively around us to see who was listening. When he realized nobody was, he said, "The only mistake I made was coming back to Germany."

That was probably the truth, and I feel certain he was innocuous. But I still didn't let my guard down or tell him anything I shouldn't. It could all have been part of his game. As the train rolled along through the picturesque farm county of Germany, I was standing in the aisle outside a row of compartments looking out of the window. Since there was no place for me to go on this German troop train, my minders allowed me freedom to roam. The train began to slow, and came to a stop beside an ancient stone wall. It obstructed my view of everything else.

The train window was open, and I could have easily jumped off the train. But where would I go? What would I do? I'd have my old problems of direction, food and lodging and the like and a chance of recapture of nearly a hundred percent. My thoughts were interrupted by an SS major who walked toward me with a look of disdain on his face.

Suddenly, the look on the major's face changed from disdain to fear, and he shouted in a voice filled with panic, "Raus, Raus!"

Grabbing me by the shirt, he literally pushed me out of the window of the train and dove out after me. Stunned by my impact with the ground, and bewildered by the major's bizarre behavior, I was trying to sort things out when I heard a sound, the hum of familiar aircraft engines. Two P-51s were approaching the train.

There was a tremendous roar as the two Packard-built engines blasted across the train at tree top level. The sound was so loud that it nearly drowned out the chattering machine guns of the aircraft.

Mixed with the receding sound of the aircraft was the incessant whine of bullets as they tore through the trains and ricocheted off solid objects. The whine was accompanied by the sound of breaking glass. In a heartbeat it was over, almost before I had time to be frightened.

Then, an awful moment of silence occurred until it was broken by the muffled whimpers, groans and cries of pain of the wounded. I had a brief view of the war as the combat soldier saw it, up close and personal instead of my usual view high above it all. It was an experience I will never forget.

The major and I huddled under the train as I waited for the rest of the attack. If this was more than a hunting party, other planes would follow these two. If not, the two marauders should make at least another pass. The attack never came. As my mind cleared and the adrenaline rush subsided, I understood why. This was a troop train. That much was obvious to me when I first boarded it and saw the entire train was full of uniforms. It carried an anti-aircraft weapon on a flat car to discourage fighter attacks like the one we had just experienced. When the P-51s ran into resistance, they were instructed to make only one pass and break off the attack. If I were leading an attack on this train, I'd have called off a second pass as well.

Badly shaken by being on the receiving end of the attacks, I crawled under the train to the side away from the stone wall. I had a new respect for the damage I had done to German trains, and for the people who were in them.

Now I was in a situation I had no idea how to handle. I owed a debt of gratitude to an unlikely source. An SS major, who was a member of the most elite and ruthless organization in the German military, had just saved my life. As I daydreamed about nothing in particular, he had heard the sound of the approaching P-51s and recognized the danger. Once he recognized it, he acted swiftly and decisively to save both our lives. He could have bailed out of the window and left me to my fate, but he didn't. Once again, the Master Pilot "way up there" had guided me to a safe landing.

When I stood up on the other side of the train, the sight that greeted me was overwhelming. A farmer's field, much like the one I had seen when I came out of the woods and in which I had been captured lay before me, this time filled with soldiers in German uniforms. It was a sea of grey and black.

Watching them cautiously get to their feet while anxiously searching the sky for more planes gave me more time to reflect on the attack. Things had happened so quickly. After the major had pushed me out the window, I had behaved instinctively rather than giving the situation much thought.

The soldiers were getting up now and coming toward the train. The SS major was gone. I was alone. I had no idea where my guard was, or if he was still alive. Escape was perhaps possible but out of the question despite the chaos as the dead were identified and taken away and the wounded cared for. Since I was a flyer, those Germans injured in the attack might take reprisals against me. It was in my best interest to be as inconspicuous as I could be.

Loitering at the back edge of the train, I continued to scan the field. To my surprise, I spotted an American uniform among the mass of humanity staggering out of the field. To my delight it was Lt. Wilhite, who had been in my flying school class.

Wilhite had gone into multi-engine training and had been flying P-38s out of Italy when he was shot down. After a brief exchange, we separated, and I never saw him again. To this day, I regret not asking him how in the world he was able to bail out of a P-38 with its boxed configuration without breaking his neck. I knew how much trouble I had getting out of a P-51 which was much more bail-out friendly. Maybe P-38 pilots got more than a manual.

When the wounded had been loaded on board, I went looking for my guard. When I found him, he had his back to me. Tapping him on the shoulder, he spun around. He seemed genuinely glad to see me. I'm not certain if he was glad to find out that I was still alive, or if he had been contemplating the consequences to him of my escape if I had not been killed. From the warmth of his smile, I like to believe it was the former.

Not knowing what else to say, I said to him, "Boom-boom, ya!"

Nodding his head he replied, "Boom-boom, ya!"

When everyone was back on board, the train began to move, but as the adrenaline wore off, I felt exhausted. I had been shuffled around half of Germany without ever having a chance to really sleep. Finding a spot to lay down, I closed my eyes.

The remainder of the trip to Frankfurt was uneventful. When we arrived at the station, it was obvious that the city had been the target of multiple air raids. As had been the case in Munich, bomb damage was everywhere, particularly near the railway station. Rail traffic was critical to both sides during the war, so I wasn't surprised. A new guard accepted me in transfer at the Frankfurt station for the short trip to the Oberussal, an internment camp for American and RAF air crews.

On arrival, I was taken to a shower room where I had my first real shower since my capture. Next, they shaved all the hair from my body; head, pubic hair, everything. The reason was obvious. It reduced the chance of lice and tick infestation.

Earlier in the war, all detainees at Oberussal were kept in solitary confinement for long periods of time. The rooms were small, cramped and hot. This had led to the place's nickname, "the sweat box." Fortunately, they had stopped that before I arrived.

I was barely finished with my shower when a colonel, the camp's ranking POW, came in. After a brief introduction, he wanted a detailed report of what was going on in the world outside. The inmates were hungry for any tidbit I could give them about the war and things that were going on in the States.

Next, I was taken to a barracks and assigned a bunk. The barracks were in decent shape, with hardly any chinks in the wall to allow the weather in. We received two meals a day, and the guards were reasonably affable. I also was subjected to my first real interrogation here.

My interrogator's English was impeccable and the questions were the same. What base? What was I flying? What were my targets? I replied each time with my standard answer.

Toying with a loose-leaf notebook in front of him, my interrogator said, "I don't know why you wish to be so stubborn. Your comrades have been very open with us. We know what bases they all came from. The information is here in this book. Would you like to see it?"

Glancing at the pages, it was readily apparent to me what these were. They were the name, rank and bases of the captured bomber crews. Bomber pilots flew planes that identified their squadron, and some of their uniform markings were clues as well. From examining the downed aircraft, German intelligence could easily identify the bases of origin of the bombers. The men had not told him any more than I had. He just had more information to piece together on the bomber crews than he did the fighter pilots.

"I'm afraid that I have not been fooled by your little charade. Our men told you nothing. You were able to deduce all this on your own. Nice try," I said and shoved the book back to him.

His facial expression darkened until it resembled summer storm clouds, and he snapped the book shut in anger.

"You will have to speak to my commanding officer!" he said coldly.

With an insolent smile on my face I replied, "That's fine. I'd really like to meet him."

I'm surprised my attitude didn't get me a trip to the sweat box, but it didn't. I might not have fared as well if the interrogator had been SS or Gestapo. German military officers treated us decently for the most part. Besides, I was only a brash young first lieutenant, and I didn't have any information that they would be interested in anyhow. After a few more questions that I didn't answer, I was sent back to my barracks.

To my disappointment, I was never able to meet the camp commandant. In two weeks, I was under guard and headed back to the train station. This time, the trip would be less than hospitable. We were herded into boxcars that were jammed with other prisoners. It was crowded, but not as bad as the Jewish trains to the concentration camps. At least we had enough room to lie down on the dirty floor.

We left after dark and traveled all night. Near dawn we stopped in a railroad yard. The train had barely come to a stop before the bomber crews among us were craning to see thorough the cracks in the slats of the car. Nervous and frightened, they talked in hushed tones to each other.

Finally, one of them said, "This is a railroad marshalling yard! We've been pounding them for weeks. They have no way of knowing what's on this train. We're a prime target for our own planes."

That's why the area around the railroad stations in every town that I had been in had been so severely damaged. My thoughts returned to screaming engines, ricocheting bullets and the cries of the wounded. I shuddered to think what a block-busting bomb would do to our flimsy little car. We all felt better as darkness approached and the train began to move again. I was finally able to nap once we were well away from the station.

That was the only stop, and the next morning we arrived in the city of Nuremberg, the seat of huge, pre-war Nazi Party rallies. Because of its significance, the city had been the target of tons of Allied bombs, and everything was heavily damaged. Nuremberg would also be the scene of the famous post-war trials.

Emptying the box cars, the Germans formed us into roughly platoon-sized groups, and we waited on the street for some time. It was an uncomfortable situation as civilians with their city in ruins around them glared and hissed at us from across the street. Only the seemingly genetic German discipline kept things from getting really ugly.

Eventually, they marched us to the edge of town and the autobahn. It was a warm day and the five-mile march to Prisoner of War Camp Number 3-D seemed even longer. Fortunately, most of us were in reasonable shape, and everyone was able to make it to the camp.

Built originally as quarters for Nazi Party dignitaries who attended functions at nearby Nuremberg, it had been turned into a camp for Italian prisoners at the outset of the war. In February of 1945, it had been re-designated to imprison American officers.

The camp was in deplorable condition. Sanitation had been non-existent for some time, and lice, fleas and bed bugs infested everything. We each received one dirty blanket and were assigned a section of floor to sleep on.

There was a single barracks for the 139 of us. Behind it was a dilapidated latrine, and the entire area was surrounded by multiple layers of barbed wire. The camp commandant was another older man with grey hair. Still, he was a spit-and-polish Nazi all the way. Each morning he marched out of his office after *appel*, or roll call, to accept a stiff Nazi salute from the sergeant in charge who gave the morning report.

"One hundred and thirty-nine American officers present and accounted for," the sergeant barked in stiff military fashion.

The sergeant was, as were most of the other guards, older. He was a particularly good guy, and we joked with him during *appel*. A favorite was reporting someone missing when the missing man was really there. But the moment the commandant showed up, he became a model example of the Wermacht.

In the barracks, there was a single, long, picnic-style table. The few bunks that still survived lined the walls like shelves. Rations at the camp were meager. They consisted of one bean can of grass soup and one slice of bread per day.

Each morning, a two-wheeled, horse-drawn cart came into the compound loaded with loaves of bread. The loaves of bread were unceremoniously dumped on the picnic table in the barracks. There was one loaf for seven prisoners. Fortunately, we were disciplined enough to behave like civilized men when this happened.

One of the men had a small knife that had somehow gone undetected by the guards, and another had a deck of cards. These simple items became indispensable tools in the daily meal ritual. We formed up in groups of seven and stood drooling as the man with the knife meticulously measured each loaf into seven precisely equal pieces. Then he cut the bread.

When each group of seven had their prized slice safely in hand, the well-worn deck of cards was placed on the table. The seven of us cut the cards. The fortunate man with the high card got the crumbs that fell on the table when the bread was cut. When the table was clean, the next group of seven stepped forward.

Drinking water was not a problem. There was plenty of that. Coupled with our watery diet, it was fortunate there was a latrine where we could urinate near the back of the barracks. Although our average age was about thirty, we looked more like a gaggle of eighty-year-olds parading to the john in the middle of the night.

Two weeks of these starvation rations and the monotony of camp life drove morale into the dumps. Everyone had lost weight. Tempers were short. Skin rashes were rampant and diarrhea commonplace. The prisoners' commanding officer was a Canadian Air Force major. Gathering the entire company in the barracks he stood on the table to address us.

"Gentlemen, I don't have to tell you how bad things are. I have no idea how many of you are religious, but the only thing left for us to do is to pray," he said.

There were no atheists in foxholes, airplanes or Prisoner of War Camp Three that night. We bowed our heads, and 139 prayers ascended to way "up there." I knew the Great Pilot was looking after me, so I felt certain He heard our anguished cry for help.

The next morning we awoke to the sound of General Motors truck engines. Rumbling in from Switzerland was a convoy of Red Cross trucks filled with prisoner of war food parcels! Divine intervention? I believe it was.

There was one parcel for every two prisoners. Inside were cans of food, ration bars and cigarettes. They were supposed to last us for two weeks, and we hoarded every crumb. Of course, our gourmet soup and bread stopped.

With the food, our spirits were up, and they bounced even higher with the arrival of a new group of prisoners. Harkening back to colonial days, they were Indian troops who were part of the British Army. They had been captives for some time and had accumulated a lot of things. Pitching a tent in the middle of the compound, they brought the essence of Middle Eastern culture into camp by opening an ersatz bazaar. It was delightful, and so were they.

During the fourth week in camp, the Germans marched us all to the showers. There were four prisoners for each shower head. Water pressure allowed only a trickle of water to each shower. There was no soap, and the showers were drafty, but it was still like heaven. The down side of the experience was seeing each other naked. The weight loss, physical deterioration, rashes and sores each of us had suffered was painfully obvious.

Several nights later, we heard the sound of aircraft overhead. We could tell by the drone of their engines that they were RAF bombers, and they plastered the town of Nuremberg only five miles away. The rumble and flashes from the exploding bombs were readily visible from the barracks. It was like a magnificent fireworks display, and it lifted our sprits and kindled a spark of hope.

Next morning, we were certain that we could hear the sound of distant artillery fire. With D-Day behind us, and the Allies moving forward, could liberation be near? The camp was abuzz with rumor and speculation the rest of the day.

After a fitful night of sky watching, we were ordered to form up. Leaving everything behind but a single, thin blanket, we evacuated Prisoner of War Camp 3-D.

We walked south from early in the morning until well into the night. The Germans had accepted our plans to try and march twelve miles per day. Still, guys were dropping from exhaustion, and the string of marchers were scattered along the road for a mile or more.

Three of us formed a little group for the march. When the German guards finally called a halt to things, we fell out on the side of the road. We sought shelter under a tree by the edge of the road. The guards allowed us to build fires and forage for food, but most of us were too tired to do it. Rolling up in our blankets, nearly everyone fell into an exhausted sleep.

When we awoke the next morning, we were soaked, and the few fires that had been built were out. It had rained during the night, and we were so exhausted that none of us had awakened. Everything was saturated. Our clothes and blankets were wringing wet. Taking pity on us, the guards allowed us to build fires and dry out our wet things before resuming the march. It was a small thing, but a welcome blessing. In the early afternoon, we moved out heading, south again.

One of my threesome was a West Point graduate, and the other one was a chemical engineer. The engineer had studied German, and spoke the language reasonably well. As we walked along, he spoke quietly to a guard about an escape.

"Look, you can walk away with us. We are your prisoners and you're taking us to a new camp. We'll go toward the American lines. When we get there, they'll accept your surrender, and we'll tell them how you helped us. You can spend the rest of the war in safety, treated better than you can believe," he said. "Cigarettes, real coffee, anything you want," he added to sweeten the pot.

The guard was definitely interested. He listened intently to the proposition, and you could see the indecision in his eyes. As we talked with him further, the indecision was gradually replaced by fear. In the end, the fear won out. He refused to help us.

Later that day, word spread quickly along the line that we were approaching a German village that was a Red Cross food parcel distribution point. It was music to our ears. Everyone was hungry. The next morning we moved eagerly into the town. There was no Red Cross station, and there was no food. Morale sank, and the hunger and fatigue we suffered seemed even worse.

It was a typical Bavarian town, and we wandered around the streets. Suddenly, we realized that there were no guards or even any other prisoners around. We were completely alone! Directly in front of us was the medieval city gate leading to freedom. Before we left Camp 3, our commanding officer released us from the charge that all Allied prisoners should attempt to resist, escape and evade.

"Guys, our troops are coming. It shouldn't be much longer. There's no good reason to risk being killed in an escape attempt at this point. Just wait it out. It's got to end soon," he told us.

Looking incredulously at each other, we arrived at a mutual decision without speaking a word. Smiling, we simply walked out of town and took off. Not as exciting as *The Great Escape*, but it worked for us.

Without a definite plan in mind, we wandered aimlessly down the road. In time, we came to a farm. At the end of the farmyard was a three-story barn. The first floor was for the animals. The second was for grain and equipment, and the third floor was the hayloft. We climbed to the hayloft and fell exhausted into the straw.

Early the next morning, noise in the yard awakened us. Peering through the cracks, we saw a group of British prisoners with an immaculately dressed German army major and a couple of enlisted men. The group seemed relaxed, and one of the British enlisted men came into the barn. He climbed up to the second level to get some grain, and we came down to talk to him.

He told us that they had made a deal with the Germans like the one we proposed to our guard on the march. The Germans were escorting them toward the Allied lines. As soon as they made contact with any Allied unit, the Germans would surrender. Wishing us well, he rejoined his group. They formed up and marched from the farmyard, the model of a prisoner of war group.

I often wondered why we hadn't been asked to join their daring plan. I wonder why we didn't come right out and ask them if we could join them. I suppose the deplorable condition of our uniforms would have been an embarrassment to the German major as he escorted his smartly clad British co-conspirators to another camp.

We slept in the barn that night. Although we were hungry, at least we stayed dry when the rain pelted down during the night. Early the next morning, we decided we should get moving.

As I stated earlier, escape and evasion were not part of our education. In a short time, we were spotted by a civilian. He alerted the Germans. A grinning guard showed up. He was amazingly affable considering the trouble we caused him and he displayed an amazing sense of humor. By his reaction I deduced that this wasn't the first time this had happened. Soon, we found ourselves back in the column of prisoners walking south. It was an ignominious end to our great escape.

Our escape had been easy and without real risk. At one of our post-war reunions, I found that we could have run into real trouble. One of the other pilots pulled a stunt like ours and got shot for his trouble.

At the end of another day of marching south, we stopped in a village with a fair sized church. We spent the night on hard wooden pews or on the cold marble floor. It wasn't the hayloft, but at least it was dry.

Back on the road, we marched south and now a little to the east. My trio reckoned we were moving in the direction of the Russian army. We didn't care who liberated us. Any of the Allies would do.

The team approach proved effective on the long march. Each of us had a job when we stopped marching for the day. One of us staked out a camp site, while another collected firewood. I was the designated thief. Euphemisms for thievery in the military are: cumshaw man, or moonlight requisitioner, depending on the branch of the military. Sugar coat it any way you want, but I was still a thief.

Since we were traveling through farm country, we scavenged whatever we could find to eat. Edible greens, a turnip, a potato, anything at all was fair game. This night, we stopped by a farmhouse. Behind the house was a henhouse. Inside the henhouse was a treasure, nine freshly laid eggs! I gave one each to my two mates and reserved one for myself. The rest I distributed to six other lucky prisoners. My behavior wasn't unique. We were all in this thing together, and we helped each other any way we could.

Another night on the march, I watched a vignette that gave me more insight into my captors' lives. Late in the evening, two young German officers came walking along toward each other. When they saw each other, they quickened their pace and closed the distance between them with delighted smiles on their faces. Obvious friends, they looked up and down the street. Satisfied no other Germans were watching, they exchanged standard Prussian military salutes, and then embraced each other in warm greeting.

No stiff Nazi salute was exchanged. This was in defiance of a direct order from Hitler. June 21, 1944, Colonel Count von Stauffenberg detonated an explosive device at a conference table at Hitler's Wolf Lair. Miraculously, a heavy wooden table leg kept Hitler from being killed. Hitler had the eight men involved in the conspiracy brutally executed in Plötzensee prison. A vengeful purge of the military and a subjugation of its generals followed, but Hitler never trusted the military again. Immediately after the June coup attempt, Hitler outlawed everything but the Nazi stiff-armed salute. In the eyes of the insane Führer any other salute was considered an act of treason that was punishable by death.

The two young officers told me by their actions that not everyone in Germany had replaced traditional values with the ideology of the Little Corporal. At least there might be some decent men left to rebuild Germany after the war.

At last we came upon the approach to a bridge that led across the Danube. On the edge of the bridge was a small tower. A young German soldier busied himself setting up a machine gun position in the tower. As we walked past him, my German-speaking friend waved to the boy and called out, "Hey, you know when the Americans get here you don't want to be sitting up there on that perch. They'll go after you first."

Looking grimly down at us, the young man set his jaw and returned to work. That look told me that he already knew the odds were stacked against him. I had to admire the kid. He was a soldier, and he would do his duty to the end. War is fought by young men, not the politicians who start them. War is such a waste.

Walking across the bridge, we looked down over the side at the river. The base of the bridge crawled with German engineers. Each pillar was being fitted with demolition charges. If the Germans were forced back from the bridge, they would blow it into the river and deny Allied forces the use of it.

After two weeks and a march of some 110 miles, we arrived at our destination. We were in the town of Moosberg, thirty kilometers northeast of

Munich. On the outskirts of Moosberg stood Stalag Seven A, our new home away from home.

This was a more typical prison camp with rows of barracks surrounded by barbed wire. Overcrowding was a problem, since the camp had been designed for 2,000 and now held 4,000 prisoners. The food was reasonable, but heavily watered down. In combination with loads of drinking water, it didn't take long for the diarrhea to become rampant. It was fortunate that the latrine was nearby. Since our barracks was at the back of the compound, we could see it through our window.

Bunks lined the walls of the barracks, but the slats and internal wood had long since been removed and consumed as firewood. So we slept on the floor again. My foraging trio stayed intact, and we slept huddled together. After a few days of sleeping on the outside of the trio, they determined that my body heat was higher than theirs, and that I should sleep in the middle for added warmth. That was fine by me, because their bodies shielded me from the mean cross drafts that eddied around the barracks from the cracks in the walls.

Each morning after roll call, we were given the German OKW news release for the day by the duty sergeant. It was upbeat and optimistic, overly so in view of what was really happening at the front. I suppose the commandant thought if we believed that the Germans were winning, we'd be more docile prisoners.

Later in the day, huddled in the barracks, with lookouts at the doors and windows, we heard the real war news from the BBC. Someone in the compound had a contraband radio and distributed the news from London every day to counteract the Germans' propaganda release. I never knew for sure who it was, but the Brits were very good at clandestine radio operations.

In a camp as big as Seven A, it was not surprising that we had a number of artists. Using whatever they could scrounge for materials, they painted a large map of Europe on the walls of the latrine. Using the BBC news reports, they turned it into a large combat map. Whenever there was a significant change in circumstances, the map was updated to show the true character of the war.

This led to a lighter moment that repeated itself periodically. Through the window that faced the latrine, we could watch the German guards who patrolled the grounds. Occasionally, one of them would stop at the door of the latrine and scan his surroundings. When he felt certain that the latrine was empty and that he wasn't being watched, he'd duck into the latrine for a quick look at our war map.

One glorious afternoon, the quiet of the countryside was shattered by the howl of an aircraft engine. To wild cheers from the entire prison population, a P-51 roared in at tree top level and buzzed the camp. As he moved away, he did a big, slow barrel roll! This was the announcement of something big, and we knew it!

Later that day we heard another glorious sound. It was machine gun fire, and it separated the infantry from the flyers in camp. The infantry guys hit the deck, while the crazy airman ran around whooping and cheering like Geronimo on the warpath. A number of artillery shells were fired, but fortunately none of them rained down on the camp. Twelve of the guards were injured, one of them fatally. To my knowledge, none of the prisoners suffered a major injury or any of our shelters a major hit.

Not long after the machine gun fire we noticed that our guard at the back of the camp was peering anxiously through binoculars into the distance. He looked worried.

"Hey Fritz, what do you see out there?" someone called out.

"Amerikanische Panzer," he replied.

American tanks were that close! We could barely contain ourselves. We waited for the sound of more gunfire, but didn't hear very much. The real clue that the end was near came from the German guard himself. He simply dropped his binoculars, turned from the fence and began walking dejectedly from his post toward the front of the camp. He was on his way to the front gate to surrender!

"Hey Fritz, throw me your helmet. You ain't gonna need it any more," someone called out to him.

To our amazement, he took off the iron helmet and tossed it into a crowd of prisoners who scrambled for the souvenir.

"I'll take the rifle," another prisoner shouted.

With a sad smile and shake of his head, the guard replied, "Nein."

He was barely out of sight when we saw the most beautiful thing we had seen in months. It was an American tank, festooned with a dozen infantry men from Combat Team Alpha of General George Patton's 14th Armored Division clinging to the sides of the vehicle and throwing K-rations to the prisoners. Most of the time, eating K-rations instead of a real meal was a reason to grumble. To us, it was cuisine straight from the kitchens of the Waldorf Astoria.

At 1:45 on April 29, 1945, Stalag 7-A surrendered to the cheers of 4,000 fellow prisoners and me. We could see the flagpole in town. As the German flag went down and the American flag went up, the cheers got even louder and there wasn't a dry eye in the camp.

The Germans were gone, but there was no American in command. There was no one to tell us what to do. We were on our own, wandering about aimlessly, waiting for something to happen. The inseparable trio decided to walk into town together. We joked about our newfound freedom and the possibility of a long vacation before we tried to find someone in charge. But it was empty chatter. We were ready to get back to the job at hand.

On the outskirts of the village, we spied a winery. It was hard to believe our good fortune, and we hurried to the door as if the building was one giant Christmas package. When we got there, our Christmas package was like the ones that contained a new pair of socks instead of a bright shiny toy. Every bottle in the winery was either empty or broken, and glass littered the floor in a thousand shards. The bins stood mockingly empty, as we dejectedly made our way back to the street.

Moosberg itself was not badly damaged. But the things I remember as we first walked into the town were the white flags. It was as if every door and window in the village had a white flag in it. The few vehicles that were not military also flew them. As townspeople passed us, the angry glare of the captor had been replaced with the downcast eyes of the beaten. A cursory look around the town told us there was nothing more to do here than in our camp. One of the passing units advised us that we should be patient. An airlift had been planned to pick us up and return us to a staging area under United States control. After several days of waiting, we had had enough.

The three of us had a conference. After some discussion, we decided that we would simply walk back across the Rhine into France. Thinking back on it now it seems insane, but at the time it appeared to be the perfectly rational thing to do.

Near the end of our first day on the road, we came to a large German airbase that had been taken over by the Americans. It was a graves registration detail. These unsung heroes had the unenviable task of cleaning up the detritus of war. They located, processed and returned the remains of those men killed in action for burial.

They greeted us warmly and treated us like long-lost comrades. There was more food there than we had seen in months, and they gave us all we could eat. And eat we did. It was hard to stop eating, even when we were full. After so many weeks of deprivation, it seemed mandatory to be nibbling on something constantly.

We also had an opportunity to get some clean clothes. Ours were beyond filthy and in rags since they were the same clothes we had been captured in. I found a pair of blue Luftwaffe pants that were just the right size, so I took those and placed my rags on the trash heap.

We walked and hitchhiked our way clear across Germany into France. The trip took us a mere three days. The liberated areas were filled with grateful citizens anxious to show appreciation to men in uniform, even with my strange pants. The first French town we came to was Rheims, where the German generals would later surrender their swords to General Eisenhower.

Dressed like vagabonds, we soon attracted the attention of the military police. When he had finished questioning us, the M.P. said, "Guys you have my respect, but party time is over. It's back to the system." He politely took us to the relocation center.

At the relocation center they had field showers with all the water pressure we could use. There was a series of seven showers in the line, with lots of soap and shampoo. We started at the first shower and used every one of them, showering over and over to wash the dirt of months of captivity from our skin. It was wonderful.

There were huge big bath towels that we used to dry off. And there was a tent where we could get new socks, underwear, uniforms and shoes. It was like Christmas. Not only could we get uniforms, but campaign ribbons and medals as well.

Sorting through the combat ribbons, I casually asked the clerk, "Do you have the medal of honor ribbon?"

The boy flushed, and stuttered, "No, sir, I'm sorry sir, we don't have that one. Do you have the medal of honor?"

"No, no, you don't understand," I reassured him. "I've never seen one, and I wanted to see what it looked like."

As contented as pigs in mud, we made our way to the train station the next morning for the trip to our embarkation station. Every POW got a free sixty-day leave. We were going home!

At the train station, there were lots of French girls. To my shock, their lips were painted screaming red, and their cheeks were pink with rouge. Some wore eyeliner and eye shadow. Since I hadn't seen a woman in makeup for quite a long time, they looked like garish trollops to me. Fortunately, that impression didn't last very long. We got used to the new look in no time.

Our embarkation station, Camp Lucky Strike, not related to the cigarettes, was on the French coast. Prisoners of war had priority, second only to men wounded in combat, for transportation home. Even with that high priority, so many men were trying to get home that there was a wait.

I didn't resent the delay. The food was outstanding and the weight I had lost gradually made its way back onto my frame. At least my mother wouldn't feel obligated to force feed me when I got home. Housed in a tent, I slept on a comfortable, warm, dry cot. Life couldn't have been much better.

There was also a nurses' tent on the base. A couple of times I went to their tent for the afternoon dances. Each afternoon, when their work was done, they helped the lonely GIs pass the time with a friendly dance. It was nice to be in the presence of someone other than another soldier, even if it was only for a few hours.

At Lucky Strike, I was finally able to send a cable to my parents to tell them I was okay. I learned later from Mrs. McGourty, the referee of my teenaged fight, that my poor mother had been a basket case when she found out I was missing in action. I soon understood why.

My wingman, Hal Falvey, saw my plane get hit. He must have been on the wrong side of the aircraft to see me bail out. He never saw my chute open. All he saw was the plane crash and burn. That's all he reported. For all my folks knew, I never got out of the doomed plane. Fortunately, as soon as I got back into the system in France the authorities cabled my folks with the report that I was alive.

The trip back across the Atlantic was not as pleasant as the trip had been coming over. This time, I was on a Liberty ship. There were four cramped bunks in each cell with barely enough room to turn around. I only stayed in the room to sleep.

This was one of the last troop convoys to cross the Atlantic. As we approached Newfoundland, we ran into the heavy fog banks that frequent that part of the North Atlantic. The ship's captain asked the officers on board if any of them would volunteer for extra fog lookout duty. I agreed at once. I was desperate to relieve the boredom.

I stood outside on the wings of the bridge in the dark, and in the cold, with fog so thick it looked as if it could be cut with a knife swirling around me. The convoy ships were in formation, and at set times, each ship in turn sounded its fog horn. It was our job to use the sound of the other fog horns to be certain that we were not too close to any of the other ships, or that they were too close to us. The ships had radar, but it was primitive by today's standards, and the extra eyes and ears were a routine precaution. It was a bit nerve-wracking at times, but better than that cramped little compartment.

In late May, we steamed into New York Harbor. Gliding past the Statue of Liberty was one of the happiest days and biggest thrills of my young life. Although I was only a few blocks from home, it still seemed like miles. But I had sixty great days of freedom at home before I went back to Atlantic City where it had all started.

As I walked the streets of Manhattan, there was no rubble. No bullet holes pockmarked the sides of building. There were no grubby children with hollow eyes poking through the debris in search of food. Smiling and laughing people were everywhere. Most of them had no concept of what I had seen or been a part of. Thank God for that. I just knew it was great to be home.

When I checked into the reassignment depot in New York, they went over my records. Reviewing my POW experience and my crash, the clerk looked at me.

"Lieutenant, you are eligible for the purple heart," he said to me.

Astonished, I asked, "Why? I wasn't wounded."

"Oh, yes. When you parachuted into the tree, you suffered a cut on your knee that was later treated by the Germans. You were indeed wounded in combat."

"No," I said firmly. "It was only a scratch. I've seen men who were really wounded, and I wasn't one of them. I do not want the Purple Heart. Save it for the real heroes who deserve it."

It was the best decision I ever made. Later, I saw many men who lost arms, legs, were in wheelchairs, or disfigured in other ways from enemy fire. Thank God I had sense enough not to disgrace their sacrifice by accepting a medal I didn't deserve.

When I had finished being processed, they sent me on leave. The brash young kid from a 109th Street was coming home to a thankful family after doing exactly what I promised them I would do. I had been the best soldier I knew to be.

Chapter 5

Career Management 101

On September 2, 1945, General Yoshijiro Umezu signed the surrender document on behalf of the Japanese Empire on the battleship *Missouri*, and World War II came to its inevitable end. When that historic event occurred, I was back where it all began, for me, in Atlantic City, New Jersey. Shortly thereafter, I was sent to Napier Field, Dothan, Alabama, to await my next assignment.

At Napier, I was reunited with an old friend from advanced flying school, the AT-6. Check-out flights in the trainer was my only way to get up there. It had been so long since I was in the pilot's seat I'd have taken up a Piper Cub if one was available. In the plane, high above it all, I was at peace with myself and at one with the machine. On the ground, things were less than crystallized.

At the peak of the war, more than one million American men and women comprised the greatest war machine in history. With the crisis over, their ranks shrank rapidly as those not interested in the military as a career gratefully returned to public life. That left me with a critical decision. Should I stay, or should I go?

In a dramatically reduced military, those who chose military life as a career would face stiff competition for advancement. Who would my competition be? They would be graduates of the military academies and graduates from traditional public and private colleges and universities. These people had credentials I couldn't match. I yearned to make the Air Force my home but realized it would be an uphill struggle. Twice I had been offered the option of getting out of the service. Twice I had declined. What should I do? One day, as I strolled along the flight line, I saw another old friend who might help me make the decision.

Striding briskly into the base operations office, I said to the duty officer, "There's a P-51 out there on the flight line. I'm a P-51 pilot with 52 combat missions under my belt. It's been a while since I was in one. I'd like to take the plane up for a flight."

Studying me for a few seconds, the man shrugged and replied, "Okay."

Walking to the flight line, I climbed into the familiar cockpit and started the engine. Roaring into the sky, I flew for two glorious hours. The exultation and freedom is hard to describe to anyone who has never experienced the privilege of piloting a combat aircraft. When I landed, my head was clear and my decision made.

That was my last flight for the Army Air Corps. When I landed, I went straight to the personnel office and told them I would like to go to Fort Dix, New Jersey, to muster out.

Nodding, the personnel officer asked me, "Do you want to have a commission in the reserves?"

After thinking about it for a couple of seconds, I said, "Yes, I do."

My stop at Fort Dix was short, and I was a civilian again. Back home in New York, I immediately got curriculum catalogues for New York University and Columbia University. If I was going to get ahead in this rapidly changing world, I needed a college education.

Reviewing the catalogs of the two schools, it became readily apparent that NYU was the school for me. Columbia required two years each of two foreign languages. NYU required two years of only one foreign language. I had two years of French in the seventh and eight grades, so I met the language requirement for NYU. No contest. It was NYU for me.

Despite my high school teacher's tutelage, I was still shy one course to gain entry into NYU. I needed trigonometry to enter the college of engineering. They gave the pre-requisite course at a local high school, but the day classes were filled, so I enrolled in the night school classes. They suited me better anyhow. I needed to support myself, and it gave me a chance to work during the day.

I went back to the Western Union Company, where I had been a messenger, and asked them for a job. They put me in the engineering laboratory as a technician. I did breadboard work for the engineer. I made the small, mock-up boards as precursors to the large components the engineers would build later. It was interesting and gave me an opportunity to learn more about small circuits and wiring techniques that were on the cutting edge of its time. Better yet, I wasn't dodging traffic and pedaling a bike from one end of Manhattan to the other. I needed my energy to hit the books.

For the first year and a half at NYU, I continued to work days and attend evening classes at the university. With so many people now in civilian life and seeking to better their status, the day classes remained jammed.

On September 18, 1947, the old Army Air Corps was replaced by the new United States Air Force, and the burgeoning air arm of the Army became its own branch of the military. As I read about the changes, that singular event only served to underscore the void in my life.

Despite a day already crammed with work, study and classes, I missed the sky. Every time I heard the drone of an aircraft overhead, I longed to be up there again. On top of everything else I was doing, I found the time to apply for a commercial pilot's license. Fortunately, I had the necessary flight time and experience for a commercial license, so all I had to do was apply for it.

Periodically, I made the tedious forty-five minute trip to Mitchel Field in Long Island. The plane was an aging AT-6, but it allowed me to keep my hand in when I could find time to fly. That wasn't often, and it made me savor each minute I was able to leave my hectic earthbound life behind me and fly. When I landed after a flight, my mind felt clearer, my step was lighter. I needed to do it more often.

Then, I figured out a way to fly a lot more. If I were a flight instructor, I could fly for free and actually get paid to do it! This was the world's perfect job. Do the thing you loved the most in life, and get someone to pay you to do it.

When I finished the requirements for my instructor's rating, I got a job on Long Island at the Hicksville Airport. That's right, Hicksville, but it was heaven to me. I got to fly. Although I loved flying, in retrospect, it was probably not the soundest decision I ever made.

Hicksville Airport was thirty-five miles out on Long Island. Getting there, working, getting back for my night classes and trying to fit in study time for the complex courses in the electrical engineering curriculum was almost more than I could handle. I had stretched myself almost beyond my limits, and although I didn't have any real problems with my academic work, had I not been so constantly fatigued and pushed for time, I could have been a better student. After three years of night classes, I had finished my first two years of college.

Another seminal event occurred in my life in 1947. Shortly after the war, I met a pert young dental hygienist named Doris Allen. Frequently visiting the office where she worked, I had the cleanest teeth in town, and in the process found a bride. We were married in February 1948.

As happens today, the first two years of college weeds out those who don't belong, or do not apply themselves to the task of getting by. The size of my junior class was considerably smaller than my freshman or sophomore classes. And the difficulty of the upper level courses increased as well. I needed to simplify my life. Spots opened up in the day college, and I jumped at the opportunity to land one of them.

Instead of easing the pressure, this maneuver seemed to make it worse.

With my responsibilities to Doris, day classes, a part-time flight instructor's job, and one weekend a month with the active reserves, I seemed to have little time for anything else. Had it not been for the flying, I don't know how I would have handled it.

With the formation of the new Air Force, the reserve unit I had joined became a troop carrier wing, flying the dependable C-46, aptly nicknamed "The Whale" due to its distinctive shape. It wasn't a fighter wing, but it gave me the chance to fly and to stay proficient in a twin-engine trainer, the AT-12.

Running at full tilt without a second to spare, the next two years melded into a blur. As March of 1951 drew to a close, the end was in sight. In one month, I would sit for my final exams and have my degree. It was a feeling of accomplishment. I had persevered, and I was going to graduate; not at the top of the class, but not the bottom either. I had fulfilled my mother's wishes, my teacher's wishes, and my own. I had a trade. That was Mom's wish. I was a skilled military pilot, my wish. Now, my high school teachers who wanted me to go to a generally academic college would have been happy, too.

With the road to the future seemingly stretching to the horizon, a detour sign suddenly appeared. My reserve unit received orders to be activated on April 1, 1951. If I deployed with them, I was going to miss my final exams! And, it was no April Fool's joke!

On June 25, 1950, the Republic of North Korea had invaded its neighbor to the south. On June 30, President Harry Truman committed U.S. forces to the United Nations to force the withdrawal of the North Koreans, and on July 7, General Douglas Macarthur was chosen to lead the United Nations command.

The early phases of the war had gone in favor of the United Nations troops and by year's end, they had advanced into North Korea, and it appeared that the conflict might be over by Christmas. Then, the Chinese Communists came to the aid of the North Koreans who were supplied MIG-15 fighters by Russia, and the tide turned against the U.N. dictating the need for more troops. That included my unit.

Due to the disruptive nature of the call-up, the unit had a delay reporting board. There was a sign-up sheet tacked to a bulletin board at the reserve unit. Members of the unit could sign up for a review by the board if the short-notice call-up presented a hardship for them. I prophetically believed that excuses and sob-stories would be legion, and I hurried to get my name on the list. My prophecy soon proved accurate.

The "board" was a solitary, impatient and bored full colonel, who didn't even give me time to introduce myself before he asked sarcastically, "And what is it that you want?"

From the tone of his voice and the expression on his face, I was certain he had already heard every excuse in the book. I saluted smartly and stood rigidly at attention. That caused him to straighten slightly in his chair.

"Twenty-eight days, sir," I replied in my best military tone.

Leaning forward with interest, he commanded, "Tell me why?"

"In one month I will have my degree in electrical engineering. My final exams will be complete twenty-eight days from now. I need to finish those exams to get my degree, sir," I replied while remaining at attention.

With a genuine smile he said, "Go ahead and finish. We'll see you in twenty-eight days."

Much later, I discovered that if I had approached the university with my dilemma, there was a reasonable chance I would have been released to deploy with my unit and granted my degree without having to sit for final exams! Although that would have been an easier way to go, I had the satisfaction of completing all the work for my degree. Nothing had been given to me in my entire life, and now was certainly not the time to start.

This little vignette taught me an important lesson in dealing with the military. When you want something, build your case, go through the appropriate chain of command, and stand up for what you want or need. I passed my first test in Career Management 101 with flying colors.

When I joined my unit, we were flying planes from Mitchel Field to Pope Air Force Base adjacent to Fort Bragg in North Carolina. The planes carried novice jumpers for training and Airborne Rangers for war games and qualifying jumps. I was appointed the maintenance officer for one of the squadrons at Pope Air Force Base, a job for which I was eminently unqualified! Fortunately, it would be only temporary duty that would last two weeks.

I was like a fish out of water. I had a crash course on my new responsibilities and was so paranoid about screwing up that I wore out a pair of shoes in one week walking the ramps, checking and rechecking to be sure I didn't miss anything. It was my best one man imitation of an ant farm. One of the other squadron commanders, who was my boss during my two weeks at Pope, took notice of my efforts and thanked me for a job well done.

He told my squadron commander back at Mitchel Field that I had done an exemplary job. His recommendation was that I be rewarded in some way and suggested a forty-eight-hour pass. Instead, my boss fired the maintenance officer for our squadron and gave me the job, pushing me yet one more rung up the unqualified ladder. It was the Peter Principle personified. I tried to learn all I could and for the next two weeks and tried to apply what I had learned to the job.

One afternoon, I was summoned, along with two other bewildered pilots, to the Wing Personnel Office to meet with a full colonel. From the look on his face, I was positive we had pulled a funeral detail, or that some terrible catastrophe had befallen the three of us. But since we had no obvious connection with each other, we remained puzzled.

"Boys, I have some really bad news," he began, and I braced myself for the worst. "We just got the word that they need P-51 pilots in Korea. Since you three are the only ones in the unit with any such experience, you're going to have to go to Korea to a P-51 squadron. I'm really sorry fellows, but I have no choice," he added, his expression somber, his voice husky with emotion.

Grim-faced to match his mood, we saluted smartly and answered in unison, "Yes sir!" and backed stone-faced out of his office.

Outside, we did a version of the high-five, laughed and celebrated as if we had all just gotten promoted. In fact we had been saved; saved from a fighter pilot's purgatory. We were on our way back to the action where fighter pilots belonged.

My reserve experience reinforced something else for me. The new Air Force was disorganized, and in the throes of rebuilding for another war. There was no such thing as a career management officer. If one considered a military career, which I did now, I would have to do a little managing on my own. That prospect didn't frighten me. I had the vast experience of one management on my side already. I suppose I still had the brashness of youth that I had carried through my German captivity.

In Japan, near Tokyo, I reported to the replacement depot. A young enlisted man clerk told me I was going to southern Japan to join a troop carrier wing. It was time to manage.

Sitting down across the desk from him I laid out my case with a New York street kid's brashness. I was a fighter pilot. I had flown over 50 combat missions in a P-51. It was a waste of taxpayer and Air Force money, not to mention my specialized training and experience in fighter planes, to turn me into a troop-carrying bus driver. I wanted to be in a fighter squadron, and that's where all logic dictated I should go. And in an attempt to woo him further I suggested that I knew the new Air Force was particularly logical and that is where they would want me to be.

After insulting the important job of the troop-carrying pilots, and firing my best shot at the bewildered looking young clerk, I sat back and resorted to my tried and true method. Firing my big gun, I breathed a silent prayer. After such a persuasive argument, the young clerk could do nothing but agree, and I was on my way to the 35th Tactical Fighter Wing at Johnson Air Force Base outside Tokyo, Japan. Career management grade: A+.

The wing consisted of three squadrons, one F-80 and one F-94 all-weather interceptors, both jets, and one P-51 squadron and a tow target unit.

I was assigned to that. My job was to fly a tow plane that towed the targets for aerial gunnery practice. Management time again! I went to see Captain Bugg, the tow target squadron commander. My presentation was simplistic.

"Sir you can get anyone to tow targets. I'm a seasoned P-51 combat pilot. I should be flying in the F-51 squadron, and I humbly request that you agree."

To my amazement, he agreed, and I was assigned to the F-51 squadron. I joined the squadron, and after the mandatory check-out flight, I was ready to fight again.

On the bulletin board in flight operations there was the ubiquitous sheet of paper. This time it was a sheet for those who wished to sign up for combat assignment to Korea. As soon as I was settled in, I put my name at the top of the list. It was a monthly sheet, so I made sure my name was first on the list the second month when I didn't get combat duty the first month. After repeated sign-ups, the commanding officer called me into his office. There, I learned one of the reasons my name was never called.

"Bob, I can understand why you want to get into the action, but let me tell you a couple of things. First, you have been there and done that in a P-51. You have nothing left to prove. Second, this squadron is full of young kids right out of flight school, and they need an experienced hand to guide them. I want you to stick with them, and effectively immediately, you'll be flight leader."

It was management time again.

"I understand that, sir. But I'm seriously considering going regular Air Force from the reserves. I'm only a first lieutenant, and combat seems a better chance for advancement," I replied.

"Bob, I'll bet you a bottle of my favorite whiskey that you're at the top of the captain's list when then next promotion list is published," he said with a conspiratorial wink.

I stayed with the squadron and assumed my new role. I wasn't dumb enough to take the bet on the whiskey. I knew a sure thing when it came my way, and my captain's bars were in the mail.

If a pilot was married, and his wife wasn't with him, the tour in Japan was eighteen months. I had another decision to make. I could have requested that Doris join me. But a month had already passed, and it would likely take at least a couple of months to get her here, since dependents crossed the Pacific by ship. And if she joined me, I would have an overseas tour lasting three years. If she didn't come, I'd be stateside again in eighteen months. Despite missing her, I opted for the eighteen months.

When I considered my future, I feared I would never see combat in Korea. It was time to plan my next career move. I was getting more experience in fighters and there was a good chance I would be checked out in jet aircraft. For the first time, the thought of test pilot school entered my psyche. I tucked it away for future reference.

At this time, each of the four flight commanders in the squadron was assigned to fly an F-80. Since I had never flown a jet, I got fifty hours in the T-33, the two-seat version of the F-80. Once I was qualified, it became my job to check out the other pilots in my flight as the P-51 squadron gradually gave way to the jet aircraft of the modern Air Force. By the time I got my orders to go home, I had 180 hours in the F-80. That wasn't a lot of hours, and it was a concern as far as my career was concerned.

The experience in Japan solidified my decision that my home was in the Air Force, and I applied for a regular commission. To my pleasure, it was granted. When my tour was over, I returned from Japan to the Development Center at Rome, New York, from Japan without ever firing a shot.

I went there with mixed emotions. On the one hand, I had completed another assignment and received excellent fitness reports from my commanding officer. I was a brand new captain, and I was now a jet-rated fighter pilot. On the other hand, I felt cheated that I had missed the opportunity to fly combat missions in my second war, even if they didn't call it a war but a conflict. I doubt any of the troops on the ground in the mud and snow of Korea would have called it anything but a war.

In Rome, someone noticed my engineering credentials, and that I was well versed in electronics. I was assigned to the Tactical Command and Control Unit. Unfortunately, it wasn't much of a job for me. Guidance systems were high on the list of priorities, and outside contractors did the active work along with the people well above me in rank.

With nothing much to do, I considered my options. I could stay here and do something to distinguish myself from the crowd. Or I could shoot for the moon, and do something that would really set me apart. I applied for the Test Pilot School at Edwards Air Force Base in California.

It was obviously a two-edged sword. It would be a great thing for my career, but the assignment would carry far more risk than the other paths open to me. My family would have to live with the real possibility that I might go to work one day and never come home. Fortunately, Doris supported my decision.

To escape the boredom, I applied for and was accepted to the ten-week Squadron Officers Training Course held at Maxwell Air Force Base near Montgomery, Alabama. It proved to be an interesting as well as an educational experience in assessment and problem solving.

Coincidentally, while I was at Maxwell, a Captain Bob Hippert from the test pilots' school came there and gave an informative lecture about the test pilot's program. After the lecture, I introduced myself to him and told him about my qualifications and my application. He told me that they would be reviewing the applications soon, and with my experience, I would stand a reasonable chance of being accepted. Bob would later be one of my instructors at the Test Pilot School.

When the last week of the Squadron Officers Training Course began, I was told that when the course was over, a request would be made to have me assigned to the school as an instructor. Apparently, my performance had attracted attention, but I was far from elated. It was career management time again.

Marching into the office of the lieutenant colonel in charge of the school, I fired my opening salvo. I was flattered that they wanted me there as an instructor, but I had applied for the Test Pilot School. That's what I really wanted to do. The fighter pilot mentality in me didn't want to contemplate being a teacher just yet in my career.

"No White, you *will* be assigned to this command as an instructor. End of discussion," he said, in a tone of voice that that suggested no response was expected.

Ignoring that, I replied, "But, sir, that's what I *want* to do. I believe the Test Pilot Program has priority," I said.

Flushing to a stroke-threatening crimson, he snapped, "We have our priorities, too! Dismissed!"

I dejectedly left his office. I was afraid that I had flunked my first Career Management 101 exam. And I had definitely paved the way for the possibility of my first less-than-glowing fitness report. Fortunately, time proved my assessment to be inaccurate. I returned to my duties at Rome, New York, and for the next seven weeks, the days dragged by. Then a letter arrived containing orders to report to the United States Air Force Test Pilot School at Edwards Air Force Base in California.

Just before we left Alabama, Doris and I got wonderful news. After a visit to the base hospital, she was informed that she was pregnant with our first child. This news made us deliriously happy. After a number of childless years, we had thought that our own children might not be in our future and had applied to the Catholic Adoption Service to adopt a child. Fortunately, on that score, we were wrong, and when we returned to Rome we advised the adoption service that we were to be blessed with a child of our own.

In June of 1954, I left Rome Air Force Base on my way cross country to Edwards Air Force Base in California for the six months of Test Pilot School. The school consisted of two phases, performance flight testing and stability and control. In the former, we would fly the aircraft and record and plot data that we were later required to analyze. These data, among other things, told us things such as how much fuel was required to fly at various speeds or the optimal speed-to-climb ratio.

In the latter, we were required to collect and record data on how well the aircraft performed specific tasks. For instance, how quickly do the controls react when the plane is rolled? Both phases were interesting, and I looked forward to every aspect of flight testing I would be able to do in the future.

We were informed that we would be evaluated in three ways: academics, flying ability and attitude. I felt I could be competitive in all three areas. Our performance evaluations would dictate our final assignment.

Class sizes were small, only ten to twelve students in each one. Everyone became quickly acquainted with each other, and the beginning of a bond that would last a lifetime was forming.

When the course began, I thanked heaven for my engineering degree. Fifty percent of the course was classroom work, and it was highly technical stuff. Without the distractions of my college days, I was able to devote my full intellectual potential to the course work. I even found time to tutor a classmate who lacked the necessary mathematics. Maybe there was a little teacher in me after all.

On our flights, we were taught to record a myriad of data. Once the data was plotted, it was our responsibility to mathematically massage it. Then we turned the data into tables and graphs that reflected parameters such as fuel consumption at various speeds, maximum and minimum power requirements for maneuvers and a host of other things reflecting the performance of the aircraft.

I found stability and control to be particularly interesting. In the school we flew more than just fighter aircraft. One stability and control exercise involved evaluating the characteristics of a B-25 during a planned roll. Then, the conditions of the aircraft, such as flaps up, flaps down or wheels up or wheels down would be altered and the test sequence repeated. Particular attention was focused on the handling characteristics of the aircraft during the roll.

On the way to the B-25, my instructor said in a voice tinged with challenge, "This is one of the most difficult parts of the training phase. It often takes a pilot more than one flight to master it."

I took that as a personal challenge and eventually completed the entire test card in thirty minutes. To prepare for the test run, I configured the aircraft in what was termed "clean configuration," In this case, that meant that the wheels and flaps were both up. Each of the flights was video recorded, so when I had the aircraft stabilized at the proper speed and altitude I gave the command, "Cameras on."

The moment I activated the camera, my flight instructor, who was acting as co-pilot, would throw the appropriate switch and the camera began to roll. Immediately, I fully deflected the wheel, which was the aileron control. The lumbering bomber would begin to roll, and the rate of roll was recorded.

There was also an on-board mechanical device that would allow the aileron to be deflected one-quarter, one-half or three-quarters of the way. Each setting was a separate test and the data recorded separately.

Next, we varied the airspeed and repeated the tests at each of the aileron deflections. After testing several different airspeeds we moved on to the next series of tests.

This time, we varied the configuration of the aircraft by putting the flaps halfway down. The tests were then repeated at different airspeeds. Then it was full flaps and landing gear down, "landing configuration." And we'd do the same test all over again.

The tests were straightforward and gave quantitative information on the rate of roll in many different configurations. These were facts that were recorded for anybody to read. But, there were still questions to be answered.

What did the pilot think? Is he pleased with the aircraft's response to lateral control inputs? Does the pilot believe that in certain circumstances the response of the aircraft is too slow? Is its performance satisfactory or unsatisfactory? Once these questions are answered, the answers become the qualitative results and are equally important to the final judgment of the aircraft's performance. If a drastic change is needed or a system just needs a tweak, there is both quantitative and qualitative information to base those changes on.

The Society of Experimental Test Pilots, of which I am a proud member, is not a singing, beer-drinking fraternity. It is a dedicated professional society whose goals are to enhance and improve the flight test world and its safety. Over the years, the Society's record is exemplary.

In the case I have just recited, a small group of test pilots worked on a system that could be universally used to further define the qualitative evaluations that the pilots use to rate the various qualities of an aircraft. They developed categories called: Unsatisfactory; Marginally Acceptable; Acceptable; Satisfactory; and lastly Very Satisfying. Next, they attached numerical scales to each category creating useful parameters that all test pilots and engineers could relate to.

Forty minutes later, I had completed the test on the first try and said to him, "You've got it."

Relaxing from the tension of the exercise, it was all I could do not to gloat.

We landed, and as we were walking away from the aircraft, the instructor looked over and me and said, "Nice job, White."

The remainder of the training was difficult, but uneventful. As the school wound down, we were asked to list our preferred post training assignments on a slip of paper.

There were three choices: Edwards, the Vatican of assignments, and the one I really wanted. But the fighter test section was a close-knit, elite group of crack pilots, and I felt I stood little chance of being invited into their fraternity. So, I placed Eglin Air Force Base in Florida, the armament and ordinance testing facility, as my first choice.

Wright Patterson Air Force Base, the other choice, was an all-weather testing center and the third choice on my list. Since the class size was limited to ten to twelve pilots, and I had done okay in training, I thought I had a good chance to land at Eglin.

The day class formally finished, each of us was handed a paper with an assignment written on it. Mine said, "Wright Patterson Air Force Base, Dayton, Ohio." That was my last choice, and my heart sank.

As I sat dejectedly in the classroom, Lt. Col. Ahman, the school commandant approached me and asked, "How do you like your assignment, Bob?"

"I'm crushed," I replied honestly and dejectedly.

It was another Career Management exam. Sensing I had nothing to lose, I stated my case in an impromptu legal summation. I felt that I had done better than average academically, and had completed the flights as well as anyone and deserved at least my first choice. I went on to explain that Edwards was my dream, but that I realized that the competition for those billets was intense. I might not qualify for Edwards but I felt I should at least get Eglin.

His face was inscrutable as he said, "Let me have that, Bob," and took the slip of paper with my assignment on it. "You were at the top of the class," he said, his expression remaining unreadable.

The next day, the colonel in charge of the entire flight test empire called me into his office for an interview.

"How much time do you have in jet aircraft?" he asked me.

"Only 180 hours, sir," I said, but quickly added, "I have 970 hours in the P-51."

I knew my limited time in jets would come back to haunt me, and it seemed that it had.

To my amazement, he said, "That won't hurt. Report to Lt Col. Everest, chief of flight test operations here at Edwards, and he'll welcome you aboard."

I had made it to Edwards, and I was certain I had cleared the last hurdle. There were thirty to thirty-five test pilots divided into three groups, fighters, bombers/cargo and helicopter. Since I had no experience in the latter, and was not cut out to be a bomber pilot, the fighter group was the right place for me. Still, as I walked toward the ops office, I wished I hadn't done the bomber roll drill so well.

When I arrived at Colonel Everest's office, he wasn't there, but his deputy Lieutenant Colonel Harold Russell was. He would later become a good friend.

"Why do you want to come to work at Edwards?" he asked.

"Sir, it's the thing I've always dreamed of doing. I consider it a privilege," I answered.

"That's the right answer. Go to fighter ops and check in with Major Child," he said.

Walking toward fighter ops, I looked up into the cobalt blue California sky. I was going up there, in the most advanced fighter planes in the world, with the best pilots in the world. Could the heaven above that crystal clear California sky be any better than that?

Chapter 6

A Pilot's Dream Job

I could hardly believe my good fortune. Here I was, at the world's premier aircraft test center. Every day, I would have an opportunity to fly the country's newest and most sophisticated fighter aircraft before anyone else. And I was getting paid to do it. That perfect job, just like when I was a flight instructor!

Like the parents of any kid with a new driver's license, they were not going to just hand me the keys to the family car and turn me loose on the highways. After all, the vehicles I was driving cost a lot more than a new Ford. They broke me in carefully. Although I was chomping at the bit to fly the newest aircraft, I appreciated that need for caution. Unlike football, in this game when you go out of bounds you don't come back!

I needed more time in the jets. The only jet planes I had flown were the T-33 trainer and the F-80. There was ample opportunity to get some seat time and to check out the other planes while flying safety chase. Safety chase is an integral part of the testing program. The contractors who were building the new planes leased base facilities and conducted their own testing and certification flights with their own pilots. Once their pilots felt the aircraft was ready for delivery to the Air Force, they turned the craft over to the military test pilots. When the company pilots did these flights, we were assigned to chase duty. It gave me not only valuable seat time in a high-performance jet fighter; it gave me time to get an idea of how the new plane performed.

When the company pilot took off, I was already in the air in a chase plane. I picked him up when he was airborne and followed him along. Since I was briefed on the extent of the test, it was a simple matter to fly with him as he executed his flight plan. My job was to be certain the airspace remained clear, to watch for trouble, and to supply visual information to the company pilot concerning the condition of his aircraft. My favorite chase plane planes were the F-86 and F-100. I got lots of hours in both performing what was usually a routine chore.

But it wasn't always routine. Once, I was flying chase for a company pilot in a Convair 880. It was a routine flutter test exercise. In the exercise, shotgun shells were inserted along the vertical tail stabilizer. Triggering the shells in a prescribed manner caused the vertical stabilizer to flutter. Records were made of the aircraft's reaction to the resultant flutter and any corrective measures needed to overcome a problem.

On this particular day, something nearly went tragically wrong. Instead of the usual controlled detonation with its characteristic pop-pop-pop as the shells went off, there was a large bang. From my vantage point above and behind the 880, I watched in horror as two-thirds of the rudder and vertical stabilizer disintegrated.

I immediately called the Convair's chief test pilot Donald Germeraad who was at the controls and said, "Chase One to Convair 880, Don, you need to hold your plane very steady. Don't make any sudden moves with any of the controls."

"Roger that, Chase One. What's my damage, Bob?" Germeraad said in a calm voice.

"Chase One to Convair 880, we need to abort the exercise. The detonation of the shells has destroyed two-thirds of your rudder and your vertical stabilizer. You need to declare an emergency and land as soon as possible."

"Roger that, Chase One," he answered, his voice portraying nothing of what he must be feeling inside.

I heard him call for an emergency landing as he began a very gradual descent. After what seemed like an eternity of breath-holding minutes, he landed the plane safely, avoiding what could have been a real tragedy.

When we had an opportunity to analyze the problem on the ground, the cause was evident. The shells had fired in the prescribed fashion, but for some reason, instead of producing a flutter that quickly dampened, the firing caused a divergent flutter in the stabilizer. This caused structural failure, and this section of the tail ripped itself apart. The loud bang that I heard was the tail section tearing off.

The episode was another example of what makes a good test pilot. During the emergency Don remained calm, attended to business and followed procedures. As a result, disaster was avoided. When I think back on it, I showed those same characteristics when my P-51 decided to do an end-over-end when I was checking it out. It was a good quality to have in this business.

The five-mile-long runway on the dry lake bed was one of our best friends. On numerous occasions, test pilots were able to land crippled aircraft and walk away from situations that would have been far more difficult to handle on a conventional runway.

While I was still a virtual neophyte at Edwards, I had my most embarrassing moment. Each year on Armed Forces Day, the base put on a special air show, and with the expertise of the pilots at the base, and the base's reputation, the public expected, and always received, a spectacular show. And so did the center commander.

I was chosen to play an integral part in the opening segment of the production. My task would be elemental, but would open the show with a dramatic flair.

The aircraft I would fly was the familiar T-33, especially equipped with jet assist takeoff or JATO bottles. I would take off and fly at a very low level, light up the JATO bottles and climb straight up, leaving a white trail of expanding gas in my wake. At the top of the climb, I would rollout to the awe of onlookers.

A second plane would swoop down through the wake I had created and break the sound barrier with a window shaking boom! Practice went smooth as silk, and the effect was just what the C.O. wanted. I couldn't wait for show time.

The day of the show dawned a typical desert summer day. It was almost unbearably hot, and there was not a cloud in the blue sky. The white of the JATO trail on that blue palate would be spectacular. By afternoon the runway was like a griddle. I felt no particular apprehension, only the excitement of being part of the production, and having a chance to be first to wow the audience.

To this day, I don't know exactly what happened. I like to think it was the heat that perhaps affected the lift of the T-33. In reality, it was my brain that was affected. But isn't that human nature? It's much easier to blame someone or something else for what is most likely your own mistake.

As I flashed down the runway, and started to lift off, I retracted the landing gear too early and bumped the trailing end of the JATO bottle on the runway, knocking it off! It went tumbling across the runway, and I took off in a most routine fashion. The show was denied a spectacular opening. My only saving grace was that I didn't belly into the runway and ignite my onboard fuel. That *would* have been a spectacular and tragic opening to what was truly a great air show. I was ordered to land at an alternative runway on North Base, well away from the action.

Edwards Air Force Base was designated the Air Force Flight Test Center. The commander was a general officer, and he was the center commander. The base commander was a colonel, and he was responsible for all the housekeeping things that kept the base running.

To say that the center commander was less than thrilled with my JATO-less take off is a gross understatement. He called my boss, Lt. Col. "Pete"

Everest, into his office and instructed him in no uncertain terms that appropriate punishment was due the culprit who, had he bellied in on the runway, would have ruined his air show.

The punishment turned out to be less than I expected or perhaps deserved. The F-100 was the first new supersonic plane to be released since I came to Edwards, and we had just received them for testing. It could break the sound barrier in level flight with afterburners. I had just been checked out in it, and was salivating to put it through its paces.

"White," Everest said to me, "for that little stunt on Armed Forces Day, you won't fly the F-100 for an entire month."

From the twinkle in his eye, I knew I owed him one. Instead of the F-100, I was still allowed to do one flight in the pre-production Convair YF-102, the precursor of the F-102. The flight was most interesting. However, the YF-102 was not quite ready for prime time.

There were some cockpit things that needed changed, but they were minor. The serious problems lay with the handling. The YF-102 wallowed and yawed terribly, and had a very slow response rate compared to the other fighters of its time. Those would be fatal flaws in combat. Based on data that test pilots accumulated, the Air Force rejected the aircraft. At least the other pilots and I who were not involved with the earlier tests on the YF-102 had an opportunity to experience what a lousy aircraft was like.

So, Convair went back to the drawing board and redesigned the aircraft using the newly discovered "area rule" aerodynamic principle of giving the fuselage a tapered "Coke Bottle" shape. To their credit, they got it right this time. I later flew the F-102, and it was a very fine aircraft. It was proof positive that if the tests were done impartially, and we recorded and reported flaws correctly, problems could be solved.

This episode illustrates the primary task of the test pilot. It is an extraordinarily expensive enterprise to design and build an airplane. What looks right to the engineer on the drawing board may not be right when the plane is in the air. Feedback, good or bad, from the test flights help make the final version of the aircraft the best it can be. That was part of the reason Test Pilot School stressed math, data collection and analysis. It allowed us to talk to the engineers in the same language. I was doubly grateful that I was an engineer and had a leg up in that category.

At this same time, England had a test pilot school called the Empire Test Pilot School. It was not uncommon to have a British pilot train at Edwards or one of our fellows to train in England. One such man was Iven Kincheloe. We were assigned to fighter test at the same time.

Iven was a captain in the United States Air Force and a young fighter ace from the Korean War. He was obviously on his way to the top. When

Iven arrived, I was assigned to test the F-86K, an air defense interceptor aircraft. Iven was assigned to another project, but we became friends from the beginning. Later on, our relationship became even closer, and I considered him my best friend at Edwards.

The North American F-86D was the Air Force air defense interceptor. The F-86K was an identical aircraft with two exceptions. On the F-86D, there was an on board intercept computer and a little different armament. The intercept computer allowed an attack at a ninety-degree angle for firing rockets. The F-86K computer lacked this capability and only allowed the pilot to track an enemy that would steer the F-86K onto the rear of the target to a fifty-caliber machine gun firing position.

My boss, Lt. Col. Everest, wanted to try out the system at night. The first night he flew the F-86K and I flew the T-33 as his target. He made several runs. The next night, I flew the F-86K and he flew the T-33 to be my target.

In each case, when the radar locked onto the target aircraft, a circle appeared in the center of the radar screen. As I approached the target, the circle got smaller. When I was 600 feet away from the target, a large X filled the screen telling me to fire and break away. At the speeds we were flying, that was a very small margin for error.

After the flight, Lt. Col. Everest asked me, "What do you think? Did you fly down to the breakaway signal?"

"No, sir, I stopped just short of the X," I replied.

"Why did you do that?" he asked.

"I was concerned for your safety, sir," I said with a straight face.

"Get out of here, White," he said with a grin and a dismissive wave of his hand.

I truly liked Pete Everest. He was a tough but fair commander, and he was a shrewd judge of people. You couldn't ask for better than that from your boss.

My next assignment was to the Northrop F-89H. It was a slight alteration of the F-89D air defense interceptor. It was subsonic with no-frills. That may sound dull, but it had some novel features that made it enjoyable to work with.

There were pods on each wingtip of the F-89 that held over 100 rockets. The object was to fly the intercept, blast away with the rockets, and by sheer numbers knock down the bad guys. It was quite a thrill to blast away with that much firepower. The H model added three Falcon missiles to each pod. Falcon missiles home onto their target with heat sensors.

My job was to test the plane's stability and control with this new modification. We did every combination imaginable; rockets in, rockets out;

On the boarding ladder of a USAF Air Research & Development Command Lockheed F-104A Starfighter.

rocket asymmetry; missile asymmetry; and every combination of rocket and missile asymmetry. With each new iteration, we recorded performance and handling data. We simulated failures of every sort, including many that would likely never happen. Then we executed strategies to work around the failures. It was a great exercise in problem solving and a lot of fun to boot.

As we finished testing the F-89H, I was sent on temporary duty to Tyndall Air Force base in Panama City, Florida, to an Air Defense Command School. There, they trained those of us who would one day sit and wait for the Russian Bear to come, and when the Bear did come, to stop him. It was an enjoyable respite from the demanding test flights. There was ample opportunity to fly ninety-degree intercepts and to fire weapons. Fighter pilots *love* to fire weapons.

I believe the purpose of my temporary duty at Tyndall was not to go through the entire course that prepared pilots for their Air Defense Command assignments. My job was to get a very abbreviated course so I had the knowledge of the intercept and firing problems they did there. I believe the

Teaching my son Greg about the F-104.

idea was to have me in position to do work with a new and future air defense aircraft, the F-102. The test pilot in fighter test who was the expert with air defense fighters was due to leave Edwards soon for another assignment. Indeed the F-102 was in my future.

In truth, the majority of my time at Edwards Air Force Base can only be descried as fun. I flew every fighter plane in our fine arsenal, switching back and forth between them. In time, I was comfortable in every one of them. What more could a fighter pilot ask for?

I was even assigned to the Ryan X-13 program. This was early in my career. I took it as a good omen, since they would assign me, as a newbie,

Greg here is perched on the F-104's nose cone and is wearing my helmet.

to an intricate aircraft development program it had to bode well for my future. And, it gave me one chance to try the controls of a helicopter.

The X-13 was one of the early breed of vertical takeoff aircraft and was powered by a jet engine. In the vertical position, it was handled like a helicopter. To get a sense of the controls of a helicopter and to try my hand at them, I scheduled several rides in a chopper with one of our helicopter test pilots. When I arrived in San Diego, I was glad I had done that.

They had a mock-up of the aircraft at Ryan Aviation in San Diego. It was rigged for a ring-toss game. There was a doughnut-like circle on a board, and a rod on the nose of the aircraft. The object, as in ring-toss was to put the rod into the doughnut. It took a little practice, but it was doable after a while.

Unfortunately, the program was short-lived. The plane was only flown by the company pilot. They had the plane tethered to a wire mounted on a truck bed that could be rotated into the vertical position. The pilot took off in a vertical fashion from the wire, and then converted to level flight to make a pass around the field. Next, he hung the plane back on the wire slick-as-a-whistle. I thought the idea had merit, but it was scrapped after only a few test flights.

Weather in the desert was seldom a problem. The sky above Edwards was almost always blue and cloudless. And, with the enormous runway for landing in an emergency, flying was as safe as it could be, considering the stresses we placed on the aircraft we were flying. But we all knew it was still risky business.

When the revised F-102 arrived, I was assigned to fly it. Between missions and chase time, both Iven and I were logging over sixty hours a month. That was well above the usual forty and on rare occasion 50 hours we normally logged. It got to be a joke with the other pilots.

"Hey, you better slow these guys down. First you didn't want White here, now you're flying him too much," one wag said.

The F-102 was a great, delta wing air defense fighter. It was easy to fly, forgiving and fun to land on the "delta cushion." We had four to five airplanes at any given time, and our task was simply to fly them; to put time on them; to stress them to their limits.

The reason for this extended flying time was to test the endurance of the aircraft and its individual components. We recorded information about lights, brakes, switches, gauges, and anything else imaginable. How long before something would fail? We also supplied information concerning the performance and handling of the aircraft under various conditions to the Using Command, the people who would take the plane for use after the testing was completed.

I spent a lot of time checking other pilots out in the 102 including many pilots from the Air Defense Command. When they were trained, they would then check out other pilots as squadrons converted to the F-102. Still, sitting on the edge of the cockpit explaining the layout, switches and gauges to another pilot unfamiliar with the aircraft was not necessarily stimulating work. Also, I had to evaluate their flying. And, since these were the men who would train those pilots who might have to go to war in a 102, I took my job seriously.

The "delta cushion" landings had a specific sequence; flair and touch the wheels down before deploying the drag chute. First you picked your landing spot. The next step was to flair the aircraft and settle on the cushion of air supplied by the Delta wings. When you felt the wheels touch, you deployed the drag chute.

A pilot always manned a little booth along the runway called Runway Control. Armed with a pair of binoculars, flare gun with assorted colors of

My son Greg sitting in the cockpit of an F-104 wearing my helmet, and living the dream of millions of young Steve Canyon fans of that generation.

flares, and a radio, it was his job to warn the landing pilot of any unusual situation. If the landing gear was not down, you could call the pilot to abort the landing. If the plane was too high or too low, the pilot could be warned of that. Of course, there was always the red flare that would abort the landing.

As I watched one of my rookies land from Runway Control, just before his wheels touched down, the drag chute popped out. I left the booth at once, and was waiting for him when he came into the operations room.

"Why you did you employ the drag chute before your wheels touched down?" I asked him.

"I knew I was only two or three feet from touching down," he replied with a confident smirk.

"Have you ever thought you were two or three feet in the air when you were really ten to fifteen feet up?" I asked. His reluctance to answer the question told me that indeed he had made that error.

"If you pop that chute at fifteen feet instead of two, we'll scrape what's left of you off the runway with a putty knife," I said, and walked away, knowing my point had been made.

During this time, I was able to fly other forms of aircraft. There were bombers, transports, as well as other fighter planes. Being able to fly made up in part for the tedium of the checkout duty.

The Republic YF-105A fighter bomber came next. It had some problems that were ironed out by the time the more advanced production B model was delivered. The company test pilots had done the preliminary phase one testing, and it was my honor to do the first phase two flights.

Over the next few weeks, I flew the usual stability and control tests, but I ran into problems. As in the F-102, it began with the cockpit and carried on from there. The lateral and longitudinal control systems were both unsatisfactory and needed redesign.

On a trip to Republic, I reinforced my written test reports that the flight control system needed redesign. The cockpit displays, switches, gauges, warning panel placement and flap controls, among others, all needed serious review and refinement. The engineers at Republic took my comments to heart without taking them personally and set about improving the aircraft.

My test flights on the F-105B were personally gratifying. This was what it was all about, being able to do a series of tests on a new aircraft that would go into production and enter the Air Force inventory. That's where the action is. It's not about whether I could fly a sloppy aircraft or put up with some poor cockpit features. My job was to be certain that the pilots out in the squadrons could get the best and safest aircraft possible. Of course, that was the criteria for the circa 1959–1960 time period. Fortunately, the testing world has changed dramatically since then, but more on that later.

This airplane also gave me one of my hairiest moments while testing fighter planes. The F-105, a fighter bomber, had nuclear weapon capabilities. On one test flight at near supersonic speeds, I ran a test to see how much stick force was required to turn the plane in a series of increasing gravitational or G-force levels.

At two Gs, I registered the force. Then, I went to three and then four Gs. As I approached four, there was a horrendous noise and alarms went off all over the place. I was not sure what happened. I didn't lose control of the aircraft, and everything seemed okay inside the cockpit.

"Edwards tower, I am declaring an emergency. I just got a big bang and my warning lights are all on. I still seem to have control, but I'm bringing it back."

"Roger that. We'll be waiting," was the reply.

I headed for home. Sweating more than usual, I landed the plane safely, taxied off the runway and stopped. I was still clueless as to the problem.

A Republic engineer was waiting for me. He took one look at the airplane and shook his head. Just in front of the air intake of the 105 was a piece of metal about the size of three or four tennis rackets and about a quarter of an inch thick. This splitter was supposed to keep the air flow laminar as it went into the air intakes.

At four Gs, the plate had ripped off and consequently was sucked into the air intake. Spinning through the intake duct, it ripped the internal portion of the engine to shreds. I profusely thanked Pratt and Whitney for making an engine strong enough to get me home, even after it had been gutted by flying metal.

I realize it sounds strange, but at no time did I feel I was in danger of crashing. That was true in the war and is true now. It was only after I had landed and surveyed the extent of the damage, that I realized how close I had come to disaster. The thoughts sobered me, but they passed quickly. If a test pilot is afraid, or worried about his safety, he will not do his job. Bad things happened to other people, but it wouldn't happen to me.

This was true of most test pilots. During a test flight, there was so much to think about, and so much to do, that I really didn't have time to be afraid. If fear entered the equation, it could disrupt my thought processes and lead to real disaster. All test pilots get anxious from time to time, but most of the real anxiety comes after the fact.

To Republic's credit, when the improved all-weather F-105D was delivered, they had corrected every technical problem, and I was certainly glad they did. Although I didn't realize it at the time, this would be the plane I would later fly in combat in Vietnam.

After the 105 tests were completed, the announcement was made that

Convair's F-106, the first really advanced supersonic air-defense fighter, was scheduled for testing. All systems were updated, and the airplane had Mach-2 capabilities. It was to replace the F-102.

Standard procedure called for the formation of a task force for the planning and testing of the plane. To my delight I was appointed director for the F-106 project. The rest of the task force involved not only the Air Force Test Center, but the User Command, the manufacturer, and any major subcontractors. I looked forward to the job.

During the planning stage for the 106, an announcement was made that the highly anticipated North American X-15 rocket plane was ready for assignments. Iven Kincheloe was designated as primary Air Force pilot, and I was to be his backup. It was a natural pairing since we were the best of friends and had done a lot of work together. Needless to say, the F-106 project quickly disappeared from my radar. It would have been fun to stay with the 106 task force and participate in the entire project of bringing a new fighter from the preliminary stages to the User Command, but the prospect of the X-15 had too much allure. Once again a small thing had changed my career path. This time it happened to be a friendship. I later learned that Iven had been instrumental in getting me second seat on the project.

The X-15 was very advanced for its time. But it had been preceded by other rocket planes, each one designed to push the envelope in incremental fashion. When the envelope is pushed, sometimes things break, bringing with it another side of the job.

Every test pilot knows that the potential for hazard and even death is always there, but every test pilot I have ever worked with accepts that as part of the job. It is not different from the modern racecar driver who knows that around the next bend there might be an accident. None of us ever dwelt on the negative. When we lost a friend, we grieved and went on with the task at hand.

My personal routine to minimize danger was preparedness. The more prepared I was for any emergency the more likely I would be able to handle it. I began that routine in flight school, as I prepared for war, and carried it with me to the rest of my career.

A prime example was my first flight in an F-86. I went supersonic, did stalls right and left, power on, power off, and left and right spins and a full series of aerobatics. It was a marvelous aircraft and a joy to fly. When I returned to base Major Childs asked me what I had done on my shakedown flight. When I told him what I had done, he told me to take it easy. I understood his point of view, but old habits die hard. I now knew every little quirk of the plane, and when something unexpected happened, I'd be as ready as I could be.

At this stage in the fighter test program, the flight characteristics of the aircraft were not significantly different from standard aircraft. But, as time passed, the Air Force knew that speeds would escalate and that aircraft would change. New skills would be required to control them. This would be part of the challenge of the X-15.

Life was not easy for the pilots' families either. By this time I had a wife and three children. While the flat terrain and the marvelous visibility around Edwards was so important to the test program, it also allowed the families to see tell-tale black smoke for miles.

A number of firefighting units were stationed at the base, and they too had to drill to keep their skill levels high. If we forgot to remind the families that it was fire drill day, the columns of black smoke from the desert meant anxious moments for them as they awaited the dreaded knock on the door.

I will not trivialize the danger. At no time did our complement of test pilots number more than thirty-six to thirty-nine with seven to nine of those being in the fighter cadre. In one year, we lost a total of nine men from the 39-men complement. Three of them were fighter test pilots. All of them were friends of mine. Some were closer than others, but they were all family in the brotherhood of test pilots. When we lost a man, it triggered a new and at times heartrending job for one of us.

A summary court officer was appointed to help the widow through this time of intense grief. It was the officer's job to help with funeral arrangements if needed, contact the benefits office, do whatever he could to help from a business or personal standpoint.

Captain Mel Apt was a good friend of mine. Mel backed Iven Kincheloe when they were flying the X-2 in September 1956, and he was set to take the airplane to Mach 3. After successfully reaching a speed of Mach 3.2 and becoming the first man to fly three times the speed of sound, Mel turned back toward the base to prepare for his routine dead stick landing. At that speed, however, the insidious effects of "inertia coupling" sent the X-2 hurtling out of control. Mel tried desperately to regain control of the tumbling aircraft but was knocked unconscious several times during the descent. When he came to at lower altitude, he ejected the nose capsule and prepared to manually bail out of that new escape device, but it was too late, and he was killed.

I accompanied his widow to Phoenix, went to the Social Security office for her, and helped her settle in. It was one of the most difficult things that the Air Force had ever asked me to do. What came next was even worse.

Contractors work on Saturdays, and as a result we pulled additional duty. Iven Kincheloe was assigned to ferry an F-104 from Edwards to nearby Palmdale on that fateful day. The F-104 had a unique T-tail configuration.

Concerned that an ejecting pilot might hit the tail, Lockheed engineers designed the aircraft with a downward-firing ejection seat. A real boon at high altitudes, the seat was less desirable close to the ground.

Shortly after Iven took off that morning, the F-104's engine quit. Since it happened when he was quite low, the hazard of ejection increased. He rolled the slowing airplane inverted and ejected upward, but was well outside the envelope for a successful bail out. Although his chute opened, he could not avoid the fireball in front of him from the crashing plane, and he was killed instantly.

When Major Childs rang my doorbell that day, I could tell by the look on his face that something was terribly wrong. I barely had time to digest the news that my best friend was dead, and I would again be the summary court officer, when I had a second visitor. It was Everest's deputy, Lt. Col. Harold Russell.

"Bob, you're now number one in the X-15. You're in the catbird's seat, and I must ask this. Do you have any second thoughts about moving into that position?" he asked.

It is difficult to describe my feelings at that moment. I had just been told that I was being given the chance of a lifetime as a pilot. But the reason I had it was that one of my good friends was dead. I knew that Iven had gone to bat for me and was instrumental in my being chosen as the backup pilot for the program. At that moment, and ever since, I would have given it all back if it could somehow bring Iven back to life. Knowing Iven's family as I did, the summary court task was doubly difficult for me.

I kept my answer simple and said, "No."

Pat Hunerwadel was a Lockheed U-2 pilot and another good friend of Iven and me. The Lockheed U-2 was the plane made infamous when Gary Powers went down in Russia. While flying in a routine three-hundred-sixty degree approach to landing, Pat lost control and crashed. The board of inquiry found no explanation for the accident.

Much to my surprise, his wife said that Pat had told her that if anything ever happened to him, he wanted me to be the summary court officer for him. For the third time I had the unpleasant task of helping a widow settle her affairs and deal with the loss of her husband. Hopefully the third time was the charm, and I wouldn't have to do it again.

Occasionally, pilot error, ego and even ignorance can be involved in a catastrophe. Two weeks into the F-89 program, a pilot wanted to try and take the aircraft supersonic. In the daring attempt to push the envelope, he would need to do a vertical dive to reach the desired speed. Ignorance came into play.

What no one took into account was a shock wave that occurred over the horizontal stabilizer at high speed. In a high-powered aircraft, the shock wave is easy to demonstrate. This time, ignoring it proved to be a fatal error. As the shock wave passed over the stabilizer, it changed the pressure over the elevator, rendering it ineffectual. The pilot pulled his control stick full back, and he was still not be able to get the F-89 out of the dive. Out of control, he cratered into the ground. This occurred during my first month of flight testing. This flight should never have happened. As a new man in flight test I realized I had a lot to listen to and learn from.

As is true of most things involving the government, politics always plays a part. The X-15 program was not without its political intrigue either.

Everyone even vaguely conversant with the history of flight knows the name Chuck Yeager, the first man to fly faster than sound in the X-1. Kit Murray, his number two, took the X-1 to over 90,000 feet. At this time Murray was stationed at Wright-Patterson Air Force Base in Dayton, Ohio.

As part of my duty as Iven's summary court officer, I read a letter from his wife at a Los Angeles conference he was supposed to attend. It was there that I first heard the rumors concerning Murray.

Murray was being rumored as a candidate for the job of primary X-15 pilot. I received the news with mixed emotions. The job was mine, and I had earned it, even though the job was given to me by tragic circumstances. But I was wise enough to understand that in programs like the X-15, other forces beyond my control could come into play. Career Management 101 was not an option this time. I had to sit on my hands and wait for things to sort themselves out. That was a really hard thing for me to do. The thought of losing my ride in the X-15 now was gut-wrenching to me.

Lt. Col. Russell was now an assistant to the commanding general of the Flight Test Center. When he heard the news, he went at once to the general's office.

"Sir, they are trying to undercut your man. Talk is they want Murray. This has to stop," Russell told the General.

General Marcus Cooper ordered his plane made ready for a flight to Washington. He told the powers-that-be in no uncertain terms that Bob White, the Test Center's man, was the X-15 pilot. When they agreed with him, I received the news with a great sense of relief.

At the same time NASA was in the preliminary process of choosing astronauts. It would be a glamorous, high-profile assignment, but I was never tempted. The 10-year-old boy inside me still sat on those stone steps in Manhattan and looked up into the sky. My destiny was linked to an airplane. The astronauts were wonderful men, and I am proud to number many of them among my friends, but I have never regretted my decision to pass up the opportunity to join that illustrious group.

Approaching the start of the X-15 test program, I had that old feeling. I knew for certain that this was the right place to be. I was living a pilot's dream, surrounded by as elite a group of flyers as I could ever have dreamed of being part of. Now it was going to be my time to ride the rocket.

Chapter 7

A Brief History Lesson

For me as an engineer, the X-15 program had to be the zenith of my flying career. From my position as a career military officer, it was an important step along the way. The history of the X-15 is an interesting study in pushing the performance envelope. The real story of the X-15 actually began during World War II.

War is a terrible thing, but from it comes some of mankind's more remarkable accomplishments in medicine, engineering, and, in my case, aviation. Army intelligence knew that the Germans were pushing the development of advanced aircraft including the development of jet-powered aircraft. We were determined to do the same. During the war, the speed of aircraft doubled from 200 to 400 knots, an amazing speed for the time.

Unfortunately, the demands of the war dictated that the industrial might of the United States focus on the development of war machines. There was neither time nor money for anything else. As various shielding and heavy armament were added in an attempt to strengthen the defense of our warplanes, they often behaved erratically or broke up during early flights. Scratching their heads, engineers blamed the extra equipment. In reality, no one could be absolutely sure that was the culprit.

As combat flights increased in speed and altitude, pilots began to notice aberrant handling characteristics. At high speeds the P-51 could suddenly become a shaking, pitching, yawing animal as difficult to handle as any bronco. This was compounded when one flight would be smooth and the next at a higher altitude or faster speed could become suddenly lethal.

Major Pete Barsodi, a fellow P-51 pilot described a number of these effects after a particularly high-speed dive. He described what looked like heat waves from a radiator coming off his wings as the wing flaps vibrated. When the brass scoffed at the idea, he took a camera aloft with him and repeated the dive. He returned with the first ever pictures of shock waves. No one knew what to make of them.

I noticed on some of my own higher altitude flights a peculiar flutter of the wing flaps associated with handling problems. After Pete's observation, I was able to see those heat signatures on my own wings radiating from the flap area. All these effects disappeared when I slowed the plane down or went to a lower altitude.

Wartime engineers came to the conclusion that they were pushing aircraft through the less dense medium of air faster than the air could get out of the way. They reasoned that as the aircraft approached the speed of sound, so much air would pile up around the nose and wings of the aircraft that the resultant pressure would slow the aircraft down so much that it would preclude flights much above Mach 1. They named this phenomenon compressibility.

Only one man, Ezra Kocher, saw the sound barrier as merely an unresolved mathematical problem. He attempted to gain support for the design and construction of special aircraft to study the problem. With the war on, that wasn't going to happen. Still, he persisted, and after the war, his idea began to gain momentum. In the next few years, his idea took root, and he became the father of the modern experimental aircraft.

Although the name Chuck Yeager is indelibly linked to supersonic flight, the first serious attempt actually began the year before. In 1946, Geoffrey de Havilland was killed when his jet-powered de Havilland DH-108 Swallow came apart in an attempt to break the sound barrier.

Interestingly, the speed of sound had been determined by artillerymen in the 17th century to be 1,140 feet per second at sea level. By firing cannons at a distance and measuring the time it took the sound to reach them, they made this calulation. The slight difference over the actual measurement (1,124 feet per second) can be accounted for by the fact that they didn't include temperature in their calculations.

The Bell X-1 was designed to assult the sound barrier and to open the envelope of supersonic flight. Three pilots were involved. Chuck Yeager was the number one Air Force pilot for the X-1 project with Bob Hoover, who became well known as a test pilot for North American Aviation and later a brilliant air show pilot, as his number two. Unfortunately for Bob, he never flew the X-1. The Bell company test pilot was Chalmers "Slick" Goodlin, a man with an ego nearly as big as Yeager's.

There was talk at the time about a $25,000 bonus for the company pilot who reached Mach 1 first. Major General Al Boyd put a halt to this immediately. He had other ideas. "The Air Force will do it," he said simply.

NACA (National Advisery Committee for Aeronautics), the precursor of NASA, agreed. They would handle the engineering in conjunction with Bell, the Air Force would do the flying, and Yeager would be the man who would break the sound barrier.

A great deal has been written about Chuck Yeager. By his own admission, he has a monumental ego, and at times it caused conflict. But I have flown with him, and he is an outstanding pilot. I can see why he was chosen for the assult on the sound barrier.

On October 14, 1947, with Chuck Yeager at the controls, the Bell X-1 broke the sound barrier in level flight for the first time in history. A later version of the airplane called the X-1A was flown by Yeager to Mach 2.5 in 1953. The Douglas D-558-I Skystreak and D-558-II Skyrocket soon followed as well as the Bell X-2. The X-2's task was to collect data to evaulate skin temperature over time, the effects of insulating material on skin temperature, actual in-flight temperatures and escape systems. These data paved the way for what we did later. All these flights were done with a rocket engine that had no throttle and couldn't be restarted after it was switched off.

An intense competion developed between Bell with Chuck Yeager, and Douglas with Scott Crossfield, who would later also fly the X-15. The race to Mach 2 was won by Scott and the bar was then raised to twice the speed of sound. The X-2 set a world altitude record at 126,000 feet with my friend, Captain Iven Kincheloe, in the cockpit. The X-2 project ended with the tragic death of Captain Mel Apt on his Mach 3 flight, a good man and a fine pilot as I have previously described.

The X-15 program actually began in June 1952. At a meeting of the NACA, flights at speeds and altitudes that could only be dreamed about when the Bell X-1 program pushed the envelope across the sound barrier were seriously debated. With rocket technology escalating at a runaway pace, flights of Mach 10 and altitudes up to fifty miles were considered definitely possible. After much discussion, NACA approved a plan to conduct that research. And they put their money where their mouths were. They approved a budget of $40,000,000, an enormous budget for a project in the early 1950s, when the average salary was $3,200 a year and you could buy a new Ford for $1,400.

In September of that year, a committee was formed and the preliminary research on space flight and the problems associated with it were begun. It became apparent that none of the aircraft in the country's arsenal at that time would be sufficient for the task. So, in February of 1954, the NACA panel discussed the need for a new research aircraft to study hypersonic flight and flight in a weightless environment. They developed and presented the proposal for the new craft to the Air Force and the Navy. Industry was added to broaden the base, and the competition between the government and the private sector was on.

The only disagreement between the Air Force and the Navy involved the number of seats in the new aircraft. The Navy wanted a two-seat craft, with a pilot in front and an engineer in the second seat. In the end, the engineers decided that newer data collection devices and monitoring capabilities could do the job without the extra weight of a second passenger. The single-seat design was agreed upon.

In December 1954, the Air Force invited contractors to submit plans for the new aircraft that would be designated X-15, in an open design competition. After an intense competition between major U.S. manufacturers, North American Aviation Company in Inglewood, California, was selected to develop the three X-15 research planes. In February 1956, Reaction Motors Company was awarded the contract to build the XLR-99 rocket engine that would propel the X-15.

The X-15 was not a large craft. In fact, it was carried over public highways on a transporter hardly larger than a conventional tractor-trailer rig. It was 52 feet long, and 13 feet high with a wing span of only 22 feet. Its gross weight topped out at 38,000 pounds. The engine that was finally developed from the

The X-15's mighty XLR-99 rocket engine (AFFTC History Office photograph).

Thiokol division of Reaction Motors, the XLR-99-RM-2 engine, could develop 57,000 pounds of thrust. It would be the first rocket engine with a throttle that allowed variable speeds and could be restarted once it was shut down.

As the development of the X-15 began, the selection of pilots for the program got underway. The first group included Scott Crossfield, who was the test pilot for North American, and the first man to eventually fly the aircraft. He made fourteen flights including the first nine in the contractor demonstration phase and LR-99 engine phase. All but three of his flights were made with the smaller LR-11 engine, however.

NASA's Joe Walker would be the government representative and the second person to pilot the new aircraft. Joe flew for 41 months from March 1960 to August 1963 making a total of twenty-five flights. He flew the flight envelope expansion phase with the LR-11 engine and LR-99 engine and research phases.

When I was the U.S. Air Force chief X-15 pilot, I posed with North American Aviation Corporation chief X-15 pilot A. Scott Crossfield (left) and National Aeronautics & Space Administration X-15 pilot Neil Armstrong (right) between the first two X-15s at Edwards Air Force Base (NASA photograph).

With the NB-52 resplendent in its bright day-glo orange high-visibility color scheme and an X-15 mated to its wing as seen in the background, the first three X-15 pilots pose for their photograph in the early morning sunlight. From left: me, Crossfield, and Walker (AFFTC History Office photograph).

I was the third person to fly the plane, and represented the Air Force. I made sixteen flights over 32 months from April 13, 1960, to December 14, 1962. I flew the flight envelope expansion phase with the LR-11 engine and LR-99 engine and research phases.

Navy Lt. Commander Forrest Petersen was the fourth to fly the aircraft and made five flights from September 1960 till January 1962. NASA's Jack McKay flew twenty-nine flights from October 28, 1960, to September 8, 1966, and my fellow Air Force pilot Bob Rushworth flew thirty-four times during the same six-year span. Before joining the space program, in the twenty months between November 1960 to July 1962, Neil Armstrong made seven flights in the X-15 including the first with the new "Q-ball" nosecone.

Air Force pilots Joe Engle, Pete Knight, and Mike Adams, plus NASA pilots Milt Thompson and Bill Dana, all flew the airplane after I left the program. I feel this was a special group of men, and not just because I was one of them. They were, to a man, as hard a working group of professionals as you will ever run across. Each of us felt a sense of honor and responsibility as we faced the challenge that had been set before us. And each of us, in our own way, did our small part to help change the face of aviation.

Chapter 8

The Fun Begins

While the X-15 was under construction, I went down to North American Aviation in Los Angeles and worked with their engineering department. I had the rare opportunity to really get into the belly of the beast. With their engineers, I was able to study the various systems of the airplane in detail and learn how they worked before I actually had to fly it.

And there was a lot to learn. A rocket engine has no rotating parts. So to provide steam to drive the turbines to produce electrical and hydraulic power hydrogen peroxide was poured over a silver catalyst to produce the necessary steam. Thanks to my critical decision to go to college after the war, I was able to speak their language and actually understand what they were talking about. When we started to fly, it was an enormous advantage when I explained to them how the aircraft was behaving.

Since computers for everyday use were still decades away, we did most of the data crunching the old-fashioned way. Our tools were slide rules, drafting tables, pens and onion-skin paper. Still, we were able to produce nearly as much information as could be done with a modern computer. There were a few of the cumbersome early computers around, and when they were available to us, we made use of them.

Around this time, Scott Crossfield, North American's primary pilot, Iven Kincheloe, who was to be the number-one Air Force pilot prior to his tragic death, and I were sent to the Johnsville, Pennsylvania, laboratory for centrifuge training. It was a far cry from the ones used later by pilots and astronauts for advanced training.

The computer that operated the centrifuge was one of the original vacuum tube models. Back then, it was a marvel of technology. It was as big as a house, and the countless vacuum tubes inside it generated enough heat to challenge a modern domed stadium's air conditioning system. If one tube failed, as they often did, the entire computer shut down and the centrifuge ground to a halt.

Fortunately, I only had to ride this beast once. Unfortunately, it was a major embarrassment for me personally. Every centrifuge ride included full, on-board video camera monitoring. Before the ride started, I was supposed to tighten a head strap that would keep my head from being pushed forward by centrifugal force, but I simply forgot to fasten it. As the machine gradually picked up speed, I realized my error. The film documented my pathetic attempts to overcome the G-forces. There I was, trying in vain to push my chin off my chest with one hand while desperately trying to complete my assigned tasks with the other. When the inevitable "crash" occurred, I was so chagrined that I didn't want to get out of the mockup and face the engineers. Worse yet, I had to face my buddies Iven and Scott. They'd never let me live this one down. And my neck was sore for a week.

The development of the fixed-base simulator evolved from the 1950s and was available for a full range of unlimited freedom flight simulations prior to the first flight of the X-15. Aside from a bunch of analog computers and other electronics, the X-15 cockpit had an accurate instrument panel and exact placement of switches and controls. It proved to be an excellent tool and a mission simulation of some ten to twenty hours could precede a nine- to eleven-minute flight. As a pilot, I considered it the most valuable time that could be spent preparing me for a flight. In addition, I had the good fortune to have Air Force engineer Bob Hoey and NASA engineer Richard Day as my mentors. They gave me the greatest insight into the many things that could go awry on a particular mission, and I owe much of my success to them.

In addition to the fixed base simulator, the "Iron Cross" simulator was used to help develop the ballistic control system that would be used to navigate the aircraft attitude outside of earth's atmosphere. Two long iron bars, about 25–30 feet, each were joined in a cruciform shape. That's where we got the colorful nickname. The bars were on a pivot at their junction and four jet thrusters were placed on the end of a bar.

Hydrogen peroxide was poured over a silver catalyst and the resultant reaction produced enormous amounts of heat. The peroxide was reduced back to its water component, and the water turned to steam by the internally generated heat. The steam jets permitted on-board adjustment of pitch, yaw, and roll, depending on which of the four thrusters was fired. Compact, efficient and self-contained, this little system would subsequently be used on board the Mercury spacecraft that the first astronauts flew.

Another facet of our preparation involved multiple trips to the David Clark Brassiere and Girdle factory in Wooster, Massachusetts. The powers-that-be considered this to be a natural fit—so-to-speak—for a company to design our full pressure suits. They would be used to protect us from Mother Nature if the cabin pressure on the X-15 failed.

Here I am sitting in the right-hand seat of a Convair JTF-102A Delta Dagger supersonic trainer at Edwards AFB and wearing my custom-made Dave Clark MC-2 full pressure suit and helmet. High-altitude flights in the "Deuce" were made to help get the X-15 pilots acclimated to cockpit ergonomics while actually wearing their pressure suits in an airborne aircraft (U.S. Air Force)

Each suit had to be custom-fitted at the factory. Scott got suit number one, and I was fitted with suit number two. Unfortunately, Iven was no longer with us at this juncture. A side benefit of these trips were visits to crooner Rudy Vallee's favorite restaurant, and we agreed with him—the food was excellent.

When the suits were finished, we were taken to an altitude chamber to test them. Mine worked fine, complete with the welts and red streaks caused by the seams and tight spots in the suit pressing into my skin. They were souvenirs of every flight.

Another task in our preparation was familiarizing ourselves with the dry lake beds that would be used for emergency landings when we were away from the friendly confines of the long runway at Edwards. Considering the speeds we were projected to reach during the program, this was a vast area. Ten dry lakes were eventually chosen. The number in parenthesis is the number of emergency landings eventually made there. In California: Ballarat, Cuddleback (2), Hidden Hills, Rosamond (1), Silver (1), and Smith Ranch (1), in Nevada: Delamar (1) and Mud (4). An emergency landing was not necessarily an emergency in the true sense of the word. For the X-15 program, it meant having to recover at a lake bed other than Rogers Dry Lake back at Edwards Air Force Base.

Another important pre-flight consideration for the X-15 was weight. In the X-2 they used an escape capsule for the pilot. In the X-15 they decided on an ejection seat with some protective covering and a two-parachute descent system. It took us no time at all to surpass the limits of the escape system, which was only good for flights up to 125,000 feet and at speeds below Mach 3. In a real emergency, we probably wouldn't have time to go that low or that slow when we needed to get out.

Finally, all the preparation was done, and the X-15 went into production. On June 8, 1959, Scott Crossfield, Joe Walker and I flew to Los Angeles for the factory rollout of the Number One airplane at the North American Facility. It was a major media event with brass bands, speeches and the whole nine yards. The Vice President of the United States, Richard M. Nixon, was there as the keynote speaker. As Mr. Nixon sat on the podium, the microphone was turned on, and he didn't know it. When the X-15 was rolled into view, Mr. Nixon remarked to the man sitting next to him, "That sure is a funny looking thing."

After the ceremony, Mr. Nixon spoke to us and said, "Well boys, if you do what they say this thing will do, it's likely I'll be seeing you again at the White House." The Vice President proved half a prophet. We did push the X-15 to its limits and beyond. As a result, we were invited to the White House to receive the prestigious Harmon International Aviators Trophy for

A rare signed portrait of all the original X-15 pilots posing with Ship 1, still fitted with its black-and-white striped nose boom in the early days of the program. From left, USAF Maj. Robert Rushworth, NASA's Jack McKay, U.S. Navy Cdr. Forrest Peterson, NASA's Joe Walker and Neil Armstrong, and me.

our work with the X-15. Unfortunately for Mr. Nixon, the president who gave it to us was John F. Kennedy.

Concurrent with this, two B-52 aircraft, designated 003 and 008, which we called Balls 3 and Balls 8, had been assigned to the project. These planes and their crews went into an intense period of adaptation and training that matched ours. Specially altered to carry the X-15 aloft for launch, they were an integral part of the project. Without them, the X-15 couldn't get off the ground.

As the representative of North American, Scott was designated to fly the first X-15 flights. In this phase, the manufacturer was to demonstrate that the airplane possessed the potential to actually do what it was designed to do. Joe, as the government representative, would fly next, followed by me, representing the Air Force.

NACA had been replaced by NASA at this point, and NASA bent over backward to be cooperative. They even offered me a desk with their test pilots, Even though I did most of my work with them, I declined, choosing instead to stay with the Air Force pilots.

Hydraulics and electronics on the X-15 were powered by auxiliary power

Aeronautical "brothers in arms" in 1960, the original X-15 pilots, Crossfield, me, Walker, and Peterson, standing next to the nose section of "Balls 8," the second of two NB-52 X-15 launch aircraft. The bomber was originally nicknamed "The High and Mighty One" during the early days of the test program (AFFTC History Office photograph).

units that turned electrical generators and pumps that were actually miniature steam engines. There were two of them, both running simultaneously to reduce the risk of failure. If both failed, hydraulics and electronics went, too. Needless to say, so would the X-15 and perhaps its pilot. It was imperative to know how well these things worked. And since the airplane spent the majority of every flight as a glider, we needed to know how well it could do that, too.

The first free flight was performed without rocket power to test the flight characteristics of the X-15, as well as the on-board flight systems. On September 7, 1959, the X-15 was attached to the wing of the B-52 for the first time. I would be piloting a chase plane for this historic flight. Takeoff was smooth, and the B-52 reached the launch altitude without a hitch.

I rendezvoused with the B-52 and made my fly-by visual inspection. Everything was in order and I radioed the information to the B-52. We held our collective breaths as the countdown inched towards zero.

The hooks holding the X-15 to the B-52 released flawlessly. Scott made the required minor adjustment away from the Mother Ship and the X-15 was airborne for the first time. There were collective whoops of joy as well as relief both silent and verbalized as we watched the black ship glide away.

But the time for celebrating was momentary. I had studied the flight plan as much as Scott, and I knew exactly what he was going to be doing before he did it. My job was to watch for any sign of external problems and alert Scott if I saw any. Secondarily, I was to give the cameraman in the back seat of my fighter plane good views as he photographed the historic event.

This first flight went smoothly and nearly without a hitch. As Scott flared out for his landing, he started through several pitch oscillations. This happens if there is the slightest mismatch between control stick input and elevator response. This is definitely not desirable when close to the ground and traveling over 200 miles an hour.

In an early flight, Scott Crossfield pilots the X-15 while I fly the chase plane (top) (NASA photograph).

Fortunately, Scott did a good job and caught the bottom of one oscillation just as his landing gear slid smoothly onto the dry lake surface. The problem lay in the calibration of the airplane's control system, and the engineers fixed the problem immediately. In my judgment, they created one of the best flight control systems in an aircraft operating at the range of speeds of the X-15.

The XLR-99-RM-1 rocket engine took longer to develop than Thiokol had originally anticipated. So, the Number One aircraft was equipped with two X-1 engines. Each engine had four thrust chambers, and they were stacked vertically. This was the XL-11 configuration. Each of the eight thrust chambers was controlled by a separate toggle switch. Each thruster could be started and shut down, but once shut down it could not be restarted. In that event, it was like the old X-1. And there was no throttle. You simply flipped a switch and held on.

The first time Scott flew under power, new issues surfaced that had not been part of the glide flight. On the second flight, the turbo pump case

Me at the controls of an F-107 chase plane (NASA photograph).

failed, there was a fire in the hydrogen peroxide compartment and engine compartment, and the lower ventral wing flaps only extended 60 percent. None of these were life threatening or caused any damage to the aircraft. These were the sorts of things that test pilots accepted as a routine part of their job and that the company pilots sort out.

On the third flight there was a fire in the engine bay. When Scott landed, the nose gear failed, but the airplane was undamaged.

I was again in the seat of the chase plane for flight number four when we had our first real scare. My F-104 flew alongside the B-52 and the cameraman in the back was cranking away. The countdown hit zero and the X-15 dropped away like a stone as I monitored the conversation between the X-15 and the B-52.

"I'm going to light her up," Scott said, and in my mind's eye I visualized him flipping a toggle switch.

Instead of the flame and smoke from the rear of the aircraft that I expected, there was a flash and a large bang that I felt in my own aircraft. The engine compartment had a major fire. Scott shut the engine down and the fire extinguished. In a careful fly around, I could see no other major damage.

"Everything looks okay, Scott, I see no structural damage," I told him.

Chief NASA X-15 pilot Joe Walker (left) and I examine the cockpit of X-15 ship 1 in the main hangar NASA's Flight Research Center on February 25, 1960. We were the first two government pilots to fly the airplane after Scott Crossfield's initial contractor proving flights (NASA photograph).

"Roger that, Bob," he replied and declared the emergency.

I followed him toward the dry lake bed as he dumped the rest of his propellants. It appeared that his luck might hold. He set up for a routine landing and prepared to set her down. He wouldn't be able to reach Rogers Dry Lake, but the smaller Rosamond Dry Lake to the west was available for the emergency landing.

The plane touched down smoothly on its main landing gear, then the nose gear slammed down and the fuselage of the Number One aircraft cracked just behind the instrument bay and folded up like a half-closed jack-knife. Scott walked away from the crash, but the Number One aircraft was definitely the worse for wear and needed major repairs. Enter the number two aircraft. Flights five and six went without incident, but on number seven there was a premature engine shut down. Flight eight was another good one. Scott was settling in.

Joe Walker flew the first NASA flight with the ninth mission. The roll damper and stable platform failed; again not life threatening malfunctions. Otherwise it was a good flight with no problems.

During Scott's next two flights, all went well.

Then, I got the word. On Friday, April 13, 1960, I would be the first Air Force pilot, and the third man overall, to fly the X-15 on mission number twelve. The first question from mission control was, "It's Friday the thirteenth, Bob. Do you have any problem flying on that day?"

Possessing not a single superstitious bone in my body, my one-word answer was, "No!" It was my turn to ride the rocket, and I wasn't letting anything as simple as a foolish superstition get in my way.

Chapter 9
Riding the Rocket

I had the luxury of flying the X-15 a total of 16 times. I've often been asked what it was like. It was my job. The X-15 was my office, so let me take you along for a day at the office.

Actually, I have to back up a bit from the day of the flight. For me, the flight didn't begin on the day it actually took place. As I had done in all my flights as a test pilot, it began two weeks before the flight date. I started the physical and mental preparation that had served me so well on the other test flights.

NAA X-15 pilot Scott Crossfield (left) handing "the keys" over to me while NASA X-15 pilot Neil Armstrong observes (AFFTC History Office photograph).

The G forces generated by the X-15 took their toll on the body, so I kept myself in reasonably good physical condition all of the time, but when I knew my next flight date, I beefed up the physical routine to be in the best physical condition possible the day I flew.

For the two weeks before the flight, I drank no stimulant at all except coffee, and I avoided alcohol for at least four days prior to flight. A clear head, steady hand and unimpaired reflexes were essential at the speeds and altitudes I worked in.

Then, like the astronauts who would come after me, I began to concentrate on and simulate the details of the specific mission I would fly. Beginning with the flight profile, I went over climb angle, rate of climb, descent rate and angle of descent until it was second nature. Next, I ingrained the knowl-

The cherished Model "A" Ford that was handed down to the chief test pilot from Col. Frank K. "Pete" Everest when he left the Bell X-2 program in 1956. The automobile provided a necessary bit of comic irony in that a pilot would drive this car to the flightline before donning a space suit and flying a rocket airplane to supersonic speeds! This photograph of me in "civvies" with the car was taken May 23, 1959 (AFFTC History Office photograph).

edge of the exact positions of the nearest dry lake beds and emergency landing areas along the way, the ones I hoped I wouldn't need. But you never knew!

Next, I ran the mission on the fixed-base simulator. It was a sophisticated simulator for its day, complete with cockpit, an actual flight control system and all the displays from the real X-15, mechanized by the analog computer. What a great help that proved to be when I actually started to fly the X-15.

I simulated flying the mission over and over until I could literally do it in my sleep. Then, with the help of the engineers, Bob Hoey of the Air Force and Dick Day of NASA, I tried to anticipate all the places something could go wrong and plot solutions for each of the problems. These were then flown in the simulator until I could handle those problems in my sleep, too! My two engineers were invaluable, and their knowledge and insight allowed me and the other X-15 pilots to have the best possible preparation for real flights.

Now that each aspect of the current mission was second nature, I flew the mission over and over again, and each time one of the engineers would throw in one of the problems randomly and unexpectedly. Soon, I was handling every emergency they sneaked in on me as smoothly as I did in the exercises where the problems were expected. Repetition is the mother of perfection, and from my combat experience, I realized the more I practiced the luckier I got.

On flight mornings, I was up earlier than usual. After finishing a light

The ground crew swarms over the X-15 as it prepares to fly (NASA photograph).

breakfast, I bid my family good-bye, at least those who were awake at that hour. For them, it would be a day of increased tension, watching and waiting. When the next man in an Air Force uniform came through the door, they prayed it would be me, and not one of my colleagues with bad news. In retrospect, I knew on a cognitive level the tension they were under, but I was so caught up in what I was doing, the real toll it took on them emotionally escaped me until I reflected on it later on.

I have often been asked if I ever felt any fear about climbing aboard the X-15. After all, isn't it really a bomb with a cockpit, and am I not supposed to light the fuse? My answer is the same as it was when I was a test pilot, "No." It's not braggadocio or macho man stuff; I just couldn't wait to climb into that cockpit. It was what I had always dreamed about doing. Why should I be afraid? I'd already watched Scott Crossfield fly the plane a number of times, and I knew what to expect. And I was as prepared as I could be for any emergency that popped up in flight.

Besides, in the ten to twelve minutes I'd actually be flying with power, and until I got the airplane back on the ground, I knew exactly where the plane would be every second of the time. I'd be so busy with the instruments, data recorders and being certain I flew the flight plan to the best of my ability that I wouldn't have time to think about being afraid.

By the time I made the short trip to the base, the flight engineers and weather people knew the exact wind speed and ambient temperature along every kilometer of the flight path. The X-15 had never been unattended for a second since the pre-flight sequence was initiated. During the night and early morning, technicians had gone over literally every inch of the aircraft. Every gauge, dial, and switch had been checked and rechecked. Every static test possible had been run. There wasn't a nick or a ding anywhere in the fuselage. Everyone knew the importance of what we were doing, the risk the pilots were taking and the enormous amount of money being spent on each flight. Everything had to be as good as it could be.

Inside the support van, I waited until the latest possible time to put on the David Clark pressure suit. Even though it was custom fitted, it was hot, confining, and pressed into my skin like a girdle that was too tight. And I always remembered to go to the bathroom just before donning the suit. It had a lot of zippers in it, but none of them was in exactly the right spot.

By the time I finished the fifteen-minute process of getting into the suit and they had attached the helmet to it, the desert heat had turned my second skin into a good imitation of a sauna. When my two minders attached the portable cooling unit to the suit, the wash of cool purified air was a welcome relief. I was ready to go, and they helped me to my feet. Carrying the cooling unit between them, we stepped from the support van.

X-15 pilots Peterson, Crossfield, me, and Walker in front of the NASA head-quarters building at what is now the Dryden Flight Research Center at Edwards Air Force Base. This grouping nicely shows the collaborative aspects of the highly-successful X-15 program utilized the best talents and capabilities of the manufacturer, the U.S. Air Force, the U.S. Navy, and NASA (NASA photograph).

Every time I walked from the support van, I felt as if I were part of a science fiction movie. The glare of the floodlights, the vapor from the propellants, and the liquid oxygen in particular, cast an eerie spell over the strange looking airplane and the dozens of jumpsuit-clad figures who ministered to it. Add to all that me in my science-fiction space suit and two handlers carrying the cooling unit and minding the hoses, the entire spectacle was surreal.

In a scene that would soon become familiar to the nation with the Mercury and Gemini flights, they assisted me to the aircraft as I smiled and waved my thanks to the support staff and ground crew. My pulse was banging a few beats faster, and I felt overwhelmed with pride for these great people who work tirelessly to get me up and back safely. They're the real heroes here, and they're great people.

A good pilot usually starts a flight with a walk-around of the plane they are to fly. But I was relieved of that duty by the support crew who had already done it meticulously. But using the imaginary features of X-ray vision, appropriate since this is the X-15, let's do an imaginary walk-around before I climb into the cockpit.

Beginning at the rear, there is the rocket engine that eats 15,000 pounds of anhydrous ammonia and liquid oxygen in 80 seconds or an incredible 178 pounds of fuel a second. That's how long it burns during an average flight, after which the X-15 becomes the world's most sophisticated and expensive glider. Around the rocket nozzle, below it on the ventral fin, and in back of both horizontal stabilizer roots are two dozen assorted vents, drains and jettisons. The turbo pump exhaust is the largest. The jettisons are for the liquid oxygen and the ammonia.

The inside of the engine, hidden from view, contains a miracle of engineering. Helium tanks are located along the left wing fairing to purge explosive gases from the engine compartment before they ignite ... most of the time. Behind it are the pipes carrying the liquid oxygen from its tank to the engine. The right fairing has the helium tank and the piping for the ammonia. I am always aware of the odor of the ammonia.

Immediately behind the engine is the turbo pump, which is actually an assortment of devices. One is a gas generator that is the X-15's catalytic converter. Hydrogen peroxide converts to superheated steam and oxygen on its catalytic bed to produce gas to drive the centrifugal turbine in the turbo pump, which in turn drives separate compressors for the ammonia and liquid oxygen.

Returning to the outside, the horizontal stabilizers are relatively simple. With a 15-degree anhedral (downward angle from root to tip), they move together to control pitch, or move differentially for roll control. This is necessitated by the fact that the wings have no ailerons. They have opposed sets of irreversible hydraulic actuators—they can be pushed, but they won't push back so the pilot feels no load on the stick A system of spring bungee cords in the cockpit compensate to bring artificial "feel" to the pitch trim.

The vertical stabilizers have triangular cross sections that help with hypersonic stability and contain adequate room for a bank of hydraulic actuators. Both the dorsal and ventral fins are divided longitudinally into one part that is fixed and one that moves. Panels on the rear third of the fixed portions spread to become speed brakes. These are never used at subsonic speeds, because the only way to close them again is to let a supersonic air load blow them back to neutral.

The top of the dorsal fin and the bottom of the ventral fin rotate to serve the function of a rudder. The ventral piece extends below the landing gear. Four explosive bolts and an initiator to jettison it before landing are attached. The pilot has to remember not to jettison the ventral above 300 knots.

The main landing gear consists of two skids locked against the aft fuselage until the pilot is ready to release them. Gravity and air loads lock them into place when they are dropped. Without wheels there are no brakes. They also don't have a device to indicate if they are up or down, but the chase plane pilots will confirm that important fact. If by chance they don't extend in the final seconds of a landing approach, the pilot has no choice but to eject from the X-15 which in seconds will become the world's fastest plow just before cartwheeling into a giant ball of smoking wreckage on the lake bed.

Nearly the entire fuselage is split into a liquid oxygen tank forward and the ammonia tank in the back. Each has a concentric cylindrical core and three interconnected chambers. The core of the liquid oxygen tank contains helium for pressurizing the peripheral ends of these propellant tanks. Propellant feeds out of large pipes at the tank end nearest the center of gravity.

Tanks for hydrogen peroxide, helium, and liquid nitrogen are crammed into the fuselage at the ends and in between the propellant tanks. Two auxiliary power units geared to alternator and hydraulic pumps are also here. There are also turbines powered by the hydrogen peroxide from their own gas generators.

The nose gear consists of two wheels that don't steer, but that's seldom a problem since landings happen on a gigantic runway that is totally empty. They drop by gravity and air load just like the skids, but there's a hitch here. Too much air rushing by the nose gear door tends to keep it closed. To prevent this, an initiator gives it a boost, and a small air scoop opens down from it allowing the stream of air to hold it open.

Eight small nozzles, the ballistic control system, are mounted in the nose to supply yaw and pitch control. With no air resistance, the regular control surfaces don't work in outer space, so these small thrusters took their place. There is a smooth metal ball at the tip of the plane's nose that measures dynamic pressure. In aerodynamic equations, this is the letter "Q," and aptly enough we called this device the "Q-ball" nose. As if it didn't have enough to do, the ball also swivels in two axes measuring angle of attack and sideslip. This is important when reentering the atmosphere and flying at low speeds when the airplane is more unstable. The airplane also carries gyroscopes and accelerometers to indicate which way the plate is pointed and which way it's actually going while above the atmosphere.

It's time to climb aboard. My minders disconnect the portable air conditioning and help me aboard. I feel at home because I have been in the simulator enough times that I know every instrument intimately. All the equipment makes the space seem confining, but there is really enough room.

There are two small rectangular double-paned windows, and on the ground when I close the canopy, there isn't a great view, but it is most adequate. On the early flights, heated nitrogen gas was pumped between the two panes to prevent icing. When that proved problematic, an electric heating element replaced the gas.

Just in front of me is that pesky head brace I forgot to use on the centrifuge ride. It folds down so I can rest my head on it. When it comes time for re-entry flights, it will really be a help.

The cockpit is air-conditioned, a real plus in the heat of the desert at Edwards. There is only ambient pressure in the cockpit until I get to 35,000 feet. At that altitude, nitrogen is used to pressurize the cockpit to 3.5 pounds per square inch. My tailored flight suit is also nitrogen fed to keep it at the same pressure.

To the uninitiated, the cockpit is a massive clutter of switches, dials, lights and gauges. Each of them is checked according to a prescribed 120-point checklist. A center stick and conventional rudders are familiar enough. Mechanically coupled to the center stick is a stick on the console near my right hand for use when high-G loads make it difficult to use the center stick. The link sums their input and sends that information to the Stability Augmentation System.

A third stick, for the ballistic control system, is near my left hand. When I arm the ballistic control rockets, I can move it left or right to control yaw. If I rotate it to fire the wing thrusters, I can control roll. When I move it up and down, I control pitch. There is additional input to this system of controls from the Reaction Augmentation System.

An important gauge is located next to the console stick. It's the horizontal stabilizer position indicator. When launching from the B-52 mother ship, and before re-entry, the position of this stabilizer is critical.

The throttle is on the left near the speed brake. It allows the thrust to be set between the minimum 50 percent and the maximum 100 percent. The throttle can also be turned off. In some of our earlier flights, we could throttle down below 50 percent but the XLR-99 engine was prone to cut out at these lower settings.

One last thing deserves mention, the ejection seat. The other time I had to bail out of an airplane, I never had a chance to practice. I had only read the manual. The same thing applies this time. Supposedly, it will eject me in a semi-capsule, and unfold fins that allow it to glide to a lower altitude. Then explosive bolts blow pieces of the capsule away to expose the parachute. The chute opens and the rest is routine. The manual said I could use it as long as I was flying below Mach 4 and under 120,000 feet. There was one small problem with this. No one had ever tested it before. I love to do things first, but this was one I was more than happy to pass on.

The X-15 is now hanging underneath the wing of the B-52, and I'm breathing 100 percent oxygen that is part of my pressure suit system. I am finished with the 120-point checklist, the last on the list being the command to close the canopy. With the canopy closed, it could be a bit claustrophobic, but that doesn't bother me, and I'm so busy I don't have time to think about it anyhow.

It's takeoff time, and the service cart is disconnected. At this point, the airstrip looks like a scramble scene from a World War II movie. The chase planes take off. There are usually three of them manned by a pilot and a photographer or engineer. I've flown chase on the first flights, but this time I'm in the driver's seat. A big C-130 cargo plane and several rescue helicopters add to the orchestrated confusion. A number of trucks and jeeps and ground vehicles are also on their way to various points along the line of flight or to dry lake beds where potential emergency landings could be made.

Up and down the range, the radar stations that covered the entire airspace cranked up to follow me every step of the way. They report that the airspace is clear all the way, but that's seldom a problem. The B-52 will release the plane at around 45,000 feet, well above and outside commercial air space. Once the rocket engine is fired, the X-15 will be out of that particular section of air space in a heartbeat.

The B-52 cranks up its big engines and its pilots run through their own check list as we begin the two-plus-mile taxi to the takeoff position. An H-21 helicopter buzzes by to make a last visual inspection of the runway. As we wait for the chopper to finish his inspection, technicians remove the safety pins from the X-15's release hooks under the wing of the bomber.

Once in the air on the way to the launch altitude of 45,000 feet, a few things will need to be heated up. My face mask heater, the ballistic rocket heater in the nose of the plane, and the windshield heater automatically activate. The crew of the B-52 will look after the heater that is on the hook holding me to the B-52.

We are roughly twelve minutes from launch at this point and it's time for another checklist, called the pre-launch. This one is only 27 points long. Its time to switch my oxygen supply from the bomber's to my internal breathing system. The liquid nitrogen, but not the nitrogen gas, is shut down, and I start the APU's. Now it's time for a new checklist.

This one has 29 items and is called the pre-countdown list. I stop the liquid oxygen from the B-52 and cycle the propellants from the tank and vent to jettison and then to pressurize.

"Three...two...one...DROP!" The exact moment of launch as the X-15 drops away from its mounting pylon under the wing of the NB-52. X-15 pilots all described this moment as being very abrupt. Launch altitudes varied with each mission, but were generally in the 45,000-ft. range. Note the F-104 chase plane just ahead of the B-52's inboard engine nacelles (AFFTC History Office photograph).

Flight controls need to be rechecked and the launch trim set. Everything but the horizontal stabilizers has to be at zero degrees. No more than a two-degree deflection of the leading edge down is allowable. Anything more than that and the X-15 can, upon release, turn into the engine of the B-52 just outboard of the rocket plane.

While I'm doing this, the B-52 is turning on its final launch heading, roughly eight minutes before launch time.

When we get down to two minutes from launch, I turn on the data recorders, check the Q-ball nose one last time and turn on the cameras that will record everything that happens. I prepare the engine for firing and then call for the countdown.

"Five, four, three, two, one .... DROP!" I drop the X-15, but it's not gentle by any means. It feels like I'm being catapulted off an aircraft carrier, only straight down. The cardiac monitors we wore showed every pilot's heart rate quickened at this point, but not nearly as much as one might expect. I go immediately from 0 Gs to 1 G and it's breathtaking. There's that tendency

I sit in the cockpit of the X-15 while it is still mated to the NB-52 mothership. The unzipped pressure suit indicates that this was probably after an aborted mission where the B-52 landed with the X-15 still attached. In-flight aborts such as this were not uncommon in the challenging early days of the famous test program (NASA photograph).

to roll left toward the B-52's fuselage. Due to the down force from the B-52's wing and the turbulence across the slab-sided body of the big bomber the amount of roll tendency is inconsistent. Today, it's not too bad, and a quick correction is followed by flicking the throttle from off to 50 percent to light the main chamber.

If the engine doesn't fire up, or dies in the first half minute of burn, I can make it back to the launch site. If it's later in the burn, one of the secondary dry lake landing sites comes into play. Given enough altitude, the X-15 could glide more than 400 miles. Not bad for a bullet with wings.

In the early flights the X-15 was launched by the B-52 crew. In later ones, I launched the plane by tripping the release button myself. I liked it better that way. I felt a little more in control when it was time to fly, or if

Dramatic photograph of the X-15 accelerating away from the launch aircraft as the mighty XLR99 rocket engine propels it forward with 57,000 pounds of thrust—enough power to drive a Navy destroyer! The white band around the aircraft's mid-fuselage is frost condensation from the super-cooled liquid oxygen fuel tank within (AFFTC History Office photograph).

something went wrong I could release the X-15 to avoid danger to the B-52 mother ship. Like Scott Crossfield always said, "If something goes wrong, it's better to lose one man than four."

And things could go wrong. Although I flew 16 times in the X-15, I actually went into the air under the B-52 a total of 32 times. Half the time I was supposed to fly, the flight was aborted. For example on one of my flights, the yaw damper went off and couldn't be reset, so we aborted the flight. But as time went on and engineering systems improved, the ratio of aborts-to-flight dropped precipitously below the 50 percent it was for all of us in the beginning.

Early flights were used to prepare for the full burn altitude flights. After release I go to full throttle and between 57,000 and 60,000 pounds of thrust start the 2 G acceleration that must be on a precise climb angle to reach the pre-determined altitude. The frost forming around the liquid oxygen tank paints the fuselage with the characteristic white band that is evident in all the photographs of the X-15 in flight. Things are slow because I still have full tanks and a gross weight of about 16 tons. Still, it is quite a kick in the pants.

Fuel burns rapidly, and in no time at all, I'm down to a mere seven-and-a-half tons and my G forces have doubled to 4 Gs against my chest. That's quite a sensation. Despite enjoying the world's highest thrill ride, I've got to fly a perfect flight plan. Lots of things are going on, and if I miss my climb attitude by as little as a degree, it produces big numbers on the other end. One little degree isn't much and the average airline pilot would call that perfect, but it could cause me to be 30,000 feet above or below the predetermined altitude target.

X-15 flights are all done on instruments. At these speeds, and climbing higher into the sky, all I can see out the window is blue or black. At this point thrust overpowers gravity and my senses lie to me. I'm positive the rotation never stopped, and I'm being pulled over backwards. I've gone past vertical, and I'm flying upside down.

Although I feel this way, my gyro-stabilized inertial platform tells me I'm not. It tells me to keep my hands off the controls. I didn't the first time it happened, and missed my altitude mark because of it. Fool me once, shame on you. Fool me twice, shame on me. I trusted the instruments on the rest of the flights.

When my later flight pattern takes me out of the atmosphere, the stick and rudder pedals are no longer effective. I go to the hydrogen peroxide thrusters for control. This was only true on the first two X-15 aircraft. The third X-15 had the MH-96 control system that had only a single stick that blended automatic aerodynamic and reaction controls together.

The rocket engine burned about 80 seconds or so and then I either shut it down or it shut down automatically when it burned off all the ammonia and liquid oxygen. That can be an important variable for peak altitude flights. An extra second of burn can make a big difference in final altitude. I used this variable when I made my highest flight in the X-15.

I'm weightless and climbing like a rifle bullet on an extended ballistic arc high above the deserts of Nevada and Southern California. Pitching over, the view is spectacular. In my flights to 217,000 feet and 314,750 feet the view of the earth's curvature was clearly visible.

At my highest altitude, I could turn my head through a 180-degree arc and wow! The earth is really round. At my peak altitude I am roughly over the Arizona/California border in the area of Las Vegas, and this was how I described it: looking to my left, I felt I could spit into the Gulf of California. Looking to my right I felt I could toss a dime into San Francisco Bay. If the coast is clear that far north, you can just about make out Puget Sound, nearly a thousand miles away.

There isn't long to enjoy the view. The reentry angle of attack is critical so it's time for me to set attitude exactly. I am now the world's fastest and most expensive glider. And this glider handles like a water buffalo, albeit a gentle one.

Recreational gliders are white to allow them to reflect solar energy, helping to keep it aloft longer. The X-15 is painted black to radiate the horrendous heat caused by friction with the air in Earth's atmosphere. As the temperature tops 1,000 degrees, the wings, nose and stabilizers glow red from the heat. Again I don't have much time to notice this since it's now time to complete the reentry.

On my higher flights I came back into the atmosphere at Mach 5.4 in a 40-degree nose down dive. When I pulled out of this dive it was by ten degrees to slow to Mach 5.3. I am whacked with 3 Gs for 20 seconds. Anything more than 40 degrees raised the G force to 5 for about 20 seconds.

As the X-15 slows down and drops, stability degrades and allowable yaw angles decrease. Once I get to 40,000 feet and Mach 0.5, minimum control speed is determined by stability. Above that, tail buffeting takes over. Stability margins allow me to fly angle of attacks up to 20 degrees, but the pre-stall buffet starts at 13 degrees. These problems are potentially deadly. The electronic stability augmentation systems that were later built into the MH-96 were really a lifesaver.

At this point, my concentration is focused on executing a no power or dead stick landing. The flight is planned to arrive directly over the runway at altitudes between 23,000 to 30,000 feet at 260 to 310 knots airspeed. This position is called the high key. I turn left, maintaining a speed of 300 knots as I begin a 360-degree spiral to the landing spot.

At 180 degrees of turn I am about four to five miles abeam of my touchdown point at nearly 20,000 feet. This is called the low key. While I am spiraling down, many other things are going on.

Chase planes have picked me up. I dump any remaining propellants, and then pressurize the empty propellant tanks to keep sand and dust out when I land. It also keeps the tanks from collapsing because the vents can't keep up with the rapid pressure changes at these low altitudes.

From the low key, my goal is to execute the last 180-degree turn in my spiral. When I exit the turn, I must have the nose of the X-15 pointed at a spot 15,000 feet, or roughly three miles, short of the intended touchdown point.

Still at 300 knots, I reach a point heading directly to the runway. It's time to jettison the ventral fin. After that, I start to flare to break my rate

Only a mere eight to ten minutes separated an X-15 launch from a landing. Here, the X-15 has rolled to a stop on Rogers Dry Lake at Edwards after another successful flight. The ground crew has just met the airplane as indicated by the still-closed canopy (AFFTC History Office photograph).

of descent, lower my flaps and drop my landing gear. Touchdown speed is 200 knots and most of the time I am within 1,000 feet of the actual touchdown spot. Two flights missed by 4,000 feet, and in the longest flight recorded by the X-15, touchdown was missed by twelve miles. Depending on the actual altitude at high key, the process from high key to touchdown takes about three minutes.

Since I can't steer once I'm firmly on the ground, and I have no brake or parachute drag to worry about, I sit back and enjoy the ride while I play with the stick. By shifting the stick as if initiating a bank, the stabilizers will shift the aircraft's weight from skid to skid and I can "steer" in the direction I pointed the stick. When the speed drops, I can't "steer" anymore, so I'm now a passenger. All in all the X-15 will skid eight to ten kilometers before it stops.

As I skid to a halt and start the last check list aptly called the "After

The original group of X-15 pilots break loose as a bit of levity strikes while they were posing for official group portraits on the sunny Edwards' ramp all afternoon long. I am supervising from the right (AFFTC History Office photograph).

Landing Checklist," the B-52 returns from its launch run and flies by in a traditional low pass salute. While I secure the cockpit and prepare to exit the X-15, the chase planes land, and another day at the office has come to a safe and successful ending.

But the flight isn't over yet. To reiterate a point, the X-15 was initiated and conducted as a *research* program. To view it as a mission to simply go high and fast would degrade the effort to the level of a grade-B Hollywood movie where the pilot in a tailor-made flying suit is daring to beat the odds and return from a wild ride to the cheers of adoring fans.

In these days before sophisticated computers, everything was recorded on board the aircraft on film. Strip chart recorders and more film cameras were used on the ground. When a flight was over, these were all rolled out on long tables and painstakingly analyzed by hand. If there had been no major problems while the data was being analyzed, another flight would go into the planning stage.

The X-15 was literally wired for sound. Hundreds of thermocouples, dozens of strain gauges and telemetry pickups adorned the aircraft. Later in the program, improved electrical pressure transducers, load sensors and improved thermocouples were added. In its time it was the most thoroughly instrumented aircraft in the world. The data the X-15 flights acquired would provide engineers with work not for a few months but for many years. The result was that a tremendous amount of information became available throughout government and industry from the most successful research aircraft in history. Everyone involved in the project, from the pilot down to the last man on the ground, was an integral part of that history.

Chapter 10

Pushing the Envelope

I suppose the first time you do anything is the time you remembered the best. That wonderful Friday, April 13, 1960, is forever etched in my memory. It was a calm morning with the chill of the desert night succumbing rapidly to the heat of the desert sun. When there was an emergency with another aircraft that morning, and our flight didn't go off on time, I was beginning to think that maybe there was something to this Friday the 13th business. The Air Force had a new supersonic bomber, the Convair B-58, which was prone to tire problems early in its flight test program. One of these jets declared an emergency and landed on the main base runway.

To emergency egress the aircraft, the crew had to climb down from the cockpit using an escape rope, and then hop to the ground. They got out pretty quickly, but then the crash crew still had to get the airplane off the runway. While this was happening, all the emergency crews were tied up and unavailable for my flight. I had to wait patiently until they were available. It didn't bump my flight, but merely delayed it. While we waited for things to clear, I remembered a question my engineer Dick Day asked me a few days earlier at the simulator before this first flight.

"Where do you think you'll land, Bob?" he asked.

It was not a rhetorical question. As I described, the X-15 had only two nose wheels and a pair of skids. As soon as the flare portion of the landing was completed, and the skids touched the ground, the nose banged down pretty hard on its two little wheels.

There was a target point on the runway that we shot for when we landed. Fortunately, on the dry lake bed at Edwards, there was plenty of room for error. Scott had missed by varying degrees during the demonstration flights, and Joe Walker the second person to fly the X-15, landed two miles down the runway on his first flight.

"I'll bet you a martini you don't come within a mile of the target," Day said with a smug grin.

"You're on," I said. "Let's make it two martinis."

142

What did I have to lose? I hadn't had a drink of alcohol for the past four days. Either way I was a winner.

Since there was no way to control the speed of the landing with engine power because it was out of fuel, the X-15 maintained 300 knots in its descent, and the pilot negotiated his flight pattern to arrive at the intended touchdown spot. Hitting the mark would have been much more difficult if we had not been able to configure an F-104 fighter with certain power settings, speed brakes and flap settings to exactly match the X-15's lift drag ratio at 300 knots. As a result, we could make practice flights in the F-104 which allowed us to consistently come within several hundred feet of the intended target. That day, at the end of my first X-15 flight, I landed within 1,000 feet of the target, and Dick had to buy.

That was another great thing about test programs. The camaraderie was second to none. While I was with the fighter test group, we had a steak-and-bottle party once a month. Each couple brought their own steaks and whatever they wanted to drink, and the host supplied the rest. They were great fun.

We had a priest named Father Clifford Stevens, who was our chaplain. One month, when the party was at my house, one of the women asked him, "Isn't what these guys do really dangerous?"

"Of course not," he reassured her, "These guys are pros. They know what they're doing."

Two weeks later, as the B-52 taxied down the runway with the X-15 attached and me in the cockpit, there, alongside the runway, was Father Stevens. As I passed, he made the sign of the cross.

I cornered him a few days later and asked, "What in the world were you doing out there?"

"Hey, you guys are good, but I want to be sure we've covered all the bases," he replied with a grin.

But, you know, I wasn't really upset to see Father Stevens standing by the runway that Friday. Every time I went up, I wanted all of my bases covered.

Later on, I got a chance to take Father Cliff for a ride in an F-104. I'll never forget his whoops of delight and the broad grin on his face.

I also had two good flight simulator engineers, Dick Day and Bob Hoey. One was a civilian engineer working for the Air Force, and the other was a NASA engineer. After the simulations were finished, we'd go outside and have a Coke and a smoke and just talk. We talked about our program and the other programs each of us had worked with. We discussed all the problems that were encountered and what was done to solve them. I learned a lot of things from them, and the level of trust and cooperation between us was invaluable to me.

During these times, and many times after, I reflected on my good fortune. I was in the right place at the right time, and to be with so many competent and personable men and women was more of a blessing than this New York street kid ever thought possible. Equally important was how easily it could all have changed at any time along the way. I know that my destiny was in the hands of Someone bigger than me.

There were plenty of things to do on the way up to the launch point, and I was so busy with my tasks that I was startled to realize we were there. We leveled off at 45,000 feet, and I was ticking off the last 30 seconds before launch. As the count neared zero, I couldn't wait to release and punch that rocket motor into action. My only fear was that some last minute glitch would prevent the launch. It didn't.

Flying the X-15 was a lot different than watching it from a chase plane. After the launch, the roll was about what I'd seen and was no surprise to me. But dropping down from under that wing was like a roller coaster ride down a long hill.

When I flipped the switch, the engine ignited flawlessly. What a kick in the pants that was. To go from 0 Gs to 1 G in the blink of an eye was an unbelievable sensation. That kind of acceleration does strange things to the body. And, I knew full well there were more Gs to come.

A minute and a half later, the engine finished its burn, and the roar of 57,000 pounds of thrust went silent as I plowed through the air at over twice the speed of sound.

The rest of the flight was routine, and as I got used to flying the aircraft, I relaxed a bit. It was just like the simulator—but a lot more fun! This was what we called a minimal profile flight.

I was required to do small tasks like pulsing various controls that would help define the inherent stability of the aircraft. This meant turning off the yaw damper, kicking out the rudder and measuring the oscillations and natural damping effect of the aircraft at that speed. Then I kicked the yaw damper back on and self corrected if necessary. This was all done during deceleration after the engine burn.

After the flight there would be a standard debriefing where I, as the pilot, could make comments about how I felt about the aircraft's responses, or anything else that merited attention. The engineers liked this because they could get a better feel for the data, and it would mean more to them when they looked at it. I guess it's much like a doctor looking at a patient's blood chemistry. He can make a diagnosis from the chemistry alone, but it will be much more accurate if he has talked to the patient about what hurts.

During the flight, I was in constant contact with the ground control room called NASA-1. The voice was that of another X-15 pilot on the ground who served as the "back-up brain." Usually it was a routine conversation, like the ones that became so familiar to the public with the advent of the Mercury, Gemini and Apollo flights. But if something untoward happened along the way, two heads were better than one. And the fact that the other head had also flown the X-15 was a real bonus.

My only problem on that first flight was a small issue with one of the controls. The all-too-short flight (they averaged ten to eleven minutes each) came to a rapid conclusion, and in what seemed like no time at all, I was aiming for the runway and the two martinis Dick Day would very shortly owe me.

All in all I was at Edwards for eighty-four of the 199 X-15 flights. I flew chase on the first eleven flights before flying for the first time on flight twelve. After that, I flew chase on another twenty-six flights. So, I flew sixteen

I am jubilant as I enjoy the cool desert breeze on the lakebed after the X-15's cockpit has been raised. This was after successfully completing another mission in the world's fastest and highest-flying aircraft. The canopy is unpowered, being manually held in the raised position by two struts, one of which can be seen on the left (NASA photograph).

as a pilot and thirty-seven as a chase pilot or forty-three of the eight-four flights that were made while I was in the program. That was pretty typical of the others who also flew the plane in the early days of the program.

My first six flights were with the smaller LR-11 engine and the last ten with the LR-99. I was involved with the X-15 test program for a total of 32 months and was fortunate enough to be involved in a significant number of milestones.

Two were with the LR-11 engine. I made the maximum speed flight with the stacked engine reaching a top speed of Mach 3.5. I was also allowed to take it to its maximum altitude of 136,000 feet.

Joe Walker took the plane on flight thirteen. It was uneventful, and then it was my turn again. On May 6, 1960, I flew flight fourteen, and outside of a roll damper failure, all was well. The next flight was part of the altitude buildup, and on flight sixteen it was my task to take the X-15 above 100,000 feet for the first time. On May 19, 1960, I flew to 108,997 feet. My target was 110,000 feet. Not bad. I was only a little over 1,000 feet shy of my mark. Considering how demanding it was to fly exact numbers for climb, course and speed, I was pleased.

Flight twenty-one, my fifth, was to collect performance and stability data, just as I had done testing conventional aircraft. It was uneventful and lasted a whopping ten minutes. In my first five flights, if I added up to flight times, I had spent a grand total of fifty minutes and forty-seven seconds of actual flying time. But even with the hours and hours of preparation and effort for each flight, it was worth every single second.

In eight of the next ten flights, I flew chase. On the other two, I was NASA-1. During this time, Scott Crossfield flew the XLR-99 engine on flight twenty-six, and throttled and restarted the engine in flight. This was an important milestone. Neil Armstrong introduced the Q-ball nose on flight thirty-one. Meanwhile, I busied myself getting ready for flight thirty-three.

This flight, lasting ten minutes twenty-eight seconds, was to test stability and control and acquired data on flight systems. On February 7, 1961, I flew the smaller XLR-11 engine for the final time.

Thanks to the flight schedule, I was living a very clean life, because my next flight was only a month away. This one would be a speed run.

On March 7, I flew flight number thirty-four. I flew ship number two on this one, and it was equipped with the ball nose for the first time. Besides the usual stability and control data, I would be collecting vital temperature data.

Moving up in altitude where there was considerably less air to provide drag, they launched the X-15, and I lit the hot engine. When all fuel had been spent, I became the first man to fly at Mach 4, or 2,905 mph. In a mere fourteen years, I was flying four times faster than Chuck Yeager's historic flight.

I got the next month off, with only a chase flight for Joe Walker on flight thirty-five. During that month, I trained for the next speed expansion.

On April 21, 1961, on flight thirty-six, I was ready to go. This time, luck was not on my side. To start with, my engine had to be re-lighted. Then, the pitch damper dropped out. When the engine shut down, the cabin pressure rose to 46,000 feet for the rest of the ten-minute flight. This left the engineers scratching their heads.

On the next flight, the first Mud Lake launch, Joe Walker's cabin pressure went to 50,000 feet. We were both thankful for the trips to Massachusetts and the effective pressure suits we were wearing. Otherwise, we might have lost consciousness with disastrous results.

On June 23, 1961, I flew ship number one with the XLR-99 engine for the first time. With the new package, and all systems go, I pushed the speed

The legendary Chuck Yeager (left), the first man to break the sound barrier, congratulates me after a successful speed record flight (NASA photograph).

envelope to Mach 5 or 3,603 mph, another new speed record. The cabin pressure was the only problem. This time it went to 56,000 feet, causing my pressure suit to inflate. What was going on?

It took a great deal of dedicated detective work on the part of the engineers before they finally located the problem. Behind the cockpit was the

I am now standing outside the airplane. The pressure suit has been unzipped, although the internal cooling device, being carried by an assistant, is still hooked up. X-15 pilots were known to have sweated so profusely in our suits that we lost as many as five pounds during a typical flight (NASA photograph).

electronics module that was cooled with liquid nitrogen. On one flight, there was a problem with the B-52, and the X-15 sat on the ground for an hour and a half prior to take off. That pinpointed the problem.

The electronics bay cooled so much while it was on the ground that once the X-15 was aloft where the air was cooler there was no demand for nitrogen. Unfortunately, the nitrogen also helped to pressurize the cabin. Readjusting the cooling sensor solved the problem of cabin pressure.

I flew chase on three of the next four flights while prepping for another altitude expansion in flight forty-three. Stability and performance data with the air brakes open, and aerodynamic heating during reentry data would be collected on this flight.

We flew on October 11, 1961, and once again, I was able to establish a new altitude record by taking the X-15 to 217,000 feet. It was the first time any aircraft had been above 200,000 feet, and the first flight that used ballistic control systems for altitude control. On the way down, I reached a speed of 3,647 mph. Everything was going perfectly until I started back into the atmosphere.

I was startled by a loud crack directly in front of me. The outer pane of the left-hand double pane windshield had failed.

I said, "Okay, my outside windshield went."

Forest Peterson, NASA-1 for the day, replied, "Outside pane?"

"That's correct," I acknowledged, and went back to work.

Once again, there was no bravado here. Both Pete and I knew that I had a second pane of glass. The plane was in no danger, and neither was I. The frame of the window as it expanded and contracted from the heating and cooling caused the tempered glass to crack. Fortunately, it was only half the window, and the break was a craze of spider web cracks. I could still see through the damaged side if I needed to. Besides, I still had the other window.

It was back to Corning, who made the windshield, to get a stronger model. They were able to get it installed before Joe's next flight, since at this point we were effectively alternating flights.

Flight forty-five, set for November 9, 1961, was to be the maximum speed flight attempt for the X-15. Fortunately, we did things incrementally. An all-out approach at the beginning, before we realized the hazards, would have been disastrous.

In preparation for the flight, the engineers worked their tails off calculating all the possibilities. The wind tunnels of the time were not built to reflect the speeds I would attempt to reach. It was up to the engineers to provide the critical data from a theoretical perspective. Once again, they came through in spades.

Here I am in my unzipped early-generation MC-2 pressure suit at the bottom of the air stairs, possibly after exiting the X-15 from a captive landing after an aborted flight. Note the X-15's nose gear is in the extended position (AFFTC History Office photograph).

Before we actually made the flight, there were a couple of aborts. The problems were minor ones, but we were attempting to push the aircraft to the upper limits of the speed for which it had been designed. Conditions had to be in my favor.

The flight plan called for me to fly the X-15 to 107,700 feet and level off or point with the nose a tad bit downhill. I would level off at the end of the burn as I reached maximum velocity. Enough above the atmosphere for minimal drag, I felt confident. As I pushed past Mach 5, the boys on the ground heard me coaxing the plane to "Go-Go-Go!" And it did! To Mach 6.04! That translates to 4,094 mph, over 6,000 fps, or the length of ten football fields every second.

On this flight, the X-15 had the entire canopy painted with a special thermal paint to help with the heat build-up. It worked very well. As I whooped with joy and slowed to a paltry Mach 2.7 to come back into the atmosphere, I heard an all too familiar sound. The crack of breaking glass!

This time it was the right windshield, and the entire pane of glass was a milky white. It was like looking through a cataract. I couldn't see a thing out of it. Fortunately, the left side was still clear.

Out loud I said, "Good Lord, not again!"

NASA-1 came back, "Say again Bob?"

"I've lost another windshield, this time the right. I can still see out of left. If that holds, I can see well enough to complete the landing pattern."

Again there was no panic in my voice. Panic is the enemy of any pilot, particularly a test pilot. In the solitude of the cramped cockpit, even more confining with half my view of the outside world gone, I begin to plot my contingencies should the other half fail.

I could see through the left side enough to make my left-hand turn, and the chase plane could talk me through any problems with my blind side. I wasn't in any trouble yet.

As I ran through my options if both sides failed, I came to a decision. I would fly the X-15 down to 300 knots on instruments. At that speed, I would jettison the canopy and see if I could fly the plane with a 300 knot wind in my face. I didn't really think that would be possible, and if it proved I could not, I would eject. Fortunately, the glass held and I landed without incident.

Later, when discussing the situation with my fellow pilots and engineers, they agreed that this seemed like a logical plan. I believe that's the key to being a success in the test pilot business. Keep your head, consider your options, and go with the best one. If everything fails, then you're allowed to panic.

The engineers quickly found another problem when the X-15 was on the ground. The heat at Mach 6 had warped one of the wing panels. It had to be redesigned to adjust to the increased heat created by flights at that speed.

The engineers came to me after the flight with egg on their faces and an explanation for broken glass. When they replaced my broken left wind-

During the X-15 program, it was not uncommon for a pilot's family to actually meet him on the lakebed after a landing. Here I am with Greg after another successful flight (NASA photograph).

shield, they had failed to replace the right one with the new Corning glass. The problem of broken glass ended with the new windshield on both sides.

Once again, I thought of how lucky I was. As it turned out, I had been fortunate enough to draw the envelope expansion flights for both altitude and speed while leapfrogging with Joe Walker. Had it been reversed, he'd be in the record books as the first man to fly Mach 4-5-6.

On flight fifty-five, I made the first Delamar Lake launch. We aborted this flight twice in May before we finally made it. The first time an inertial platform and telemetry failure caused the abort, and the second time it was the inertial platform cooling. On June 1, 1962, we were airborne. At 30 percent thrust, I had a significant engine vibration similar to one that Joe would have on the next flight. His came during boost. The problem was quickly solved by the engineers.

My next two flights were only ten days apart and both were uneventful. Much to my delight, on the next flight after that, flight fifty-nine, Joe Walker set the unofficial world absolute speed record at 4,105 miles an hour.

I didn't fly the next three missions as I prepared the flight plan to reach 280,000 feet. My main task would be to define the reentry corridor from space. This was flight 3-7-14 set for the fourteenth of July, 1962. It was to be a special flight for me and the X-15.

To give it added incentive, which none of us needed, the Air Force had re-classified pilot ratings. And the speeds and altitudes the X-15 was reaching were responsible for it. The usual ratings were pilot, senior pilot and command pilot. One advanced to command pilot over the years as experience was gained. New ratings of pilot astronaut, senior pilot astronaut, and command pilot astronaut would be added. To become a command pilot astronaut, I had to go 264,000 feet, which is 50 miles, straight up. If I reached the altitude prescribed in the flight plan, I'd be the first man to fly a winged aircraft into space and to gain the rank of command pilot astronaut. This would allow me to become only the fifth American to attain astronaut wings and only the second Air Force pilot to do this. Alan Shepard, Gus Grissom, John Glenn and Wally Schirra of the Project Mercury program went first.

This time, my preflight preparation hit a glitch. In the midst of physical training and simulations, a full colonel, the public information officer, called me into his office. His name was Charlie Brown, a really good name for a really good guy.

"Bob, I want you to fly over to Los Angeles next week and give a speech to a civic organization about the X-15 program."

"Respectfully sir, I won't go," I said almost without thinking. "I am going for a high altitude run in less than a week, and I need to give the mission my total attention. You can take it up with the general if you want to, but I just won't go. This is too important for me to disrupt my training. I have to be totally prepared."

I told you Charlie Brown was a great guy. I didn't have to go.

It was customary to do static tests on the rocket engine prior to each flight. There was an Air Force captain monitoring the tests for this flight. With the engine tied down it was fired and the thrust measured.

I ask him, "What have we got?"

"It's a hot one, Bob. You'll get all you can out of this one," he replied.

I also had another idea. On the way to the launch point under the B-52, the tanks are not pressurized. The liquid oxygen is gasifying. There are several minutes before the last top off before the tanks are finally pressurized. I talked to the engineers about modifying the checklist. I asked if we couldn't pressurize immediately after the last top off. If we did that, I could get all the oxygen possible in the tank. They agreed, and we set it up on this flight.

As I prepared for the flight, I reviewed my experience on the previous high-altitude flights. At the climb angle I would be flying, I would definitely have to fight the feeling of disorientation that plagued all of us. For reasons I don't understand, as you climb to the higher altitudes, even though your instruments tell you are on course, there is the distinct feeling that the aircraft is continuing to rotate. It feels like you are going over backwards.

The first time it happened to me I couldn't resist the temptation to push the nose down until I could see the horizon. I never did see the horizon, but the drop in pitch decreased my climb angle so much that I missed my mark by 21,400 feet. Nine days later I fought the sensation, believed my instruments, and missed by mark by only 3, 300 feet. The latter was an acceptable margin. In this circumstance, it was reassuring to hear NASA-1 say, "You are on track and on profile," even though their ability to monitor your exact pitch and attitude from the ground was not foolproof.

The flight plan was simple. The climb out of the atmosphere was steep. When the engine stopped, I would coast over the top on a ballistic trajectory then establish an angle of attack for the reentry. I would be in a weightless environment for roughly five minutes. The ballistic control system allowed me to control my attitude, and it would get a real workout on this flight. Flying the prescribed plan would be critical and I knew it, particularly during reentry into the atmosphere.

Things had not gone smoothly as we prepared for flight sixty-two. During a number of previous attempts to complete this particular flight, we had been dogged by a series of maddening minor malfunctions, which had resulted in the launch having to be aborted. On July 10, there was a problem with the B-52's landing gear, so we aborted. The next day the number one APU pressure regulator malfunctioned causing a second abort. On the 16th of July, the B-52's umbilical unplugged, causing a third abort. On the last sortie, we had got to within a few seconds of the launch point before a last-minute component failure had forced yet another cancellation. In the philosophy of the Far East, uneven numbers are considered unlucky. That wasn't the case here, because that fourth abort was the last one, and on this try we would fly.

With this flight being something of a milestone in the program, everyone was edgy about the run of forced aborts. I had geared myself up, time and again, for the launch, only to have to call it off, and drag back to Edwards. It was exasperating. During his reentry maneuver, I was going to have to fly the X-15 at an angle of attack of about twenty-six degrees to keep within the structural and heating limitations of the aircraft; at just over twenty-seven degrees, the controllability of the aircraft was judged to be "questionable." That didn't leave me much of a margin to play with, in a completely new, and previously unexplored, regime of flight. Oddly enough, those around commented that I appeared to be the calmest of all concerned. But that's the way I always handled things. I just took each abort as a fact of life, and got on with planning the next attempt. Those around me at the time have commented that if I was feeling any strain, it certainly wasn't evident to them.

As I neared the flight line, most of the buildings were still closed and dark, but I could make out the familiar splashes of lights that marked the areas of early morning activity on a "launch" day. The cargo/helicopter and fighter hangers were well lit up, as the ground crews worked to prepare the transport aircraft, helicopters, and fighter "chase" planes that would fly the various support missions. At the far end of Flight Test Operations, the bomber section lights were already on—some thoughtful soul getting the coffee pot on! Along Contractors Row, only the windows of the North American facility were showing any lights. Their specialist support team worked round the clock prior to every launch.

At the far end of the ramp, there was an absolute blaze of arc-lights around the "mating area," where the X-15 had already been loaded onto its mounting below the wing of the B-52. This area was the focal point of the pre-launch activity, as the final systems checks were carried out on both aircraft, last-minute snags rectified, and a veritable army of technicians and specialists assured themselves that every piece of equipment that could be checked on the ground had been meticulously checked. And then re-checked! Then re-checked again. This area always reminded me of the pit-stop area before a major motor car race. One got the impression of chaotic and frenzied activity, but in fact, every single operation by each of the individuals involved was planned down to the last detail, and slotted into its proper place in the three-day preparation sequence.

Pilots Doug Benefield and John Campbell were just about ready to leave. They would fly the C-130 support aircraft which would take the fire tender and medical and emergency personnel up to Delamar Lake, the dry lake nearest to the launch point, which would serve as an emergency landing ground for the X-15 in the event of any malfunction in the launch area. They would stay on the ground at Delamar, listening on their radio, until the B-52 got airborne from Edwards. Then they would get airborne again with a team of paramedics whose job it would be to parachute directly to the aid of the X-15 pilot in the event of a crash landing, or bail-out, away from one of the nominated emergency lake landing sites.

Across the hall, two of the helicopter section pilots were also on their way out, one to Delamar Lake and the other to Hidden Hills Lake, almost half-way between Delamar and Edwards. They were trained to get rescue personnel to the scene of an emergency in double-quick time, and also to use the rotor downwash to blow any smoke or flames away from the emergency crews operating in a crash situation.

The third helicopter, to cover the take-off and landing at Edwards, wouldn't be required until later, when the B-52 taxied out. The lucky pilot who had drawn the Edwards slot could plan to arrive on the scene at a rather more gentlemanly hour than the "early birds," who had to be in position at their distant locations by the time the B-52 was ready to take off.

While pilot Jack Allavie got on with the weather briefing and flight authorization, the other pilot of the B-52 mother ship, Harry Archer, made the coffee and phoned down to the mating area to confirm that the pre-launch sequence was running on time. While they drank their coffee, Jack reviewed, as he did for every launch flight the two men made together in the B-52, the normal and emergency procedures they would use during the forthcoming flight.

They had been over these same procedures countless times before, but Jack, under a boisterous, extrovert exterior, was a professional test pilot to his finger-tips. Nothing, absolutely nothing, was left to chance on any X-15 launches he flew. Accordingly, and even though they both knew the procedures by heart, they worked their way through each phase of the flight, and each possible emergency situation, reviewing the normal, back-up, and emergency techniques that they might have to use.

On this particular flight, Jack would be in the left-hand seat, and would fly the take-off and climb to altitude. He would then turn the aircraft over to Harry to fly the actual launch, so that he could give his undivided attention to monitoring the vital launch indicator panel, and the manual back-up launch system, which would be used in the event that the three electrically operated shackles which held the X-15 in place failed to function normally.

Picking up their parachutes and flight gear, Harry and Jack headed down the ramp towards the mating area and found Jim McDivitt and Jack McKay arriving at the Fighter Section to prepare for their "chase" missions. They would stay with the X-15 from takeoff until launch, to monitor the control and system checks in the air, and to provide visual back-up during the pre-launch engine prime and start sequences. Each would have a photographer in the back seat of their aircraft to record every stage of the operation. Later, when the X-15 had re-entered the atmosphere, and descended to something like 50,000 feet in the Edwards area, it would be picked up by another two chase planes, piloted by NASA pilots Bill Dana and Milt Thompson, and shepherded back for its landing on the North Lake bed.

At the mating area, the whole scene was dominated by the enormous 200-plus ton bulk of the B-52, its huge vertical tail towering forty feet in the air. Under the right wing, amid an apparent jumble of access ladders, hoses, and electrical connections, hung the squat, black dart-like shape of the X-15 cocooned in clouds of vapor from the web of fuel and chemicals vent pipes, its fuselage already coated in a thick covering of frost in the vicinity of the liquid oxygen tank.

The liquid oxygen, or LOX, was cooled to nearly minus 300 degrees Fahrenheit, and "boiled off" continuously up to the instant of launch. To keep the tank fully topped up, it would be replenished continuously from a huge supply tank in the bomb-bay of the B-52. The characteristic pungent smell of ammonia hung heavily in the air, and Jack and Harry were provided with small breathing masks to wear during their pre-flight inspection of the mother ship. Without them, you could really clear your head in a hurry by taking in a few sniffs of the ammonia vapor.

It was always tense in and around the mating area. Liquid oxygen and anhydrous ammonia are extremely sensitive and volatile propellants. Brought together, they ignite spontaneously with explosive effect. Everyone in the mating area was warily conscious that the X-15 was loaded with nine tons of the stuff, the B-52 carried the replenishment tanks, and there were plenty of re-supply vehicles within the area, all the ingredients for a major disaster if the propellants were brought into contact prematurely. At this stage in the proceedings, the X-15 was literally a very large and very powerful bomb. Little wonder that everyone involved was doubly and triply careful, and that the faces under the harsh arc-lights looked drawn and strained.

By the time mother ship pilots Jack Allavie and Harry Archer finished the external inspection of their B-52, the sun was already up over the rim of the desert, and it was becoming comfortably warmer. After a check of the documentation, Jack signed for the aircraft, and they donned their parachutes and made their way into the aircraft, and up to the flight deck.

Once they were settled in, they worked their way steadily through the aircraft checklist up to the engine start checks. At the same time, Stan Butchart, the rear crew X-15 "panel" operator, ran through his checks on the B-52/X-15 umbilical system which would provide the X-15 with propellant top-up, radio links, and oxygen supply up to the moment of launch.

During their check sequence, I came out of the physiological caravan where I had been "suiting up" and in my full pressure suit and helmet made my way awkwardly across the ramp to the access ladder of the X-15 cockpit. When I was settled in and connected up to the umbilical oxygen and radio links, Jack and Harry were able to say "good morning" and listen in as I went through my own set of checks—monitored by the launch controller in his van at the edge of the mating area. Eventually, with all checks completed on both aircraft, Jack obtained clearance to start the engines on the B-52. As, one by one, the eight engines thundered into life, the mass of equipment, vehicles and personnel withdrew rapidly from the mating area until, with the last starter trolley wheeled away, we were on our own and almost ready to move out.

A number of vehicles containing emergency and control personnel hoisted orange and white checkered flags on small poles attached to their rear bumpers, and forming themselves into a loose line, prepared to follow us out to the runway. This was the "caravan" which attended every X-15 launch. If anything were to go wrong up to the take-off point, these essential personnel wanted to be as close as possible to the event so that they could render assistance with the absolute minimum of delay. After about another half an hour of post-start checks, further checks of the umbilical system, and X-15 system checks, we were ready to taxi out.

"Eddy Tower, this is zero-zero-three. Taxi."

"Roger, zero-zero-three. Cleared taxi to runway four. Winds are light and variable, less than five knots. Surface temperature is sixty-three degrees and rising. Altimeter is three-zero-zero-six."

Jack and Harry leaned forward to set their altimeter sub-scales to the airfield pressure setting before Jack keyed his microphone

"Ready to roll, buddy?" he asked me.

"Ready when you are," I came back quietly with my standard reply.

Jack released the parking brake, and slowly brought up the throttles to get the mother ship moving. As soon as the aircraft began to inch its way forward, he throttled back for a gentle check of the wheel brakes before bringing the power up again to roll onto the main taxiway.

Settled down on the long stretch of taxiway leading out to the end of the main runway, we could all see the starters and ladders being pulled away from a two-seat F-104 and a T-38 on the ramp in front of the Fighter Section.

Leaving pre-flight on the way to the X-15 for my second record-breaking altitude flight (NASA photograph).

Jim McDivitt and Jack McKay were ready to follow us out to the take-off point. To our left, we could see assorted fire tenders and crash rescue vehicles in position off the sides of the main runway and the base rescue helicopter, already airborne, hovering lazily in a position halfway down, and to the side of, the runway.

As we proceeded slowly down the taxiway, Jack keyed his microphone again. "Say, Bob, the temperature's up a bit. Its going to be a long run to unstick [pilot jargon for take-off speed] today," he said.

I came right back with the good-humored needle that exists between fighter and bomber pilots, "Sure you and Harry can manage, Jack? I'll be happy to crawl over and give you a hand if you have any little problems."

Kicking himself for giving me the opening, Jack snapped back, "Dammit, Bob, you know we never let beginners into this thing. You just stick to your toy airplanes, and leave the real flying to the pros."

I knew what was on Jack's mind. In his usual relaxed manner, he was alerting me to the fact that the ground air temperature was high enough to lengthen our take-off roll considerably. Because the X-15 was hung under the wing of the B-52, the mother-ship's right inboard flap had been cut away to accommodate the X-15 tail. Accordingly, it had been necessary to de-activate the inboard flap sections on both sides of the aircraft. As a safety measure, both outboard flap sections had been de-activated as well. Consequently, the B-52 took off and landed without any flap at all. This meant an unstick speed and touchdown speed up to forty knots faster than on a standard B-52 and a much longer run to take off. Moreover, the hotter the day, the longer the run. The Edwards runway was 15,000 feet long—a good three miles—and we would be using most of it to get us off the ground.

As we approached the end of the taxiway, Edwards Tower cleared us directly onto the active runway, and Jack swung the huge bomber gently around to point straight down the center line. All around us were the black tire marks of a thousand previous landings, and at the far end the runway shimmered in the fast rising heat. Jack applied the parking brake, and spoke on the intercom system, "All OK in here?" Glancing around to confirm that everyone was giving him a thumbs-up, he called me again with a last minute check. "You all set, Bob?"

I came back with, "Ready when you are."

Jack keyed his microphone again, "Eddy Tower, zero-zero-three. Ready to roll."

As the tower came back with take-off clearance, Jack took a firm grip of the throttles with his right hand, and slowly eased all eight forward. The bomber nosed gently down as the power increased until Jack released the parking brake.

Shuddering slightly, the great aircraft lurched forward as Jack brought the throttles fully open, and switched in the water-methanol power boost. Slowly at first, then with rapidly increasing speed, my "ferry boat" started off down the runway.

As we picked up speed, the runway markers raced past: Five thousand feet ... seven thousand ... nine thousand." At ten thousand feet, we stormed past the gaggle of control vehicles off to the right of the runway, deafening the occupants with the thunder of our passage.

Eleven thousand feet down the runway, I felt the forward landing gear leave the concrete as the nose rose steeply into climbing attitude. Seconds later, the rear landing gear unstuck and we were airborne. The ground fell away rapidly below as the eight engines of the B-52 bore us effortlessly aloft into the cloudless blue above.

From everyone's standpoint, this was the most dangerous phase of the entire flight. Until we passed 26,000 feet, the X-15 couldn't be released to make a piloted recovery in the event of any emergency. It was designed to be landed empty of all fuel, and the pilot needed a minimum of 26,000 feet to jettison his propellants. On two occasions earlier in the program, pilots had tried to save the aircraft by landing with residual propellants in the tanks, and both times, the landing gear had collapsed, not a pleasant prospect at a touchdown speed of over 200 miles an hour.

Above 26,000 feet, Jack could jettison the X-15 immediately in the event of an emergency, and leave me to either bail-out or attempt to land, if I could. Below 26,000 feet, the mother-ship pilots wouldn't jettison the X-15 until I ejected. Until I did, there was only about thirty feet of air, and some few hundredths of an inch of aluminum, separating the men in the B-52 from a nine-ton bomb. Even a relatively minor explosion would blow the starboard wing clear off the B-52.

As we passed through 26,000 feet in the climb, we settled down to the familiar routine of the slow climb up to 45,000 feet. We were heading out almost due northeast and could already pick out the outline of Hidden Hills dry lake just off the nose and far below to the left. Further off to the left stretched the sterile expanse of Death Valley and rapidly coming into view just off to the right, the glittering sprawl of Las Vegas and the blue waters of Lake Mead beyond.

As we leveled out at 45,000 feet, the B-52 pilots tuned their navigation direction finding indicator to the VOR/TACAN facility at Mormon Mesa, which lay directly ahead on our track. By checking our radial bearing from the facility, they were able to check that we were holding a good outbound track.

This was important on all X-15 launches, because the actual "drop" was

The B-52 with me in the X-15 under the wing, roars skyward for my first record altitude flight (NASA photograph).

made almost as soon as the turn back towards Edwards had been completed. Since so many of the X-15 flights were made on a ballistic trajectory, it was crucial to make the launch as close as possible to the planned launch point, and on the right heading. Otherwise, on re-entry, I could find myself considerably displaced from the planned recovery position and with not a lot of hope for recovering the situation in this high-speed glider. Today, I would go ballistic almost immediately after the drop, and it would be doubly important to get off to an accurate start.

Throughout the outbound leg, the radio was alive almost continuously with the long litany of the X-15 pre-launch check list. I worked my way steadily through the list strapped to my knee, and reported on the temperatures and pressures showing on my system indicators, on the operation of my various controls, on the operation of my telemetry equipment, and on the engine status during the warm-up and prime operations.

Every item on the long list was confirmed either by Launch Control back at Edwards, by the telemetry range station at Beatty Nevada, or by the chase planes which had been flying close formation since take-off. The function of the chase plane pilots was particularly crucial to the operation, in that they were all intimately familiar with the X-15 and its systems and, most importantly, they were actually on the spot, a matter of a few feet away from the aircraft, and observing every operation as it happened.

This was one of the lessons that we learned the hard way during our research programs. You can have all of the telemetry and radio links in the world, but there is just no substitute for a pair of expert eyes watching what is going on as it happens.

On the left hand side of the B-52 cockpit was a small panel with five green bulbs on it—the launch panel. Three of the bulbs indicated the status of the three bomb shackles which held the X-15 in place under the mother-ship's wing. The fourth bulb was the "ready-to-launch" indicator that I actuated when I was ready to be dropped. The fifth bulb was the "launch" light which came on when the "drop" switch was actuated.

In the early days of the X-15 program, the aircraft was actually "dropped" by the pilot of the B-52, the same procedure that had been used in all of the previous air-launch programs. Experience told us that this wasn't the best or safest technique. Bill Bridgeman was launched once in the Douglas Skyrocket with an on-board fire in the rocket engine because he couldn't break in on the mother-ship pilot's countdown. Today, I would initiate the drop myself on Jack's countdown. If I wasn't happy about the launch, I simply wouldn't press the button. Just beside the launch panel in the B-52 were two back-up launch switches. One was a duplicate electrical switch to enable Jack to make the drop in the event that my cockpit switch failed to operate. The other was a hydraulic actuator to operate the release shackles mechanically in the event that the electrical release system became totally inoperative. Because the positioning of the aircraft at launch was so critical, the left-hand seat pilot of the B-52 concentrated exclusively on the launch panel and the back-up switches during the final stages of the launch sequence so that he could react instantly to any malfunction in the release mechanisms.

As the VORTAC indicator needle swung drunkenly around the dial to mark our passage directly over the Mormon Mesa station, Jack waved to Harry to take control of the aircraft for the ten minutes or so up to the launch point. Harry held the control column gently as the VORTAC needle steadied down to point directly behind us on 217 degrees—putting us dead on our track of 037 degrees outbound. He caressed the throttles gently to hold our Mach number on 0.8, and fiddled with the trimmers. All pilots do this when they take over control of an aircraft from another pilot. From long experience, Harry knew that Jack would never hand over control with the aircraft even slightly off speed or out of trim, but it was a way of getting the feel of the machine as quickly as possible. After his first few seconds of fiddling with the controls, Harry knew that the aircraft would be exactly as it was when Jack handed it over.

As we continued the run outbound, Jack picked up the countdown at the twelve-minute mark. I immediately responded with my twelve-minute checks, confirmed by either the panel operator, or by one of the chase pilots. At the eleven-minute mark, I initiated engine pre-cool, and confirmed my inertial velocity and attitude gauge indicators. At ten minutes, Harry called a check on the B-52 magnetic heading and eased the control column gently to the left to start us into a slow, wide, ten-degree bank turn. As the left wing started to dip, he eased the throttles forward to hold our speed steady on Mach 0.8.

At six minutes to go, Jack called, "Six minute mark, Bob. Please confirm all remaining time checks."

I calmly responded, "Roger six minutes, auxiliary cabin pressure on."

At five minutes, the propellant top-off was completed, and the X-15 disconnected from all B-52 umbilical systems except for the radio link. As the last few time checks were called, and the appropriate checks completed, Harry eased off the left bank and steadied the B-52 down on the launch heading of 222 degrees. He left the throttles where they were and eased in a little nose-down trim to let the speed build up to launch speed of Mach 0.82. From now on, he would concentrate solely on holding height, speed, and heading absolutely rock steady up to the instant of release.

At one minute to go, Jack selected the launch master switch ON, and I initiated the engine prime sequence that was immediately confirmed by Chase 1.

In these last seconds before launch, the thoughts of every single person involved in the project are on the man in the cockpit of the X-15. This is the time when I am truly and absolutely alone. Part of my mind attends methodically to the last few items on the checklist, but I am already gearing up for the sudden, lurching drop into the emptiness below, and the awesome, raging burst to heights and speeds which no one has ever experienced before.

The flight was absolutely routine until we reached the one minute count down. My MH-96, the adaptive flight control system, dropped out, and my heart sank. It was completely off line.

Jack Allavie immediately called NASA-1 and asked, "Shall I execute a 360 while we sort this out?"

Before NASA-1 could answer, I had re-set the circuit breaker and the MH-96 system came back on line. In retrospect, the flight probably should have been aborted at this point. Since the MH-96 system handled the entire electronic flight control system, it would have been disastrous had it failed later. I never even thought about that. After four straight aborts, I was ready to go.

Jack's level monotone continued steadily in my ears. "Ten ... Nine ... Eight ... Seven ... Six ... Five ..."—the green "ready-to-launch" light winked from the panel—"Four ... Three ... Two ... One ... LAUNCH!"

The release from the B-52 was perfect, and I fired the engine and immediately established a 41 degree climb angle. As the X-15 dropped away, the B-52 began to nose up sharply and move off quickly to the left. The second Harry felt the drop, he was already moving the control column forward and to the right and easing the trimmers to get the mother ship back into balanced flight. Their actions were routine, almost automatic from dozens of other launch flights.

Jack and Harry were both straining forward to pick up their first sight of the X-15, and by now I was well below them with the engine already lit and coming up to full power. In a matter of seconds, they could see me, rising dead ahead of them, climbing on a trail of fire from the rocket exhaust. The angle of climb was staggering. I was programmed to go up at an attitude of more than forty degrees but from the cockpit of the B-52, it must have looked like I was going almost straight up.

The boost portion of the flight went well, and the engine burn was longer than usual due to my topped-off oxygen tank. In seconds I was out of sight, but the B-52 crew could still follow the trail of flame and vapor up to the instant of burnout which seemed to take place almost directly above the mother ship. I shot out of the atmosphere as the engine burn stopped.

As I came over the top of the ballistic profile, the view was unbelievable. I could see farther than I ever imagined. I looked in both directions and could see nothing but Earth. I could see its curve. It was just tremendous. The sky above was an inky black. I could see San Francisco Bay off my right wing. Incredible! Since then, pictures from space have become commonplace. When I see them, I know that's exactly what it looked like, because I was fortunate enough to have been there in the beginning.

My enthusiasm was audible on the radio when the crew of the B-52 heard me say, "Jesus, this is really going up," then later, "I can see all the way from north of San Francisco to well into Mexico." Then the call faded. I was too far away for them to pick up my re-entry and landing back at Edwards where I would touch down almost exactly ten minutes after leaving the shackles on the B-52. The boys in the mother ship still had something over an hour to go to get home!

There wasn't much time for sightseeing. It was time to come back. Besides, for the first time I had the feeling of extreme height.

It was time to reenter the atmosphere. Once the angle of attack is estab-

The earth from 220,000 feet on my record altitude flight (NASA photograph).

lished, the process of reentry into the atmosphere begins. Very soon the G-forces begin to build and increase until you have five Gs pushing you down into your seat and about five Gs trying to throw you into the instrument panel. The resultant vector is about seven Gs that want to drive you to the floor at the bottom of the instrument panel. Of course our restraining devices prohibit that, since we knew from the centrifuge that we could not control the aircraft without them.

The first thing I noticed from the increased G-forces was a gradual pain behind my eyes that quickly became severe. Blood quickly pooled in my right arm, and the ache was bad enough to take my mind off the pain in my eyes. Fortunately, the pain was short-lived as the G-forces decreased.

While these forces were at work, I was intent on controlling my angle of attack and at five times the normal force of gravity. The result is that gradually it pulls you out of the dive, and I came level at eighty thousand feet at a speed of Mach 3.5.

Now I had a recovery situation. I knew I had a hot engine, and I was about one-half degree high on the pitch angle while climbing to altitude, and I also had a second or two longer on the engine burn. All these factors added together resulted in my arriving level over the landing runway, but at 80,000 feet and Mach 3.5, I was where I should be but with way too much energy. There was consternation at NASA-1 control center where Joe Walker was on the radio and a room full of engineers was monitoring the flight.

The question they had, spoken or unspoken, was simply, "Where is he going to land?"

Joe called and said, "Bob, I recommend a right turn."

I was already turning when he called. With the Edwards dry lakes below me and another large lake off to the right of my flight path, I had that option for landing if I couldn't get back to the lake bed at Edwards. When I turned, I held as much G force as I could. I lowered the nose a bit so I could keep descending into denser atmosphere which allowed me to maintain the G forces as I was scrubbing off speed.

It was the largest 360-degree turn I had ever made. Joe kept me informed of my altitude as I made my way around. My altimeter was not very good until I got to lower altitudes, and Joe's calls allowed me to judge whether or not I could make it back to the intended runway to land. I did and landed right where I was supposed to.

Over my headset, Joe Walker's voice said simply, "Good shot chief."

Then he ended the flight by saying, "This is your controller going off the air."

At the debriefing, as I sipped my dry martini, the Physiological Section's prize for every successful launch, the initial data came in "hot off the press" from the telemetry stations. That day, I reached an altitude of 314,750 feet—less than half a mile short of sixty miles STRAIGHT UP! It is still an FAI (Fédération Aéronautique Internationale) record for winged aircraft, and it may never be surpassed. To do so, the flight would have to stay below 328,000 feet where space actually begins. If anyone goes for the new record, they would need to surpass my height by 3 percent or about 10,000 feet. The margin of error would be between 324,000 feet and 328,000 feet or about 4,000 feet. Even today that would be too small a target to hit. Besides, with the emphasis on space, there is no major priority for flight expansion, and a new altitude record would be a moot point in the real world of aviation research.

I had just become the first man in history to "fly" an aircraft into space and back again. That made me the first winged astronaut, and only the fifth American to qualify for astronaut's "wings."

I have been accused by some of plotting to overshoot my attack angle on purpose to establish an unbeatable altitude record. Nothing is further from the truth! If the flight records from other altitude flights (not only mine) are examined, it is perfectly clear that overage and underage of the prescribed altitude targets were common. This flight did overshoot the altitude targets by 32,250 feet. I feel that was due to the hot engine, the long burn and the topped-off tanks. It was nothing I did on purpose.

I hold my pressure suit helmet and gesture "Number One" while posing next to the airplane that has just carried me to the edge of space (AFFTC History Office archives).

All I did was to try to do the best that I could with the task assigned to me. It was my job to push the X-15 to its altitude limits, and to prove that the airplane was capable of performing at that altitude. I did it, and I'm proud of that.

In fact, I am equally as proud of the way I flew the flight as I was with the altitude I was able to reach. When the flight was analyzed, I was exactly on target on both ascent and descent. I was so close to the actual plan that the engineers used data from this flight as a standard to check the accuracy of the simulators for later altitude flights.

I had flown the first aircraft flight above 300,000 feet and completed the first flight above 50 miles. By the new criteria, I was now a command pilot astronaut. I would fly the X-15 one last time on flight 75, December 14, 1962. It was a routine flight that contained some experiments on the Earth's ultraviolet background. But the flight I'll always remember in detail will be Flight 62.

British-born Harry Archer summed up the feeling of everyone involved in that historic flight when he said, "I am still proud of my small part in the X-15 program. Very few pilots indeed get the chance to work on a program that is so far ahead of its time, and which is continually breaking new ground in so many aspects of aerospace research.

"In all, I suppose I flew something like twenty or thirty successful launch missions, and I flew every type of support mission associated with the program. If I never did anything else in the flying business, I could reasonably claim to have earned my pay with the X-15 project. I was at Edwards at the right time and, foreigner or not, they treated me exactly as they would have treated any American pilot filling my 'slot' in Bomber Test, Harry concluded.

Shortly after my flight, it was announced that the X-15 team had been awarded the NASA Outstanding Achievement Award and the pilot team had been considered for the Collier Trophy for Achievement in Astronautics. We all flew to Washington for the various presentations which marked a sort of "grand slam" for me. I was promoted, awarded the Distinguished Service

President John F. Kennedy, with Crossfield (center) and me (right), and the other X-15 pilots during the Robert J. Collier Trophy Award presentation outside the White House on July 18, 1962 (NASA photograph).

Medal, and awarded my Astronaut's wings, pinned on by President Kennedy at a ceremony at the White House.

Following the ceremony, President Kennedy slyly insisted on pointing out to Harry some damage to the fabric of the building which he said, with an absolutely straight face, was a relic from "the last time the Brits were here in force." Fortunately, he didn't ask Harry to pay up for the repairs.

Chapter 11

Distractions, Decorations, and Disasters

Apart from being the lead X-15 pilot for the Air Force, I was expected to do a number of other things. One of them was public relations. That meant a giving a lot of speeches about the X-15 program. I actually enjoyed doing it, but the travel was at times a hassle, and it took my mind away from the business at hand, flying the airplane. To be perfectly honest, I haven't a clue as to the exact number of speeches I gave. I spoke to colleges and universities, veterans groups and civic organizations to name but a few. It was not an unpleasant task.

In the early sixties, there was still respect for the uniform and a confidence in our government's activities. The people who came to the lectures were interested in what we were doing and in what I had to say. The technology fascinated them and the speeds and altitudes we were flying seemed almost like science fiction to them. The majority of the questions were good ones presented courteously. I answered each one the same way, regardless of how elementary the question might be.

Another advantage of the time was a lack of detractors and protestors. There simply weren't any. I was never confronted, insulted or verbally castigated. Not once did a picket line form outside a place where I was scheduled to speak. No one tried to spray paint my uniform. The only negative thing I ever got came courtesy of the United States Mail. It was a letter from a disturbed individual who believed our project was science fiction. He accused the Air Force of an elaborate conspiracy plot.

He wrote: "I know you are not really doing all those things they put in the newspaper and in the magazines. Nobody could really do that. I know you went to Hollywood and used their special effects."

His diatribe went on and on. I don't know if it was the same individual who later accused the lunar astronauts of the same thing, but I had a good chuckle and pitched it into the waste basket. He must not have been alone, because the plot was later picked up by Hollywood and used as the basis for a Grade-C movie concerning a Mars landing.

An added benefit to the lecture circuit was my transportation. You might think that someone who flew as much as I did wouldn't get excited about flying a T-33 trainer a couple of states away to give a talk to the Rotary Club. But I did. That was my ride to the long-distance speeches and was the main reason I enjoyed giving those speeches. I'd fly anything they put in front of me.

We were also involved with the print media. *National Geographic* magazine covered the X-15 program. They contacted Joe Walker and asked him to do an article on the speed flights. They called me and asked me to do a similar one for the altitude flights. For our efforts, we would be paid $1,000, a princely sum in those days. To a young officer with three children that sounded like a windfall.

Since Joe was a civilian, he could just pocket the check. As a military man, I had to obtain approval from the chain of command before I accepted any honorarium. I didn't have much experience with gratuities at this point in my career. The only one I had ever encountered came from a small college where I gave an address. Not certain if I should accept it, I gave it back to the college for its scholarship fund. This one was much bigger and could be put to good use. So I sent my request up the chain.

Their response was immediate and negative. We received the word that no X-15 military pilot could accept any money for promoting the program. I was disappointed, but I suspect Doris and the kids were even more disappointed. None the less, we accepted their decision.

There is one thing about honorariums and the military that I'll never understand. About that time, seven young men had been chosen to be the Mercury astronauts. They were allowed to negotiate a $50,000 contract for exclusive rights to their story. And each of them received a new Corvette.

I am often asked if I was interested in becoming a Mercury astronaut. The truthful answer is no, I was not. The only thing I ever wanted to do was fly airplanes. However, I would have appreciated equal treatment from the Air Force when it came to the rules on ancillary income. Oh, well!

Shortly after this episode, *The Ladies' Home Journal* contacted me for a personal-type article. They wanted shots of the family; our quarters; the officer's club and Doris and I at a dance there. And they would pay the going rate for such an article, $1,000.

"We will be happy to do the article, but I cannot accept any money for doing it. It is against Air Force policy," I responded.

They came to the base and took their pictures. Then they handed me a check. I was about to protest when the magazine's representative said, "We know that you can't accept any money for doing this article, but we hadn't intended to pay you anything. This check is for Mrs. White."

Final score on honorariums, Air Force one, Mrs. White one.

I also came into contact with two Hollywood productions while with the X-15 program. The first movie was about a downed B-25 crew, and they used one of our emergency dry lake bed landing zones to simulate a North African desert.

When we had time, we visited the production site and spoke to the stars and the technical people. It seemed strange to see the shell of an old B-25 all riddled with bullets lying on a dry Nevada lake bed. The visits were

Hollywood meets the real thing. Posing in front of a very convincing X-15 mock-up mated to one of the NB-52 launch aircraft in April 1961, I am surrounded by two actors (Ralph Taeger and Charles Bronson) literally playing my part in the aviation epic *X-15*. Definitely not an Oscar contender, the movie nevertheless featured stunning color inflight footage shot during actual X-15 missions. Two newcomers to the silver screen made their debut in this film: Mary Tyler Moore (playing a test pilot's girlfriend) and tough-guy Bronson, seen here wearing a mock X-15 pressure suit (AFFTC History Office archives).

enjoyable, and the Hollywood people knew who we were and what we were doing and always treated us kindly.

The second brush with Hollywood was nearly my downfall. Hollywood decided to make a movie about the X-15. The film starred David Mclean, James Gregory, Richard Kirby, and was to be the motion picture debut of a young actor named Charles Bronson.

They obtained permission to come to Edwards and use a stripped down X-15 as a prop for a number of their shots. They also had a simulated pressure suit for Mr. Bronson and the other actors portraying pilots in the film. I don't believe their suits left any of the tell-tale seam lines on their skin because they were never subjected to any G-force, but they were certainly tailor-made for the actors.

Another component of the suit, the cumbersome backpack that we wore, was different on the Hollywood model. Ours contained the hardware and controls that activated the suit. The thing weighed at ton. Hollywood's version was practically weightless. Straw, however, is not a good suit activation system.

When the film was completed, they invited all the real X-15 pilots to the gala opening in Hollywood. Afterwards, there was an invitation to a reception at Chasen's Restaurant, the really "in" watering hole for the Hollywood crowd in those days.

Joe Walker, Neil Armstrong and a few of the other guys decided to go, and I joined them. When the movie was over, we congregated outside on the sidewalk. Naturally opinions concerning the production were expressed.

The picture made a valiant attempt to create realism, a trend in motion pictures at that time, and the actors did a credible job. For those of us flying the airplane on a day-to-day basis, the movie left a lot to be desired. In all fairness, I'm certain that's not unique to test pilots. Physicians view medical films, scuba divers underwater sequences and real soldiers see combat films in an altogether different light than the average person who is not involved in these activities. Unfortunately, I expressed my opinion a bit too forcefully.

"What did you think of the movie, Bob?" one of the guys asked me.

"It was a turkey," I said, louder than I should have.

By this time, I was feeling tired, and going to a party wasn't at the top of my "to do list." I bid the gang good night and drove home to the desert.

The next morning I received an unexpected call from the public affairs officer. The colonel would like to see me. Supposing I would be off to the hinterlands for another speech, I went to his office whistling a happy tune.

"Good morning, Bob. Come in please, and close the door," he said in a tone that let me know this was no social call and motioned me to a chair across the desk from him.

"I understand that you went to the premiere of the movie *X-15* last night," he said.

"That's right, sir. A bunch of us went over," I said, shifting uncomfortably.

"And what did you think of it?" he asked.

"Frankly sir, it was a turkey," I said.

Grimacing, he shoved a copy of the local Bakersfield newspaper toward me. It was opened to an article on the premiere, and I scanned it quickly.

> A number of X-15 pilots attended the premiere. All but one of them attended the post preview gala reception at Chasen's. Outside the theater when asked about the film, someone was heard to remark, "It was a turkey." Those interviewed at the reception did not seem to share this less than enthusiastic opinion.

"They didn't name any names in this article, did they?" I asked hesitantly.

"Not that I can see," the colonel replied.

"They didn't actually *say* it was a pilot, did they?" I continued.

"That's very fortunate for the person who said it. Now, get out of here, White," the colonel said with a dismissive wave of his hand.

That was a close one. Had I been quoted directly, I'd have been in deep trouble. Lesson learned. I would not repeat that error again. Henceforth, if I didn't have anything good to say, I would keep my big mouth shut.

Thanks to the X-15 project, I also had the privilege to meet three sitting presidents of the United States, and a fourth who would later become president. I have already described my contact with Vice President Nixon at the X-15 roll out. The other three were Presidents Eisenhower, Kennedy and Johnson. As a member of the armed forces, to be able to meet four commanders-in-chief is an unusual honor. Not too bad for a street kid from New York.

Jacqueline Cochran, the first female aviator to break the sound barrier, was a friend of mine. She and her husband, Floyd Odlum, invited me to an informal dinner party at their home in California. There were about a dozen people there. One of them was Dwight David Eisenhower.

He was a consummate gentleman. Gracious and charming, it was easy to see why he was picked to head the Supreme Headquarters Allied Forces Europe (SHAFE). That job, like the presidency, required the penultimate politician, and from where I sat, Ike filled the bill.

I met President Kennedy for awards ceremonies I will describe later, but my first encounter with him was at an official Air Force function. An annual event for the military in those days was a function called the Fire Power Demonstration at Eglin Air Force Base in Florida. Along with the B-52 crew, I was assigned to take the X-15 to Florida for the big day.

President John F. Kennedy hosts the X-15 pilots (including me, speaking) after the Collier Trophy Award presentation at the White House in 1962. General Curtis LeMay is in the center (NASA photograph).

The ground crew stripped down an X-15 aircraft and we tucked it under the wing of the B-52. We flew it to Florida to set up a display that spotlighted the aircraft. No, I didn't ride in the X-15, I took the more comfortable seats with the bomber crew.

As was his custom, JFK drove by in an open-top limousine. When he stopped in front of the aircraft, I gave him a short presentation. When I finished, I saluted smartly. He nodded his approval and drove on. The procedure was repeated in front of each of the displays.

Later, I was invited to sit on the reviewing stand. The president was there in his famous rocking chair in deference to his bad back. Beside him was General Curtis Lemay. We watched a demonstration of Air Force fire power culminating in a B-52 flyover, dropping bombs as they went. The president was duly impressed.

Since we had not disconnected the X-15 from the B-52, when the show was over we simply flew home.

I met President Lyndon Johnson on two occasions, once at a White House awards ceremony that NASA held in Washington and a second time when he presented me with a medal in Vietnam that I will describe later.

In publicizing the X-15, I came into contact with a number of radio, television and film personalities. A few stand out. One of them was Walter Cronkite. He interviewed me for his news program. When it was over, we had lunch. He was a solid person who respected my uniform and seemed genuinely interested in the program and in me as a person.

When he was leaving, he shook my hand and said, "Bob, if you are ever in New York, give me a call. We'll have lunch."

From the look in his eyes and the firmness of the handshake, I truly believed it was a sincere invitation. I have no doubt he would have honored it if I had taken him up on it.

Another man who was the real deal was Ed Sullivan. I was asked to be on his show along with the incomparable Ella Fitzgerald and the star of the

In this Air Force publicity photograph, I was posed next to the Flying Tigers Pilot Achievement Award trophy with a model of a Curtiss P-40 mounted on top. Madame Chiang Kai-Shek is on the right (U.S. Air Force).

television show, *Paladin*, Richard Boone. The show's opening was taped while the show itself was live. I went to this one as a solo flight without any of my fellow pilots for company.

They started off with a photo session for everyone and then went into rehearsal for the show. Richard Boone and Ella Fitzgerald were laughing and joking with each other and making a bit of noise.

From across the room, the familiar baritone voice boomed, "Dick, Ella, knock it off."

The set immediately became as quiet as a mortuary at midnight. *The Ed Sullivan Show* was the top variety show in the country, and Mr. Sullivan paid his guests top dollar. When he spoke everyone listened.

Of course, I wasn't allowed to accept a reimbursement, so after the show I went backstage to thank Mr. Sullivan for his hospitality. I had been treated like royalty. All airline flights were first class, and I stayed in the finest hotel in New York.

After I thanked him, he asked, "Everything okay?"

"Yes, sir. Couldn't have been better. Thank you again," I replied.

"Well, before you leave town, if you have a favorite restaurant go there. If not eat at the hotel. Either way, the bill is on us. You guys in uniform do a great job. Don't you worry about the expense. It's my pleasure," he said with a warm smile and a firm handshake.

Yes, Ed Sullivan was the real deal.

Another show that Joe Walker and I did was the old classic, *What's My Line*. The show had many stars over the years, but the night we were on, the stars were Bennett Cerf, Alan King, Dorothy Kilgallen and Arlene Francis. Ms. Francis had to rescue herself, because I had met her on a previous trip to Los Angeles. The other three panelists were unable to guess our occupation.

Usually, the show had only one guest, but in this instance, there were two of us. So Joe and I had to share a stool meant for one, cheek to cheek, so to speak.

The pay for being on the show was fifty dollars. This time, the Air Force had said I was allowed to take the money. When payday came, they wanted to give each of us twenty-five dollars. After a bit of persuasion, they gave us each fifty dollars. Not quite like the *Ladies Home Journal*, but remember the value of a dollar in the early sixties.

Countless men and women in the armed forces can recall having met, shook hands with, had their pictures taken with, or been to a performance of the legendary Bob Hope. I am one of those, too. It was my good fortune to meet him on several occasions and had the opportunity to talk with him more than the average serviceman. He was every bit as gracious and as much

Joe Walker and I sit in the back seat of a convertible during a parade, one of the many peripheral activities to our more rigorous test pilot duties (NASA photograph)

of a friend of the military as his shows to entertain the troops portrayed him to be.

Another remarkable figure, and to me, a really good guy and supporter of military people was the Michigan football legend Tom Harmon. He was a sportscaster in the Los Angeles area during and after the time I worked with the X-15 program. We had lunch together to talk about flying. It was a bit after the X-15 years, and I was a bit older. But it was because of the X-15 that Harmon knew who I was. He was a really nice man who was also a World War II bomber pilot. Tommy was surprised to find that I was still flying.

"That's amazing. I just can't understand how you can still do that," he said.

I didn't answer him, but in my heart I understood then, and in my mind I understand now something that is at the core of my being. I was still flying, and would fly as long as I could, for one simple reason. I was, am and always will be a pilot, even though I'm not in the driver's seat of an airplane cockpit anymore.

Another notable evening at the Odlum's New York Apartment began with cocktails. Afterwards, we adjourned to a private club that Floyd and his wife, the famed aviatrix Jackie Cochran, belonged to for a magnificent lobster dinner.

It was a delightful evening. Among the guests was one very attractive and personable young movie starlet. Besides her good looks, she was a down-to-earth person conversationally, until a camera came by. Like a chameleon, she changed into the starlet complete with pose, frozen smile and come-hither look. As soon as the flash bulb popped, it was back to the delightful person she really was. Just like a test pilot, she had a job, and she knew how to do it.

At the end of the evening, the club president came over to me and handed me an envelope.

"I understand that you and Mrs. White have tickets to see *Peter Pan* starring Mary Martin," he said, smiling.

"Yes, we do. And, we're looking forward to it," I replied.

"When you go to the theater, would you give this to the usher who seats you and ask him to give it to Ms. Martin," he asked, handing me the sealed envelope with her name on it.

Puzzled, I pocketed the envelope. The night we went to the performance, I delivered the envelope as instructed. Although my curiosity was killing me, since the envelope was sealed, I never opened it.

At intermission, the smiling usher came back with an envelope for me. I opened it and read the note inside.

It read, "Ms. Martin will be pleased to see you backstage after the show."

When the spectacular performance concluded, I took the note to the usher, and it became our passport to the backstage area and her dressing room.

Mary Martin was as warm, personable and animated off stage as she was on stage. After a wonderful conversation, she signed pictures of herself as Peter Pan for each of our children, and I left the theater with a deeper appreciation of a truly talented performer and another genuinely warm human being.

To be sure, not everyone was as nice as Ed Sullivan or Mary Martin. Some believed they really were the larger-than-life parts they played in their films. Some believed they really were important. When I watched them in action it made me sad. I'm sure at some time in their lives, most of them were folks just like me. But, they had forgotten that. I hoped for their sake, their charade wouldn't end.

Yes, I was fortunate to rub shoulders with the rich and the famous, but I never let it affect me. Shortly after World War II, while I was in the process of trying to decide what to do with my life, I tried selling vacuum cleaners for a little while. I gave it the old college try, but I wasn't very good at it. I sold a few, but my heart wasn't in it. But I never forgot the experience.

As I climbed those stairs to apartment after apartment, some nicer, some the same and some not as nice as the one we lived in, I became acutely aware of who I was. I was one of these people to whom I was trying to sell a vacuum cleaner. Yes, I might have my fifteen minutes of fame, but in the end, I was just Bob White, a boy from the streets of Manhattan. I'd never be anything different.

So as I met those celebrities and politicians, and was wined and dined as though I were one of them, I knew it was fleeting. In a few short months I'd be back in the seat of a fighter plane where I really belonged along with all the other New York or Chicago or hometown USA men and women who were doing the same thing.

I was just a New York vacuum cleaner salesman. Had I tried to pretend I belonged to the same circle as the rich and famous, I'd only have made an ass of myself. So I enjoyed it while it lasted, but I never forgot who I was.

Another thing that came with the X-15 program was the awards. Many of my fellow pilots received well-deserved awards for their part in the program. As the lead Air Force pilot, a number came my way.

But, and this is not false modesty, these awards are not to the pilots alone, although we were the ones who accepted them. They also belong to the countless men and women, engineers and technicians, and an army of specialists down to the guys who cleaned the X-15's windshield who helped us to fly. All of my awards are their awards, too.

President John F. Kennedy and the X-15 pilots during Harmon Trophy Award presentation at the White House in 1961 (NASA photograph).

In 1961, Joe Walker representing NASA, Scott Crossfield representing North American Aviation Corporation, Forrest Peterson representing the Navy and me as the Air Force representative went to the White House to receive the Harmon International Aviation Trophy for outstanding achievement as pilots. This award was presented to us by President John Fitzgerald Kennedy.

In 1962, the quartet of White, Walker, Crossfield and Petersen returned for an encore, and the Collier Trophy given for Outstanding Achievement in Aviation for that year. It is one of the most prestigious awards that can be given to a pilot. President Kennedy repeated his performance and presented us with that award as well.

In 1962, I also met Vice President Lyndon Johnson who presented me with the NASA Distinguished Service Medal at a ceremony in Washington, D.C. We would meet later in Vietnam where then President Johnson presented me with the Air Force Cross.

Not to diminish being given awards by presidents, I think perhaps I am most proud of the medal pinned on me by the Secretary of the Air Force, Eugene M. Zuckert. In a ceremony at Edwards Air Force Base, I was given the Distinguished Service Medal by the Air Force. It is the highest non-

Above: President Lyndon B. Johnson being presented with a scale model of the X-15 at the NASA Headquarters Awards. From left are: me, two unknown gentlemen, President Johnson, NASA X-15 program director Paul Bikle, Joe Walker, and Navy Commander Forrest Peterson (NASA photograph). *Right:* As a major I attended an Air Force news conference denoting my X-15 achievements (U.S. Air Force).

combat award that can be bestowed by the Air Force. The medal is usually reserved for someone with the rank of full colonel or general. Since I was still a major at the time, I was doubly proud.

To be recognized by one's peers

is a singular reward, and Joe, Scott, Forrest and I were so honored by the Society of Experimental Test Pilots. This group, formed in the late 1940s presented us with the Iven Kincheloe Award for outstanding achievement as a pilot. The award touched us all, since Iven had not only been a colleague but a dear friend as well.

In 1962, after my altitude flights, I was given the Thomas G. White Air Force Space Trophy for outstanding contributions to aerospace progress. It is a large trophy. In fact, it is a *very* large trophy, and it now resides in the Smithsonian National Aerospace Museum in Washington, D.C.

David Shilling was a top ace in World War II and an annual award for outstanding achievement in flight is presented in his memory. I received that honor for the 1961–1962 period. To my delight, it was presented to me by General James "Jimmy" Doolittle, whose carrier-launched bombing raid on Japan in World War II is forever engraved in the annals of military aviation.

My alma mater, New York University, presented me with their Distin-

X-15 pilots Crossfield (nearest seal), Walker (behind model), and I (front right) presented President Kennedy with a 1/40-scale display model of the X-15 at a White House ceremony (NASA photograph).

guished Alumnus Medal. Villanova University also presented me a medal, although I never went to school there. They gave it annually to a Catholic who did something they considered outstanding. Since I was still a Catholic in good standing, I qualified.

After the ceremony, Villanova's president, who was also a priest, said to me, "Come up to the office of a poor priest for a toast." By some university standards, that office may have been poor, but it was far nicer than any of the other priest's offices I have visited.

Shortly after my last X-15 flight on December 14, 1962, I left the program. The X-15 continued to fly for another 125 flights ending on December 20, 1968. I followed the progress of the program from my subsequent postings.

Soon after I left, they began to modify the flights and more critically, the aircraft. They added external fuel tanks for longer engine burn and married a dummy scram jet to the X-15. This and the new challenges they laid out for the X-15 were definitely more difficult as well as more hazardous, but were intended to assist the airplane in reaching its maximum performance potential.

Standing next to my monument display after being inducted into the Aerospace Walk of Honor in Lancaster, California, in 1992. The Aerospace Walk of Honor along Lancaster Boulevard pays tribute to distinguished Edwards Air Force Base test pilots whose history of achievement in the field has been continuously outstanding (Flight Test Historical Foundation).

The experimental aircraft of the Edwards' era bridged the gap between the sound barrier and space. It proved to the aviation world and to the politicians who would fund it that space exploration was not only probable but a feasible reality. And it was my honor to be a small part of that historic endeavor. While I flew the X-15 I was fortunate enough to be a part of the following records:

For Speed

Date	Height	Mach	Speed
February 7, 1961	78,150	3.5	2,275 mph
March 7, 1961	77,450	4.43	2,405 mph
April 21, 1961	105,000	4.6	2,3074 mph
June 23, 1961	107,700	5.27	3,603 mph
November 9, 1961	101,000	6.05	4,093 mph

For Altitude

Date	Height	Mach	Speed
August 12, 1960	136, 500	2.52	1,772 mph
October 11, 1961	217,000	5.21	3,647 mph
July 17, 1962	314,750	5.45	3,832 mph

Even though many people might think I had done enough and should have retired to a quieter life after this great adventure, I had other ideas. Now, it was time for this New York street kid to get back where he belonged; in the seat of a fighter plane!

Chapter 12
Goodbye Edwards, Hello Bitburg

It was now 1963, and my time at Edwards Air Force Base was drawing to a close. I had been ensconced at Edwards for nine challenging and professionally rewarding years. As a pilot, I could have stayed there forever. But the X-15 project was moving into a new era, and as a career military officer, it was time to move on.

I flew only one more X-15 flight after the altitude flight, and my time was up for reassignment. The big boss at Edwards, Major General Branch, sent word that General Bernard Schriever, the four-star general in charge of the Air Force Systems Command, had said I was to go to Cape Canaveral in Florida. My new assignment was to train to be the flight director of the Titan Two project. The word was passed to Major General Branch who gave me the news.

Time for career management advanced course. I spoke up and told General Branch that my heart was still in flying. I didn't want to go to a static job, even though it would be challenging and something I could do well. That little boy on the steps was still inside me longing to be "up there." When my request was denied, I was down but not out.

Since I knew General Schriever, I requested permission from General Branch to talk to General Schriever about the decision. With my rank, I had that option, so long as I did it through the appropriate channels. Fortunately for me, my request was granted.

When General Schriever was commander of Air Force Systems Command, he had come to Edwards. While he was there, he wanted to take a ride in an F-104. He had a talk to give in Albuquerque, New Mexico, and would use that opportunity to get his ride. I drew the assignment to be his pilot.

The first order of business was to get him suited up in a flight suit and chart a course for our destination, Kirtland Air Force Base. It was a typical desert day. There wasn't a cloud in the sky, and a balmy little zephyr of wind. It was perfect flying weather.

I knew that once a man became a general officer, they seldom got to fly an airplane of any sort, let alone a supersonic fighter. When we were over the mountains of New Mexico, I said, "Okay, you've got it."

He started to protest, but he needed only a modicum of coaxing for him to take the stick. I took a last glance at the fuel load and hit the afterburner. The F-104 jumped to Mach 1.5 in a heartbeat.

Since the general was unfamiliar with the aircraft, I talked him through it all the way. He was a good pilot; he'd just never flown a supersonic fighter plane before. As the highlight of his supersonic experience, I talked him through a barrel roll and then cut the after burner to conserve fuel. I had more than enough to get us there, but I was taking no chances. With the big boss on board, conservatism was the rule of the day.

When we reached the base, the usual reception committee was waiting for the general. They asked him about his flight, and I was appreciative of his glowing description of the trip.

"Of course the flight was great. I was with one of the best pilots in the Air Force," he said.

It's always nice to please the boss. I gassed up the F-104 and flew back to Edwards with the feeling I had done a good day's work.

With that kind of history with the general and my boss's permission, I called General Schriever's executive officer to set up the meeting. "The general will be here tomorrow. See you at noon," he told me.

I went down to Los Angeles to the Ballistic Missile Division to see him. I was ushered into an empty conference room. In a few minutes, he came in, sat down, put his feet up on the desk and indicated that I should proceed.

Feeling pretty comfortable with the situation, I pleaded my case as eloquently as I could. "Sir, I'm a fighter pilot. I realize that the missile program is important, and I take nothing away from the job the folks there are doing, or their value to the overall mission of the Air Force. But I love to fly. It's what I'm good at, and it's what I want to do," I said. After some chit-chat, I also pointed out that I wanted to get back to tactical aviation.

He looked at me for a long moment, then asked, "What kind of equipment do you want?"

"I really don't care, sir. I would take the last F-84 in the Air Force if it would let me fly and get me a command one day," I replied.

After some small talk, I went back to the base. Four days later, I received my orders for Bitburg, Germany, and its three squadrons of Republic F-105s. Being the newest fighter bomber in the Air Force, I got way more than I wished for by offering to take that company's last F-84!

As soon as I got the word, I called a friend at Nellis Air Force Base in

Nevada and arranged an F-105 refresher session so I could hit the ground running in Germany. I needed to drop a few bombs, hook up with the tankers, things that I would be doing every day in my new assignment. I still had that "be prepared" attitude. Why not? It had worked through a couple of wars and the X-15 program.

In those days before I could go overseas, I was required to go to Reno, Nevada, and the Air Force Survival School. I figured survival training was two wars too late, but I had no choice. And there was always the chance that I might have to use it in another war, or police action, or whatever they decided to call the next conflict.

Shortly after my arrival at Nellis, I got a welcome message from General Branch at Edwards. He told me that I was on the list for promotion to lieutenant colonel. I would go to Bitburg as the squadron operations officer, which was usually a major's job. It was time for some of the folks at Bitburg to rotate, and it wouldn't be long until I would be moved into a job appropriate to my new rank.

Survival training began with physical training and education segments. Lots of calisthenics, running and other physical activity were involved to get us ready for the mountains. We ran everywhere: to class, to chow, to the barracks. It wasn't a problem for me. I was in good shape the entire time I was at Edwards. I trained routinely and even harder when a mission was imminent. Those habits die hard, and I continued my workout routine while I was between duty stations.

The classes were aimed at teaching us useful survival skills. They taught us how to hunt with traps and snares, navigate in the wild, start fires, and fish with primitive equipment. For a city boy, this was new stuff, and I kind of enjoyed it. It was more like a supervised camping trip. I had to keep reminding myself that these skills might one day save my life.

After the preliminaries, we began in earnest. The most memorable was the live fire exercise. We were required to crawl under barbed wire with machine gun bullets whizzing overhead and explosive charges going off all around us. If this is what the ground troops were subject to, I was certainly glad to be a pilot.

Following this exercise, we were marched off to the prisoner-of-war camp. The "guards," I found out later, were all enlisted men who spoke a camp language that was supposed to represent a foreign language. They wore strange uniforms and acted toward us as one might expect a captor to act.

Our confinement began with a very thorough search. This included drawers at half mast. They wanted to be certain we weren't bringing in any dangerous contraband, anything we could use to escape, or creature comforts. I kind of missed my paraffin-coated hacksaw blade.

The first order of business was to fall into formation with our canteen cups. Then we were ordered to throw them all into a pile. I was puzzled about the order but complied.

There were three officers among us "prisoners" in the camp who were all lieutenant colonels, but since my promotion was the most recent, I was the junior in grade. The senior man was the camp commander. I was in charge of resistance and escape.

The guards were quite adept at separating the three of us and trying to drive wedges between us. Their primary goals were to undermine the commander's authority and to try and demoralize us. It didn't work. We had a strong leader, and he kept that from happening.

Escape from camp had its inherent reward. If an escape was planned and successfully executed, the escapee was rewarded with a hot shower, a cup of coffee and a piece of pie in a nearby mess hall. Then it was back to the camp for the rest of the "experience." After all, it was a game, and we had to play the game.

The interrogation techniques they used were pretty standard. They separated the three officers and put us into underground cells. They were more like storage bins. Once separated, they tried to play one of us against the other. Pumping us for information was standard. "Who is the prison camp commander? Who is in charge of escapes? Are there any escape plans currently?" they asked over and over.

Just like I did in World War II, I answered with name, rank and serial number. They used sleep deprivation, minimal rations, physical discomfort and harassment. They did stop short of any actual physical abuse or brutality, something that could occur if this were a real prison camp,

I had no flashbacks to my German internment. There was no comparison between the two in my mind. This was an exercise. It was a school to teach modern airmen skills needed to survive in today's prison camps. That was in my mind most of the time. I was able to ignore their barbs, insults and degrading commentary most of the time. Only on one occasion did I nearly lose it.

One evening, I was in my cell and one of the guards came in.

"Who are you?" he screamed at me.

I responded with name, rank and serial number.

Getting even closer, he screamed again, "I said, who are you?"

I gave him the same answer.

Moving closer until his nose was only an inch from mine he screamed, "I asked you, who are you? You're nothing! You're nobody! You have nothing! Now, answer me!"

I had enough. I looked down at the man's throat and then back up at him. I was getting ready to go for his throat when he suddenly backed up. It must have been the look on my face or in my eyes. Something told him I was ready to boil over. Fortunately for me, and him, the guard was an experienced tormentor and recognized the impending explosion. I dread to think what would have happened with a new or inexperienced man who would have kept pushing. In any event, the crisis was over and no harm done.

That night a guard opened my cell door in the middle of the night while I was asleep. He shined a light in my eyes, and when I stirred, he threw a can of liquid into my face and slammed the door shut leaving me in the darkness. It was diluted tobacco juice! The stuff was disgusting. It burned my eyes, but there was no permanent damage.

The next morning, the camp portion of the experience came to an end. An officer came in to debrief me. My first question was about the purpose of the tobacco juice.

"Remember the first formation when you were required to deposit your canteen cup in the big pile?" he asked.

I nodded in response.

"One of the prisoner's cups had a false bottom in it. Beneath it were cigarettes and matches. We used it to make a little tobacco tea and served some to everyone," he said with a malevolent chuckle.

I told him what I thought of the camp, the way it was run and the effectiveness of the interrogation techniques. All in all, I told him I thought the camp was useful. But I felt they missed an opportunity when they didn't use my X-15 experience against me. He agreed that was probably an error on their part.

Breaking camp, the guards took immediate leave and cleared the area. That was a good choice to prevent hard feelings. I often wondered what would happen if any of us ran across a former guard at another duty station. I hope nothing, but you never know. After we were divided into groups of nine or ten to represent downed bomber crews, we headed into the mountains.

There were no provisions. The only thing we took with us were the newly learned skills we had been taught. We were given a geographic point we were supposed to reach in a specified time. To do it, we had to cross a couple of significant mountains.

The terrain was inhospitable to say the least. It was a rough climb, requiring at times that we pull ourselves hand over hand by grabbing onto rocks, scrub brush or anything else that we could find that might afford us a purchase. I tried to gauge the physical conditions of my crew. It was obvious that some of them were in better shape than others. After a particularly tough stretch, I called a halt to the climb.

At the back of my little band were a first lieutenant and a specialist technical sergeant.

"Well, lieutenant, how are you doing?" the sergeant asked.

Gritting his teeth, the young lieutenant answered, "If White can make it, I've got to make it, too."

That was enough for me. I said, "Okay you guys, let's go. Rest time is over."

There was also a captain in the group who was a little overweight and a fair amount out of shape. I noticed by noon of the first day that he was struggling. By late afternoon, I had serious doubts he that he would be able to keep up.

I took him aside, away from the others, and said, "Captain, I can see that you are having a hard time. There's no disgrace in not finishing this little hike. If you can't make it, go ahead and bow out."

He simply nodded. The next morning he did drop out, and the minders who were following us arranged for him to be taken back.

Food on the trail was scarce. They gave us each two sticks of stuff called Pemmican. It was a beef jerky that tasted so horrible that I figured hunger was a better option than that. We had a couple of guys who would eat anything, so I gave mine to them.

The trip was short. It only took us three days to complete our run over the mountain. That left us out for two nights so there was little time to trap game. One of the nights, a couple of the fellows did trap a rabbit.

Fortunately for this city boy, we had some hunters in the group. It was barbarous, but one of them smashed the poor creature's skull with a rock. They skinned it and cleaned it while the rest of us made a fire. We roasted it on a spit and each of us had our share of the cooked meat. It reminded me of dividing the loaf when I was in the German POW camp. No one complained about being too full, but it tasted pretty good.

It was cold and uncomfortable in the mountains, and none of us shed any tears when the exercise came to an end. That last morning when I awoke, there was a young doe standing at the edge of our campsite. She never knew how lucky she was. Had this been the real thing instead of an exercise, she would have been dinner.

At the end of the line there was coffee and doughnuts which to us tasted like ambrosia and nectar. Afterwards, I threw away the boots I had been wearing. The rocks and the shale on the mountains had ruined them. Two rooms in the barracks were equipped with showers, and we took full advantage of them. After a shave and a change of clothes, it was off to town for a whopping breakfast. Next, we went to Harrah's Casino in Reno where we were given "WE SURVIVED" stickers and ten dollars in chips to play with.

Ten dollars doesn't sound like much today, but it was a fair amount compared to our salaries then. It really didn't matter. Fortunately for me, I saved all my luck for the air. I lost my ten spot in a flash at the casino.

I left for my new assignment alone. Doris and the three children would come later on a Military Air Transport (MATS) flight. When the time came for them to arrive, I went to Frankfurt to meet their plane. As I waited expectantly by the gate, the time for their arrival came and went. No family arrived. Unlike a commercial airport, there was no airline representative or TV screen in the lounge to keep me updated. Going to the flight desk, I asked the enlisted man about my family's flight.

Checking his sheet, he replied, "That flight landed in the Azores. It won't be in until tomorrow."

So I cooled my heels for another twenty-four hours, and they came in the next day.

I was assigned to the 22nd Fighter Squadron, as the operations officer. My squadron's commanding officer was Dick Ransbottom, a classmate of mine from test pilot school. After the school, he was assigned to Wright Patterson Air Force Base for duty. Later on he was assigned to Bitberg as a squadron commander. He still had five months to go when I got there. When he left at the end of the summer, I took over as squadron commander. Winter and the wonderful Bitburg weather weren't far away.

Bitburg was a wonderful place to live with my family, but it was a terrible place to fly. The air was filled with freezing rain, snow and winter fog. Our base had the second worst weather of all aviation stations reporting back in the United States.

The wing commander was Colonel Blood, and the wing consisted of the Twenty-Second, Twenty-Third and Fifty-Third fighter squadrons. When it came time for Dick Ransbottom to leave, Colonel Blood called me into his office.

I was told that after Dick Ransbottom left, I would command the Twenty-Second for several months. The commander of the Fifty-Third Squadron was also on the promotion list to go to full colonel, and was only waiting for the promotion to become official. The Fifty-Third had a good group of experienced pilots many of whom would also be leaving in the months ahead.

Just before the commander of the Fifty-Third departed for a new assignment, Colonel Blood called me into his office and said, "Bob, I want you to take command of the Fifty-Third."

Surprised, I said, "Gosh, I've only been with the Twenty-Second five months, and only two of which were as commander."

"Yes, but a lot of new pilots will be replacing the more experienced ones.

Winter is coming on, and you know what kind of weather that brings. I want you to lead that squadron of rookies and get us through an accident-free year," he responded.

Gee thanks, boss, I thought to myself.

Of course, I accepted the job and was able to see it though without the loss of a man or even a serious incident. Flying over Bitburg can best be summed up by my thoughts one day when I was landing through a pea soup sky with visibility near zero.

"You know, Bob," I said to myself. "You're getting pretty good at this instrument flying. But that's no surprise since you never see the ground except when you take off or land."

Despite the bad weather, I loved the flying at Bitburg. The Cold War was in full swing, and we were constantly honing our fighter and bombing skills. It was a first-class refresher course in wartime flying. Since I had been away from combat flying for a number of years, it was good for me.

We practiced with the Gatling gun, a twenty-millimeter cannon, on both air and ground targets. There were also lots of bomb runs with both conventional and nuclear bombs. We dropped the conventional ones and of course only pretended to drop the nuclear ones. Since I had little experience with nuclear weapons, I was glad to get in the practice time while hoping I'd never really have to drop one.

All the practice was conducted over the Libyan Desert and the Mediterranean Sea. As part of those exercises, I took my turn as wing detachment commander at Wheelus Air Base in Libya for one month twice a year. The detachment consisted of pilots from all three of our fighter squadrons.

Although the training in Libya was fun, the paperwork certainly wasn't. There was no direct communication with Bitburg. There were no satellites to bounce off of or internet to log on to. We had to file our nightly reports by telephone and a radio network over the Mediterranean Sea, and that took well over an hour to complete. They were a pain. But they had to be done before I could reward myself with dinner and a beer.

Part of the reason I enjoyed flying at Bitburg was my fellow pilots. There were some good men, good leaders and really good pilots.

With Germany being a divided country, we had to be careful where we flew. While I was there, a T-33 from another wing strayed off course and crossed the invisible line into East Germany. The Russians forced him down. Shortly after, another incident occurred. These incidents led to the establishment of a no-fly buffer zone to reduce the possibility of another incident.

We had little contact with Berlin except for the military trains that passed through Frankfurt on their way to the isolated city. I could take that

Wearing my G-suit and survival gear, I prepare to board the ladder to my Republic F-105D Thunderchief fighter bomber in Bitburg, Germany (U.S. Air Force).

train safely because as a military train it could pass without harassment thorough the occupied zone and into the city. But I was never allowed to visit East Berlin.

Another advantage of the Thirty-Sixth Tactical Fighter wing was that it had a reputation for getting its commanding officers promoted. And we got every new airplane that came down the pike. After I had been there about one year, Colonel Blood was promoted to brigadier general and replaced by a West Point graduate, Colonel Hackler. Although it wasn't as common then, occasionally a member of the other two service academies transferred to the Air Force. That became less common with the addition of our own service academy.

One of the first things I had done when I moved in was to transfer my personal office to the back of our building to make more room for the pilots in the operations room. It was a lot quieter and made it easier to do the paperwork that at times seemed to reproduce of its own accord in my inbox. It was such a civilized working environment that Colonel Hackler came down on occasion to use my office and to get away from distractions of his office so he could do his own paper pushing.

The normal tour at Bitburg was three years. When I had been there nearly two years, Colonel Hackler came into the office with a stack of folders under his arm and plunked down at my desk.

"Bob, how would you like to go to the War College?" he asked.

The National War College is now called the National Defense University. In those days, it was two separate schools, the War College and the Industrial College of the Armed Forces.

"It's a good assignment. You're responsible to no one but yourself. All you have to do is go to class and study. D.C. is a nice place to live," Hackler said.

Needless to say, I availed myself of the opportunity. As usual, I was given a going-away party by my fellow officers. As I looked around the room, I saw a number of men I knew were the kind of leaders the modern Air Force needed.

In my remarks I said, "In the group in front of me, I see at least three or four men who I believe will one day be general officers."

My statement proved prophetic. Colonel Hackler followed Colonel Blood to brigadier general, and three more of us got our stars years later.

The relocation to Washington went smoothly for the family and me. My first day at Fort McNair and the Industrial College of the Armed Forces (ICAF) was a memorable one. We met often in joint session with the War College in the huge on-campus auditorium.

Our commandant was a three-star Army general. He introduced himself and asked for the first slide. It was the softball schedule between the ICAF and the War College.

"This is the most important tradition here at the ICAF. We are the perennial softball champions, and that will not change on my watch," he said seriously.

I would love to have played on the team, but we had recently held a colonels and lieutenant colonels versus sergeants softball game at Bitburg. Unfortunately, I had broken a finger catching a fly ball, and it was still in a sorry state when I arrived at ICAF.

In that game in Bitburg, I slid into a base and beat the throw, and my son Greg, who was ten, said in amazement, "I didn't know my dad could do that!"

At nearby Andrews Air Force Base, they had a T-33 trainer. To keep from getting too rusty, one of my classmates and I periodically arranged to take overnight flights with it. I'd fly one way, and he'd fly on the way back.

Another advantage of being at the ICAF was their arrangement with George Washington University. As part of the curriculum, with some extra work, I could get a master's degree. I opted to do that. This would extend my stay for a couple of months at the conclusion of the ICAF to finish the required courses and take the exams.

First I had to draft a thesis. Once it was approved by the thesis advisory board, permission from the ICAF was a given. Then it was also accepted by George Washington University for their thesis requirement. The orders came for my extension at the end of the course, and I was a student again.

With my background, I decided to do a thesis entitled, "Need for an Advanced Manned Research Aircraft." In it, I proposed an aircraft capable of flying in the Mach nine to thirteen range.

How does that compute to a master's degree in business administration? In it, I proposed the need for dedicated research in both materials and propulsion. The economics of this work was an important part of the body of the document.

I thought I did a reasonable job and was proud of the final product. But due to the nature of the material in the thesis, it was immediately classified since the bibliography contained classified documents I had been privy to. I'm not certain if it was ever declassified. The thesis dealt with supersonic ram jets and scram jets, a line that was not tested until 2005 when a vehicle was launched from a B-52 that had a ram/scram combination.

After the thesis and our classroom courses were finished, we were required to sit for comprehensive exams as were the regular students from George Washington. It was a multiple part examination, and if I failed any part of the exam, I would have to take it again. Twenty-seven percent of those who took the exam from the ICAF failed it the first time.

To prepare, I sent Doris and the kids back to her parents' place in Pennsylvania, and checked myself into the bachelor officer's quarters at Bolling Air Force Base. I pounded the books long into the night. When the day of the test arrived, I was as ready as I could be. Just like preparing for a test flight, I did the best I could to get ready.

It was an old fashioned Blue Book exam. We were given essay questions and blank Blue Books to write in. As soon as I read the questions, I began to write furiously. If I didn't pass, I'd have to wait a full year to take the exam again. I didn't know if I could do that or not. I paused to give my cramped fingers a rest and looked around. A lot of people were sitting glumly, looking as if they were trying to pull answers from the air. Heartened by what I'd seen, I went back to work.

I passed the exam, and when I found out, I went to the officer's club dinning room for a celebratory breakfast. As I was eating, I noticed a little mouse march out from the corner of the room toward a table where some female guests were seated. Considering the commotion he might cause if they saw him, I called the mouse to the manager's attention.

Somewhere, in the brain trust of the Air Force in the bowels of a Washington office building, an Air Force personnel officer was considering a little mouse named Lieutenant Colonel Robert White and deciding what they should do with him.

Chapter 13

Another War

At Bitburg, when I joined the squadron, one of the other pilots grumbled, "Looks like they're bringing in another hero here." I suppose that's the price the command paid for its record of being the source of so many general officers.

I wondered what he would say when he found out I had just been promoted to full colonel after only two years in grade as a lieutenant colonel. He'd probably say it was preferential hero treatment. I like to think it was career management and hard work. And it was time for career management again. With my new degree and my new promotion, it was time for re-assignment. There is an assignment branch for colonels at the Pentagon so I stopped by the office.

One possibility was the C-5 Systems Program Office at Wright Patterson Air Force Base in Dayton, Ohio. The C-5 was a big, lumbering transport plane. I had flown it once, and it was pleasant and easy to handle. But it wasn't my cup of tea. After a discussion with the assignment office, I was off to Wright Patterson anyhow, but in the Systems Program Office for the new F-111.

Then Secretary of Defense Robert McNamara had decreed that a modern fighter plane should be built so that both the Air Force and the Navy could use the same plane. Of course, each service had specific ideas in mind about how their version of the new aircraft should be built.

I was given a small office designated the Tactical Systems Office. There was a one-star Navy admiral there to represent the Navy's interests. He was a really good guy, but he always wore sunglasses. He never took them off. It made me wonder what went on behind those glasses. I could never see his eyes, and eyes are ordinarily the easiest part of a person to read. He could have been a spy, or he could have been asleep. I never knew. Maybe I had just seen too many espionage movies. Either way, he was a good guy so in the end it didn't matter.

One of the major issues with the F-111's development concerned the armament. The plane was designed to carry bombs, both conventional and nuclear, as well as the heat-seeking AIM-9 Sidewinder air-to-air missile. That all made sense, considering the design capabilities and mission of the aircraft.

The primary mission of the F-111 was to be able to deliver a nuclear weapon. A secondary mission was to deliver conventional weapons. The AIM-9 was in sufficient supply in the Air Force inventory, and since the F-111 was not considered a dogfighter, the AIM-9 was really in an ancillary role in the F-111's secondary mission.

Hughes Aircraft had the radar-guided AIM-4D Falcon missile, a highly sophisticated weapon that carried a ton of extra electronics. It was being considered not as an addition to the F-111, but to replace the AIM-9, something that didn't make sense to any of us on the project, Air Force or Navy.

Space was already at a premium on the aircraft and some of the dogfighting ability of the plane was already limited. Although it never was intended to be a dogfighter, it had to at least be able to hold its own if things got hot. The AIM-4D would be a secondary weapon at best. To fit it on board the aircraft would require a great deal of modification and design changes. And it would be a highly sophisticated weapon on board an aircraft that didn't need it in the first place.

The powers that be, namely the Air Staff, seemed hell-bent on proceeding anyhow despite the fact that a new procurement would come with a high cost. To prevent what all of us on the F-111 project thought would be a monumental mistake, it was evident a full court press lobby would have to be started. The command decided I should get my feet wet.

As a new colonel, I was sent to Washington to lead the SPO's effort to get the Air Staff to change its decision on the AIM-4D. There were a number of briefings where I presented our case to the members of the Air Staff. In each instance our request to not add the AIM-4D to the plane was rejected. Finally, we reached the court of last resort.

The ultimate decision in the matter usually lies in the hands of the Air Force Air Staff Board, composed of two- and three-star generals. By the time I made my presentation to them, I had been over it so many times I could have given it in my sleep. Not having to worry about the presentation eased any tension I might have felt with so much brass in the room. On behalf of the project team, I gave it my best shot. Despite my eloquence, the result was the same. The board turned us down.

Frustrated and dejected, I returned to Wright Patterson where I was greeted by a message to give the presentation again. This time, it would be on the base at Wright Patterson, and my audience would be the commanding officer of the Air Force Tactical Air Command (TAC) and the commanding officer of the Air Force Systems Command (AFSC), both four-star generals.

Stone faced, they came into the conference room and sat down. General Ferguson of Systems Command said, "Let's hear the exact same briefing you gave to the board in Washington."

When I was finished, he asked me, "Are you sure that was exactly the way you presented it to the generals in Washington?"

"Yes, sir. It is! I have given the presentation a number of times, and I'm certain," I replied confidently.

General Ferguson looked at his contemporary from the Tactical Air Command, General Disosway, and said, "Sounds good to me."

"Sounds good to me, too," the other general replied.

I'm not exactly sure what they did, but the AIM-4D never made it on board the F-111, to the delight of the entire project team. As I said, the ultimate decision in the matter *usually* lay in the hands of the Air Force Air Staff Board, but four-star major Air Command bosses do get heard.

Although my work at Wright Patterson was rewarding, and I was doing something important for the Air Force, something else that was going on in the world distracted me. In a place called Vietnam, my buddies from Bitburg were flying actual combat missions. Some had gone down and some had been captured. Others were lost. It might be hard for some people to understand, but I felt it was my *duty* to be there, too. I was a combat pilot, and I should be there with them, doing what I do best.

In the military the old saying, "Rank has its privilege," was true in my case. As a full colonel, I could contact the assignment office for colonels directly. It was not required that I go through my commanding officer first. That was fortunate for me, because if I *had* asked him, after my success with the F-111 controversy, I am certain he would have turned down my request.

Finally, I could stand it no longer. I called the assignment office for colonels to see if there might be a spot open in Southeast Asia for a guy with F-105 experience. There was indeed a need for someone with my qualifications, and the assignment officer was overjoyed to find there was someone who might actually want the job.

The assignment still wasn't a lock. The Seventh Air Force Command, which conducted the air war in Southeast Asia, had to approve the assignment. All I could do was wait and check the news for more information about my friends from Bitburg.

One day, my secretary answered a phone call, and then said to me, "The boss wants to see you."

The general and his deputy were sad-eyed and almost hesitant to tell me that I was being sent to Vietnam. It conjured up images of another office in another war when three young fighter pilots were given the news that they were headed for Korea. They told me I had done a good job, and that both of them were sorry to see me go.

I thanked them and kept my solemn demeanor until I was outside. Then, feeling like a schoolboy at recess, I could hardly keep from whooping for joy. I was on my way back "up there" where combat pilots belong. No longer would I read the news of another downed flyer and feel guilty that I wasn't there doing my part.

As the reality of the situation sank in, my elation faded. The selfishness of my decision weighed heavily on me. I was about to become a father for the fourth time, and I hadn't mentioned any of this to Doris. I would have to do it tonight.

She took the news as well as any military wife does when she finds out her husband will be going once again into harm's way. I believe living through the time at Edwards, with both the test-pilot segment and the X-15 project, she had found a way to cope with the fact that each day when I went to work I might not come back. I still don't know how she did it. In any event, she was a trooper. And I didn't fool her one bit.

Shortly before I left, she asked, "When did you volunteer?"

"What makes you think I volunteered?" I asked.

"I know you. I see you read the names in the paper. I see the look on your face when another of them gets shot down. I know you have to go," she said.

When the time came to go, in April of 1967, the usual transportation was via the Military Air Transport Service that had brought my family to Bitburg. Unlike peacetime, they didn't have enough planes to ferry everyone to Southeast Asia that needed to go there. So they chartered commercial airliners to help out. Regardless if the plane was military or civilian, they were jam-packed with people. I didn't fancy a sixteen- to eighteen-hour trip under those conditions, so I called the "Young Tigers."

They were the tanker wings making regular runs to Southeast Asia. The planes only carried the tanker crew, and there was plenty of room for a hitchhiker. There was room to stretch out and move around. It was almost as good as going first class, minus the cocktails and attractive flight attendants, of course.

I was able to catch a lift and made my way to Castle Air Force Base in California to meet the plane. We stopped first in Hawaii and later in Guam to refuel. Then, at the end of April, it was on to Takli Air Base and my fighter wing.

Many people on their way to Southeast Asia were required to stop off at the Philippine Islands for jungle survival training. Fortunately for me, my trip to the mountains near Reno, and a good commanding officer, kept me from a government-paid trip to the jungle to dine on insects and other reprehensible creatures the military had decided you could eat if you were desperate enough.

The 355th Tactical Fighter Wing had been the 355th Fighter Group in World War II. Two of the fighter groups even had the same designation as they did then. It was the end of April 1967 when a C-47 ferried me from where the tanker had landed to my new home away from home, Tahkli, Thailand.

One might wonder why the base was in Thailand and not in Vietnam. The answer was elemental. Geography dictated only a short flight to our major targets in North Vietnam, and the aircraft were much safer on the ground away from the Vietcong sappers. The base itself was out in the middle of the jungle. There was a small town nearby that I never visited socially. From the description of the fellows that did, I don't think I missed anything.

It was always easy to tell who was flying the next day and who was not. After dinner at the officer's club, there was a noticeable drop-off in the number of people at the bar. Those who had to get up early were off to bed, while those who had already flown had an extra pint in celebration.

My wing commander turned out to be an old friend from the states, Colonel Bob Scott. Bob was a liaison officer at Edwards when the F-105 came in for testing. We also shared an enjoyable experience when I went to Las Vegas after survival school. I knew Bob was in Las Vegas on TDY, and I contacted him. He invited me to dinner with Brigadier General Charles Blair, a reserve officer who was a senior captain for Pan American Airlines and a real-life version of John Wayne. He was also a consultant for the Air Force on air navigation systems. His many aviation accomplishments included being the first man to fly a fighter plane over the North Pole. With the general was his date, a dynamite-looking, red-haired movie star named Maureen O'Hara. Seeing Bob again brought that night back to me in vivid detail.

Dinner was delicious, the show was fantastic, and Ms. O'Hara was a dream. She was personable, charming and possessed a wonderful sense of humor.

During the show, I said to her, "This looks like something from one of your movies."

"Yes, and the costumes are still the same," she replied with a smile.

She married the general in 1973, and, he retired again from Pan American Airlines. Together they moved to the Antilles and ran a small passenger airline service. Tragically, Blair was killed in a seaplane crash in 1978. Maureen pulled things together and managed the service for a few years after that before selling it.

When I got settled in at my new base in Thailand, Bob said, "I just got a call from the Philippine Survival School. They say you must be there for the jungle survival school. They want you to complete their course."

"The Reno school was enough. Been there, done that in World War II. I've been in real prison camps. I don't need to practice suffering anymore," I replied glumly.

It may have been a rash decision. Had I been forced down in the jungle, I might have had a difficult time staying out of trouble and figuring out which bug to eat. Fortunately, I never had to find out.

Breaking into an expansive grin, Scott said, "I told them that I was short-handed and needed you here and that you couldn't come."

I certainly did feel welcome. And the welcome was added to by some of my old friends from Germany. One of them said to me, "Bob, we didn't know *when* you would be here, but we knew you'd be here." That's the best kind of praise, when it's heartfelt and comes from one of your peers.

When I think about flying, there are two kinds. The first is fun flying. That's when I fly from point A to point B with loops, rolls and aerobatics thrown in for good measure. No pressure, just fun. Business flying is what I did in the X-15. It was grueling preparation leading up to fifteen to twenty minutes of intensity and flying a machine to the edge. It was followed by an emotional release and letdown with the satisfaction that a very difficult task had been completed successfully.

Flying a fighter-bomber out of Thailand was a combination of the two. It was relatively safe flying from point A to point B, but with the loops, rolls and aerobatics there just in case we came into contact with a hostile fighter. Although we saw a few Soviet-built MIGs, we never engaged in any dog fights. An occasional pilot was able to launch an AIM-9 missile and get a kill, although it was rare for F-105 pilots.

Over the target, it was a few minutes of intensity until the bombs were away and we had turned safely toward home with the satisfaction of a job well done. Since we controlled the sky, the major danger was from 85mm anti-aircraft guns and surface to air missiles that caused the most casualties for the F-105s.

A standard tour for a combat pilot in Thailand consisted of flying 100 missions. Most of the guys wore bush hats and kept track of the number of missions by placing a mark on the hat at the end of each flight. For me, it was a little different. My tour would be for one year, regardless of my number of combat missions.

The F-105 Thunderchief carried the nickname Thud, and a Thud mission followed a standard format. They began in Saigon where orders were issued to the combat operations centers of the fighter wings based in Thailand.

The pensive-looking colonel (me), commander of the 355th Tactical Fighter Wing at Tahkli Air Base, Thailand, sits in the cockpit of my F-105D prior to launching an attack mission over North Vietnam, the most heavily defended airspace in the history of military aviation (U.S. Air Force).

Staff officers at the fighter wings broke the complex orders down to specific instructions for each of the three squadrons in the wing. These fragmentary orders, or FRAGS, included the time of the mission, number of aircraft and the weapons they were to carry. On the night before the mission, we got our FRAG orders specifying the target or targets for the mission, navigational details for the primary target and two alternative targets.

With those in hand, we had a meeting for all pilots flying the mission to discuss ingress, the way in to the target, and egress, the best way to get back out after the bombs were away. Alternate ingress and egress routs, sometimes several, were planned in case of an emergency. Careful consideration was always given to where the tankers might be and roughly the times they would be there. This information would be updated in flight. I treated this portion of the mission like I had every X-15 flight. The devil is in the details, and I wanted to know every detail when my life might depend on it.

Then it was early to bed before the pre-dawn launch of usually twelve fighter-bombers. We dressed without deodorants, aftershave or any other tell-tale scent that might help a North Vietnamese patrol find a downed flier, although I had heard the rumor that because of our largely red meat protein diet we smelled differently anyhow. A last-minute meeting in the briefing room updated us on the weather, potential enemy defenses along the way, and any other details that might help the mission succeed. A call sign was then given to each flight of four aircraft.

Next, we suited up. The G-suit was tight, but not as bad as the one I used with the X-15. It did the same job. It inflated automatically during high speed maneuvers to keep the increased gravitational pull from causing a blackout. I also wore a survival vest with lots of pockets for flares, a two-way radio, a .38 pistol, maps, matches and a dozen other provisions that might help if I went down. Instead of the heavy backpack I wore on the X-15 suit, I had a fifty-pound parachute. Carrying half my weight in gear, I toddled to my airplane.

I would start my engine with the ground crew and double-check the systems with the crew chief. Then it was time to taxi to the end of the taxiway where the arming crew was standing by. The last ground function was performed here when the arming crew pulled the red safety clips off the bombs and rockets loaded under my aircraft. In the air, we flew in three standard combat formations of four planes each, just as we did in World War II.

The major difference from other wars I had been in was the function of the fourth flight of four planes called the Wild Weasels. Instead of flying in formation with the twelve other planes, these brave pilots would go in low and fast to locate the surface to air missile batteries and neutralize them before we arrived on the scene. It's a very tough mission and they did a magnificent job for us.

Missions to North Vietnam were designated "out country" missions because we were leaving South Vietnamese airspace. If the target was in the western part of North Vietnam, or Hanoi and its environs, we flew over Laos to get there. If the target was in the northeast of Vietnam, we went in over the Gulf of Tonkin. Along the way, I was given the coordinates for the refueling tanker's position, and its time of arrival at the coordinates.

There was an invisible line in the Gulf of Tonkin and Laos above which the tankers were not allowed to fly. If they did, they became vulnerable to the few MiG-15 aircraft the Vietnamese possessed. We met the tankers as close to the line as we could and topped off for a raid to the north or for the trip to Hanoi. On the way home we met them again for another sip of petrol. Each trip to the tanker for fuel took about six minutes. The coupling mechanism was in the top of the nose, and it took a light touch on the controls to stay hooked up.

Over North Vietnam, we went in from the west over the Black River. Then it was a right turn to the east where we skirted a small mountain range that shielded us from the enemy radar. We called the protective barrier Thud Ridge, short for Thunderchief Ridge.

The first command before we reached Thud Ridge was "music on." No, it wasn't the dramatic sound of loudspeakers blaring "The Ride of the Valkyries" by Richard Wagner as Robert Duval did in the classic war movie *Apocalypse Now*. Ours had a practical use. The countermeasure signals emanating from the electronic pods on our planes jammed Charlie's radar.

We were told that it made our planes look like clouds. I'm sure it did! However, when a North Vietnamese radar man saw the sudden appearance of a group of supersonic clouds round the corner of Thud Ridge, he must have reached for his red phone because once we rounded Thud Ridge, the high intensity phase of the mission began, and everything lit up.

Next, as force commander, which was my only job now, I called for command switches on to ready the bomb release mechanisms on each of the planes.

We had a Doppler navigation system on board. It was not very accurate, but it could get us in the vicinity of the target. We also had maps and navigated visually. When I had the target in sight, I called it out to the flight. Once I rolled into my dive, everyone rolled in at the same time. We followed the age-old dictum, in and out fast!

There were plenty of details to attend to once the bomb run commenced. Things weren't as high tech then as they are now. We used a bomb sight that was altitude- and speed-dependent. I needed to put the aircraft into a forty-five degree dive and then release the bombs at a given altitude and speed. I had roughly nine seconds to do this while still flying the airplane. I couldn't watch for surface-to-air missile threats while trying to hit my target, so I just ignored them for the moment. Since we stayed above 4,000 feet, machine gun fire from the ground was routinely not a problem. Just as on the X-15 flights, there were a lot of things to do. The intensity of concentration on an attack or bomb run precluded any feeling of fear or nerves. It was always a feeling of accomplishment to hit the "pickle button" that released the bombs. Then it was time to pull out of the dive and get out of the target area. With my back to the target, I climbed to the rendezvous altitude and counted the noses of the rest of my guys.

When multiple high-speed aircraft attack a target, things can get a bit chaotic. I remember watching films of our attack on a rail yard. It was easy to see the bombs leave the airplane but nearly impossible to tell which bombs were from which planes when they reached the target below. Occasionally, it became obvious which plane dropped a specific payload of bombs.

On one particular run, I did notice that one of our guys, a young major, had missed the target by a literal mile. It was my duty to call him in and chastise him for his grossly poor aim. Being well aware of his mistake, he took the comments sheepishly and promised to do better. He was eventually shot down and captured, but later returned home, thank God.

As I sit in front of my television today and watch smart bombs literally go through the door of a house, it boggles my mind. I wonder if things would have turned out differently if we had had that technology back in 1967.

After the bomb run, we rejoined in formation and flew to the place where we knew the tanker would be waiting, and they always were. After gassing up, the rest of the trip was a relaxing flight from point B back to point A.

The success of the mission was determined by an evaluation of aerial photography of the site. This was the major topic of discussion at the standard after-action report. Then there was down time until the next flight, either the next day or the day after.

While in Thailand, I had two especially memorable flights. The first was on August 1, 1967, when I led the attack on the Long Bien Bridge, also known as the Paul Doumer Bridge.

Built at the turn of the century, the 5,532-foot-long bridge was the key to the rail system developed by a French governor of Indonesia, Paul Doumer, after whom the bridge was named. It was the sole bridge across the Red River within fifty kilometers of Hanoi and carried the only railroad tracks into the city for trains from China and Haiphong. Two highways sat atop the bridge and it was surrounded by over 100 anti-aircraft guns.

Until this time, we had not been able to attack all the targets we wanted to attack in the North due to restraints placed on us from Washington. That afternoon, we got the signal that President Johnson had taken the gloves off. Colonel John Girado, our wing commander, received the news from General Momyer that a strike was to be made on the bridge immediately. The decision was made to attack the previously untouched bridge at once to minimize the possibility of security leaks. But, that only gave us four hours to prepare the planes for the attack.

I was overjoyed despite the short warning. Tons of cargo flowed over that bridge every day. If we knocked it into the river, it would seriously disrupt their supply line into Hanoi and assist our GIs in the south. Now we'd get our chance. However, I still had an issue with the way the air war was being waged. They had the B-52 strategic bombers down south pounding the jungle, while we flew the fighter bombers to strategic targets in the north. Never did reconcile that one.

This mission presented a problem for our ground crew who had just loaded the twenty F-105 aircraft with the normal load of six, 750 pound bombs usually carried by the planes. Some time earlier, the Dragon Jaw Bridge at Thanh Hoa was attacked with medium-sized bombs with less-than-adequate results. The decision was made to attack the Paul Doumer span with 3,000 pound bombs! The ground crew had only had four hours to change the bombs.

Every available man was assigned to the task. Colonel Girado helped them out by taking a risk and allowing bombs and fuel to be loaded onto the planes at the same time. That was ordinarily strictly forbidden due to the risk of explosion. Working like demons in mid-90s tropical heat, the ground crews stripped off the old bombs and added the new ones. In an incredible three hours, the job was done.

As Girado's deputy commander for operations, I had been set to command the next day's mission, and when I received word of the target change, I had the same four hours to prepare my pilots. I told my boys to expect the heaviest flak and SAM missile attacks they had ever seen as we planned our ingress and egress. The possibility of casualties would be real.

At 2:18 P.M. we took off. There were three flights of F-105's with a total of seventy-two tons of 3,000 pound bombs. The bombs were World War II bridge-busters and still had their original wire-trip fuses that had been know to blow up the airplane carrying them a time or two in the past. But we were more concerned about the heavy fire we would come under than that.

In front of us were four Wild Weasels and four more F-105's assigned to flak suppression. For backup, an identical force of 105's from the 388th Tactical Fighter Wing at Korat trailed us. Around us, Colonel Robin Olds led a fighter escort of F-4 Phantoms also carrying heavy bomb loads.

I can't describe the thrill I had when we were in the air. I was about to lead a potent strike force into the heart of enemy territory to do something truly important to the war effort. It was the same feeling I had in Word War II when we attacked the enemy on the ground. Hopefully, it would go better than mission fifty-three. We headed north over Laos and the waiting tankers.

Since we had lost our two wing fuel tanks to lighten our load for the heavier bombs, we needed more than a top-off of fuel this time. So we rendezvoused with the tankers to be completely refueled before the actual bomb run. The tankers were waiting as close to the no-fly zone as they could get, and now with a full fuel load, we headed for Hanoi.

Once we cleared Thud Ridge, things got dicey at once. The weather was clear, too clear for our purposes today. We could have used some real clouds that day, aside from the electronic clouds we were supposedly making. Thirty miles out, we saw the first surface-to-air missiles arch up from the ground. The strike force evaded them without incident.

Major James F. McInerny with the 388th Tactical Fighter Wing and his four Wild Weasels sprang into action. They eliminated two SAM sites and forced four more to launch sporadically, with no damage to the attackers.

Ten miles from the target, I saw four MIGs above and to our right. They were firing at us. Dogfighting with a full bomb load would be impossible.

"Hold on to the bombs," I called to the rest of the pilots, as we readied our weapons.

The four enemy planes passed well to our rear and with our afterburners on, we were outrunning them. As it turned out, no one was hit by any gunfire. I'll never understand that one.

Now we were over the flat delta leading to the bridge. The flak was so thick, it looked like a roadway. One of our guys said that it was like trying to run several blocks through a rainstorm without letting any of the raindrops hit you, and that was a pretty accurate description.

Somehow, I made it to the bridge with no "raindrops" hitting my plane. I went into attack mode and hit the pickle button. My guys followed suit.

My radio crackled and Colonel Robin Olds' voice filled my headset as he said, "Great work, guys. I saw the bombs hit. You got a direct hit on one span. It just dropped into the Red River!"

That was music to my ears. The bombing run had been perfect. Any damage the 105's from the 388th Tactical Fighter Wing behind us did would be icing on the cake. The bridge was out of commission. That's what we came for.

It was time to get out of Dodge. Everybody was present and accounted for. Two planes were badly damaged, but both pilots would be able to make it safely back to Thailand. From Olds' description, the bridge was cut and it remained to be seen if any of the flights after us did any more damage.

Over the Gulf, as I waited my turn for the tanker, I had an immense feeling of pride and accomplishment. It wasn't a personal sense of pride, it was the pride of patriotism for my team; all those American men had risk their lives and done their best, and in this case it was certainly good enough. Best of all, we were all going home together. No parachutes. No one left behind.

In the after-action report, my sense of what had happened over the target and Robin's visual report was verified. During the night we received photos from our reconnaissance aircraft. We had dropped nearly 100 tons of high explosives on that bridge and put it out of operation.

The next morning, John Girado said, "Take these pictures of that bridge in the water to your ground crew. Show them the results of their hard work. They did a damn fine job, and they should know it was worth it all."

I did as commanded, and when they saw the pictures, I had never seen a happier bunch of guys. It is always rewarding to know that your hard work produced the results you had hoped for, particularly when you're one of the guys doing the grunt work that makes it all happen.

A day or so later, Colonel Girado informed me that he was recommending me for the Air Force Cross, the second highest combat medal that can be given, and one that ranks just below the Medal of Honor.

Around the twenty-sixth of August, I participated in a second memorable flight. On our way back from a mission over North Vietnam, I called the base control tower when I was 100 miles out as was standard operating procedure. The call was used to alert the field about casualties, badly damaged aircraft, or anything else that might demand immediate attention when we landed. My call sign was Shark.

"Takhli tower, this is Shark One, over," I said.

"Roger Shark One and congrats. Father, seven-pound, five-ounce boy," he continued.

"Roger that," I said and broke into an expansive grin.

Since the transmission was on an open frequency, all the guys heard it, and the chatter started.

"Not bad, Pappy," my wing man said.

"Not bad for an old guy," someone else piped in.

"Okay, you guys. Knock it off," I said, but with a smile in my voice.

I requested permission to do an Immelman over the base, and it was granted. When I got on the ground my commanding officer, Colonel Girado, was there with a bottle of champagne. It was one of the most wonderful days in my life, and one that I will always cherish.

Another mission close to Hanoi stands out in my memory. We had received photos from the recon squadron that showed Russian heavy lift helicopters out in the open. In the trees and brush surrounding them there were six other helicopters' blades sticking out.

I got an artist to make a sketch from the grainy film of the recon planes cameras, and he sketched in the positions of the blades in the trees and the helicopters on the ground. Using these sketches, I assigned specific pilots to take out each of the Russian choppers. The attack force would be the usual sixteen aircraft. We also had a rail yard to attack, not just the helicopters. I had eight aircraft with bombs. As we approached our targets, my deputy would take the bombers to the rail yards, and I would split off with my eight planes to attack the choppers.

The attacks were successful. The railroad yard took a pounding, all the Russian helicopters were destroyed and we returned to our base with no losses. I always felt an enormous sense of relief when I came back with all my men.

Although we were constantly taking losses, missions were routinely uneventful. We tried not to get into machine gun or stray ground fire range as we did in World War II. Instead, we stayed above 4,000 feet. I was thankful for that. The last time I came blasting in on the deck with guns blazing things didn't turn out so well.

The surface-to-air missile sites were very mobile so they were here today and gone tomorrow. Save for missions like the Paul Doumer Bridge, the only concentrated fire we usually faced occurred as we approached, were over, or were leaving the target area. An accidental hit could occur, but in my seventy missions, I never took a single hit. No skill in that, just good luck.

A frightening and amusing anecdote happened to one young man that underscored how potentially harrowing any given flight could become. He called for an emergency landing in Thailand. When he was on the ground, what observers saw left them open-mouthed and shaking their heads. A SAM had tracked the heat of the exhaust of his F-105 and embedded itself in the fuselage just above the tailpipe! Inexplicably, the missile didn't detonate, and the young man walked away without a scratch.

Things could get dicey at the end of the mission when we were landing at the base. Occasionally a bomb got hung up and didn't release when the "pickle button" was pushed. Just like the ventral on my old X-15, they had a penchant to drop off when the landing gear touched down. It was an exciting few minutes as a runaway 700-pound bomb bounced and skidded to a halt somewhere along the runway. Fortunately, detonation was rare and none went off during my tour.

Before my year was up, I received orders to go to Seventh Air Force Headquarters at Tan Son Nhut to run Alpha Division. That division was responsible for developing and sending out the FRAG orders for missions the next day over Laos and North Vietnam. I didn't want to go and protested to my commanding officer.

"Bob, you've done enough. With all you know, and the things you've done in the past, we can't afford to get you shot down," he said to me.

Despite further pleas, it didn't do any good. I was headed for the 7th Air Force Headquarters.

A few weeks before I left the wing at Takhli, the base commander, Colonel Lewis told me he was going to a shop called Johnny's Gems in Bangkok to purchase some jewelry for his wife. He asked if I'd like to go along, and I agreed. As the base commander, he was responsible for all the housekeeping and security at the base.

I had become friends with the colonel when solving a problem with the runway at Takhli. Our airfield had a runway and a parallel taxiway. If there was an accident on the runway, returning aircraft would have to land on the parallel taxiway. There was often a lot of vehicular traffic on that taxiway. I told Lewis about this, and he said he would have a plan in place by the next morning. His plan was simple. If an emergency blocked the active runway, his security police would immediately clear the taxiway and block all entrances to the taxiway to vehicular traffic thus allowing no delays in recovering aircraft. I thanked Lewis, and he told me that anything I needed or wanted that would insure greater safety or enhance our combat operations would have his top priority.

When I told our wing commander, Colonel Girado, that I wanted one day off to go shopping with Lewis in Bangkok, he said, "Sure, and I'm surprised the two of you get along so well."

"Is there anything wrong with that?" I asked.

"Oh no, it's just good to see the base commander and the deputy of operations communicate so well. That's a rare occurrence," he said with a smile.

Off we went to Bangkok. Johnny's Gems was a nice shop, and Johnny was a very personable chap as well as a good salesman. He invited us to dinner that night at a cabaret; good food and the entertainment was a number of young, pretty Siamese girls dancing about the stage with their gowns and veils moving softly as if in a light breeze.

When the time came for me to leave the base at Takhli, I was told there was to be a farewell party for me. That night, the club was filled with pilots from our three squadrons. The music began and, to my shock and surprise, out came those same young dancing women with their exotic movements and their flowing veils. I laughed out loud while the pilots, who loved the show as much as I did, cheered and applauded wildly.

I knew from their reactions that I had earned the respect of the men I had led into combat. There is an old saying that you never forget the guys you went to war with. I didn't forget, and I loved them all.

Shortly thereafter, I left the wing in Thailand and went to my new assignment, the Seventh Air Force Base at Tan Son Nhut Air Base in Viet Nam. I was in a hooch with two other full colonels. There was a sitting room and a kitchen attached. It was a comfortable arrangement. Tex Peebles, obviously from Texas, was the base commander at Tan Son Nhut Airbase. He was a good cook which was a Godsend. My other roommate was Lou, the Seventh Air Force public information officer, who unfortunately is no longer among us.

Tex handled the food and the drinks. At the end of the month, he presented each of us with a bill for our share of the supplies. I think the biggest bill we ever had was still under thirty dollars, and that included the lobster, steak and cognac. Lou would needle Tex about the size of the bill, and Tex's response was standard.

"Do you want the job?" he would scream at us, his face getting red.

Of course we didn't. We all knew it was a joke, but the same scenario always played out. Tex had Navy ships he visited as well as his own base supply and engineers. He could get anything done, and anything he needed. We couldn't possibly have handled the job as well as he did, but at times we just couldn't resist pulling his chain.

Around that time, my Air Force Cross came through, and it was pinned on me by President Lyndon B. Johnson. I am proud of that medal, but I know it belongs as much to the other pilots who participated in the raid, and the ground crew that made it all possible, as it did to me.

My new job title was chief of attack division for Laos and North Vietnam. My staff was composed of veteran pilots who had flown combat missions just like the ones I had done. We met every day, consulted, reviewed data, the results of the latest strikes, picked new targets and assigned them to the wings.

At 1,700 hours each day, seven a days a week, I briefed General Momyer and gave him the mission plan for the next day. The general was fair, but he was definitely in charge. Once, an F-4 pilot I knew called me and said that the armament on the plane was not quite a proper fit. A small suggested change would solve the problem. I gave him the go-ahead and reported what I had done to the general at our evening briefing.

"I don't have any objections to the change, colonel. It's simple and it makes sense. But let's get one thing straight. In the future, I have to approve all changes before they are made. Is that clear?"

"Yes, sir. It is," I replied, and made certain that I never made that mistake again.

The general was good. He knew all the guys on the base and what they were doing. He'd even fly a simple mission himself on occasion, but he wouldn't let any of the rest of us fly one. He seldom vetoed one of my suggestions if it made good sense. I truly enjoyed the time I worked for him.

And I liked the guys who worked for me. One day, one of my young men came back to work after a weekend off. The work space was small, and the other men were scattered around the office at various work stations.

"I hate this fucking place!" he yelled enthusiastically and at the top of his lungs.

"Son, how many days do you have left?" I barked out from my office.

"One hundred ten," he replied quietly, waiting for me to chew him out.

In the expectant hush of the office I said, "Well, you have no right to say anything like that until you are down to 100 days!"

The tension in the office broke, and I think my men decided that perhaps I would be an okay boss. Of course, as each man reached the magic 100-day

Doris and I attend an award ceremony where Brigadier General Bernard Shriver admires the Air Force Cross, the nation's second highest combat commendation for service in Vietnam (U.S. Air Force).

mark, he came into the office and bellowed out the catch phrase in resounding tones.

I also had the pleasure of being on the base during the Tet offensive of 1968. There were no windows in our hooch, so I almost missed it.

The base had been relatively quiet, and we were not flying because of the Vietnamese New Year. All night long it sounded as if someone randomly banged the walls and the doors with a ball peen hammer. Since the Vietnamese celebrated their new year with fireworks, we didn't think much of it, although the noise was annoying.

The next morning, when I opened the door to the hooch, the way was blocked by a gigantic African-American sergeant, who looked as if he would be equally at home in a National Football League uniform as he was in his military fatigues.

"I wouldn't come out here if I were you, sir," he said politely.

"I've got to get to my office," I replied.

"But sir, there are V.C. on the base," he said.

"It's okay, Sergeant, I know the drill," I said.

As much as possible, I kept myself covered by keeping a building at my back, and my eyes peeled for trouble. Slowly, and safely, I worked my way back to the office. When I got there, I got the bad news. Since the attack had occurred on Sunday, and some of my men lived in town, they had no way of getting back. I had to find a way to get them myself and went looking for transportation.

My boss, Brigadier General Dale Sweat, said, "The only vehicle available is my car."

"May I borrow it?" I asked.

"Just don't scratch the paint!" he joked. "And take somebody with you."

"I'll go. I know where they live," said a very large young man that I knew flew the back seater in a Wild Weasel F-105.

This type of guy loved to get into the action, in the air or on the ground. At least since I was going to have to go, I'd have someone with me who knew how to shoot. He was a brave kid, and I spent half my time during the trip telling him to keep his head down. We made it into town. It was my only trip there, and under the circumstances I didn't have much time to check things out. We picked up my men and made it back to the base without incident.

My time in Vietnam was winding down. My year was nearly finished when my new orders came through. I knew it was time to go. It had been a rewarding year. Since I had the opportunity to fly combat, and then work at a high level in the planning and execution of missions, I felt I had two years experience in one.

On an April morning in 1968, Tex Peebles drove me to the airport in his staff car. He took it right onto the tarmac and up to the stairs leading aboard the World Airways Boeing 707 MAC charter jetliner.

We shook hands and Tex said, "Do well."

I looked toward heaven and said, "thanks," as I went up the stairs and into the aircraft. I was on my way home. There was a young man waiting there for a father he had never seen and I couldn't wait to change that.

Chapter 14
The FX Program

When I returned to the States from Vietnam, I finally got to see my youngest son, Dennis. It was a happy reunion with Doris and the rest of the children who were ensconced in our house in Dayton, Ohio. In those days, Wright Patterson essentially consisted of two components with Patterson Field being the larger of the two. It was the commercial hub of the base with longer runways, and all of the aircraft operating from the base flew out of the Patterson Field.

Wright Field, with a historic connection to the birth of flight in the bicycle shop of two Dayton bothers, Orville and Wilbur Wright, was smaller, with shorter runways, and housed the Aeronautical Systems Division. A system is Air Force parlance for a new aircraft or weapon. Each part of the base was a hive of activity.

Wright Field was eventually closed. It is still part of the Air Force complex in Dayton, but now it is the home of the National Museum of the Air Force and the National Aviation Hall of Fame.

The Air Force Systems Command is one of the major Air Force commands. It has a number of bases and the Aeronautical System's division at Wright Field was responsible for overseeing a number of systems that were in the developmental process for the operational or combat commands. A system might be one for air defense, new weapons, fighters, bombers or new radar equipment. It is big business on a grand scale. And as a program director for a new system, I'd be on the hot seat. I found my master's degree experience quite essential in costing out projects.

I knew the key to the success of the project would not be just what I did or said, but how those around me performed. So I brought to the job the same philosophy I had used as a squadron commander when I commanded twenty-six or twenty-seven talented and temperamental fighter pilots.

Fitness reports are a fact of military life. These are the critical evaluations of one's performance as viewed by your immediate superior. Based on the contents of these reports, careers hang in the balance.

I knew all my pilots were dedicated, hard-working young men. They all flew well, hit their targets and could be counted on to cover my behind as a wing man. But what makes some men leaders and others followers? What makes some men aspire to become generals with multiple stars while others will happily retire as a colonel or lieutenant colonel? I'm not saying I had the answer to that question, but I had developed a style that seemed to work for me.

Periodically, I got everyone together and asked them if they had any suggestions, pro or con, that would improve the way we operated, or if there were any problems they could see that we could fix. Reluctantly at first, but later more freely, members of my systems program office began to pop up with ideas.

I must be honest and clear about this. I was new in the business of systems program management, and I was fortunate to have good people with the experience in that line of work. I particularly think of Colonel Floyd Wenzel who gave me a number of briefings right after my arrival on the job. He was my engine manager and a darned good one. I also had talented people in our program contract office, procurement, and contracting. After going through a couple of engineers, I got Fred Ralls as our chief engineer. He was bright, articulate and a huge help when it came to dealing with someone like Al Flax, whom I will speak of a bit later.

I think all military leaders, at least the successful ones, are among those who pop up when the situation calls for it, and stay out of the way when a more qualified underling is doing the job just fine. I used that technique in dealing with the numerous department heads on the FX project.

Likewise, I think the Air Force does the same thing. Their potential leaders are placed in a situation that tries their mettle and sees which of them will pop up as the generals of tomorrow, and if I was going to pop up, I'd take all the help I could get in solving problems regardless of rank. I believe I was chosen for this job to see if I could handle the administrative side of the Air Force. That's what general officers do. They don't fly fighter aircraft in combat, and they don't test experimental rocket planes. Despite all of my accomplishments in the air, my future in the military would directly depend on how well I ran the FX Systems Office.

Why were we the "FX" Systems Office? Although the Air Force had identified the need for an air superiority fighter aircraft, they had yet to give the airplane a number designation. They were all F series planes, but until we got a number we were the FX Systems Program Office.

By this time I had gained a fair amount of seniority in grade as a colonel, so I was informed that base housing was now available for me. That presented a dilemma for the White family. We loved our house, and the rest of my brood was settled in there. On the other hand, the availability of base housing presented us with a unique opportunity.

We could sell the house for a profit and free up some cash for a growing young brood. It was doubtful that we would return to Dayton after this assignment, and it would not be a retirement destination for us. And I would be on base and closer to the FX Program Office. After some consternation, the decision was made to sell and move on base. Due to the lifestyle, career military families become experts at moving.

I often wonder if I priced the house correctly. It was a lovely little split-level, and Doris had kept it in good shape during my absence. The first people who came to look at it bought it for the asking price. A second family who had been given an appointment to view the house, was heartbroken when they found it had already been sold. In either instance, the house would have gone to a family who really wanted it, and that was okay with us.

The job of a system program director is a combination of senior executive, project ramrod and referee. Some decisions are made by consensus. Others have to be directed. That's the executive part. Once a decision is made, deadlines must be met and tasks organized and accomplished in an efficient manner. I put on my ramrod hat to be certain that part of the job ran smoothly. When dealing with so many different departments and a host of people, military and otherwise, disputes naturally arrive. Call in Referee Bob in striped shirt, black cap with whistle in hand.

My first task was to acquaint myself with the thirty to thirty-five people who would be working with me, as well as to begin lining up a veritable army of consultants from both civilian and military arenas to help in finalizing the project. It was a crack team of individuals from start to finish.

Like any business about to make a multi-million dollar investment, we had to decide exactly what it was we wanted. We had to have a game plan. And this plan was for a fighter jet that would dominate the skies not only now but for years to come. That was no small undertaking.

This led to the implementation of the first of many developmental flow charts or story boards. Though it was intended to be a graphic demonstration of what we were attempting to accomplish, at times it felt more like the cartoon someone put up in the office.

The picture showed two construction teams building a bridge from opposite sides of a river. Unlike the Biblical water tunnel of King Hezekiah of Israel that was chiseled through solid rock starting from two sides and meeting perfectly in the middle, the one in the cartoon did not. The two ends of the span were wide apart, each containing a group of head-scratching workmen staring across the void at each other. I kept the cartoon in mind as the various divisions worked from different directions toward their common goal.

Our first order of business was to consider the various components that we would want in the FX and how these components would relate to each other. Grinding through the design and engineering phases, we debated weight-to-thrust ratios, size, design speed and a myriad of electronics and engineering possibilities.

At each step along the way, I was off to the Pentagon in Washington for an informational briefing to the men who would make the final decisions about the project. One man to whom I briefed often was the assistant secretary of the Air Force for research and development, Mr. Al Flax, a civilian appointee. When the briefings were informational, Mr. Flax was an okay guy.

Once the general idea of the aircraft had some flesh on it, we developed a wish list of the things we wanted on board. Each department looked for the newest and best of the modern equipment available and brought their ideas to the table. We looked at the most modern jet engine, radar systems, insulation, cockpit instrumentation and weapon systems, to name a few.

Under the latter category of weapons, we had a marvelous opportunity to really improve the function of our aircraft. We already had the Gatling gun that had proven its worth in Vietnam. One of its major drawbacks was the weight of the large amount of ammunition needed for such a rapid-fire weapon. Our armament people insisted on the new caseless ammunition that would decrease the weight of the combat-loaded fighter significantly.

Finally, after countless man hours of preparation and dozens of informational briefings, we were ready to submit our Request for Proposal. The RFP is a document that describes in general terms what we were looking for in our airplane. Once that document is complete, the call goes out to contractors to submit bids to do business with the Air Force. After a final meeting with all my departments, I was back in Al Flax's office. This time I was giving him a decision briefing. We needed a thumbs up or thumbs down on the RFP. Nothing moves forward in the Air Force Systems Command without an RFP. I was after a thumbs-up.

During informational visits at the R&D office, Flax could be affable. When it came to decisions, he was a bulldog, to be polite. But I had to get past him. If he approved the project, then the RFP could be released and the aircraft companies could submit their proposals for what they deemed to be the best air superiority fighter plane.

As I entered these contentious discussions, I remember a previous meeting with Johnny Foster. He was an assistant in the Secretary of Defense Office on the third floor of the Pentagon. One day, after a briefing, we were chatting in his office as he changed his shirt and cleaned up for another meeting.

"Bob, can you be an advocate and impartial at the same time?" he asked me.

"Yes, I really think I can," I assured him.

"Then do it, and be patient," he added.

He didn't tell me that I would need all my patience and more when it came to dealing with Flax. I was patient, even if I had to do it through gritted teeth!

Johnny was a great guy compared to some of the guys on the third floor and Al Flax was at the other end of the scale. He asked all the technical questions, and when I'd answered them, he asked a variation of the question that was even more technical and harder to answer. Fortunately, I had engineering back-up for those.

At the RFP briefing, Flax sat rocked back in his chair, rolling his trademark cigar in his teeth. There was also a three-star general in the room. For what seemed like an eternity, he grilled me with one technical question after another. I think my irritation may have been starting to show a little when the general took pity on me.

The general said, "Al, what the hell do you want? You've been hammering this guy for the last half hour. Just what are you after?"

The tenor of the meeting changed immediately, and I survived it. The RFP was approved for release and the game was on.

Three industry heavy hitters stepped forward to accept the challenge outlined in the RFP. North American Aviation in Los Angeles, McDonnell Douglas in St. Louis and Republic Aviation Corporation in Farmingdale, Long Island, the same town where I was certified as a flight instructor though it seemed like a million years ago. Each of the giant corporations went to work on plans for their version of an air superiority fighter.

It was "deja vu all over again," as Yogi Berra might say. The navy was looking for an air defense fighter plane to protect their carrier task force. As was the case with the F-111, the talk on the street was that the Department of Defense wanted one fighter for both jobs. *Nightmare on Elm Street*, part two.

When the rumor mill began to bear a semblance to reality, I met with my counterpart from the Navy, an affable captain. Although he had no part in the F-111 controversy, he knew all the reasons why that chain of logic was a bad idea. He was as much against the idea of one plane for both services as I was. After an intense lobbying effort, in which I didn't participate, each service was allowed to develop its own fighter aircraft, thank goodness.

We still didn't have a designation for the new aircraft. We were still the FX airplane. Hoping to energize the effort, we petitioned the Department of The Air Force for a designation. Fortuitously, the Navy beat us to the punch. Their aircraft was labeled the F-14. We were designated the F-15. I had an affinity for the number fifteen.

I was also given inappropriate credit for the decision. Since I was with the X-15, the F-15 designation was more coincidental than my crew could stand. They were sure I had had something to do with it. Like any good commanding officer, I didn't try to convince them otherwise.

Getting the name reenergized the crew. We channeled that energy into evaluating the proposals as the three industrial combatants competed for what amounted to millions of dollars in business. Properly evaluating their efforts would take a lot of time and expertise. I made sure we got it.

Our intimate group of thirty expanded into triple digits as specialists in every imaginable discipline were mobilized as we implemented the consultant list developed in the planning stage. There were firefighters, fuel experts, insulation gurus, radar specialists, armament people and engine aficionados. You name it, we had the expertise.

A secure building, complete with iron bars on the windows, was requisitioned for the task. Tons of papers were loaded into the building, and the experts went to work.

There were subcontractors for the specialty areas. General Electric and Pratt & Whitney vied for the engine contract. Hughes and Westinghouse would compete for the radar system. There was no competition for the gun system. Our only choice was the Gatling gun, because the development of the caseless ammunition appeared to have too many problems. At least it had been a good idea.

One day, I got a phone call from the four-star general who was Chief of Staff of the Air Force, John Ryan. I met him when he was commanding officer of the Pacific Air Force. There were over a hundred people working in the building and in minutes everyone in the place knew about the call.

"Hi, Bob," he said, and we exchanged pleasantries.

"Bob, my old crew chief's son works for you, and he'd like me to give him a special job. I need to know what kind of guy he is," John said.

The young man, a lieutenant colonel, was a nice, competent, hard-working executive officer for me, and I gave him a good recommendation. In a few minutes, it was apparent to me that this was merely a friendly personnel request. After some more small talk, we wished each other well and hung up.

Colonel Wenzle, my chief engine man, was quickest to the office, and he asked me, "What was the general's call all about?"

"He was just checking up to see how we're doing and to wish us well," I lied.

This little ruse pumped even more energy into my team. I never did tell them the truth about the phone call. Why should I spoil it for them? It gave them a lift when they were mired in a pile of technical minutia.

The evaluation of the proposals was not all on paper. There was a lot of sophisticated testing involved as well. In the old days, we built a set of aircraft wings and bent them till they broke. Not so this time. We had special machines and specialists to man them to test the possibilities offered by the contractors. After countless hours of evaluation, we were ready to go forward with the results of the source selection process.

I walked into the conference room of the secretary of the Air Force on the fourth floor of the Pentagon. Thirty to forty stern faces greeted me. I was absolutely certain I could see blood on the carpet from previous presenters.

It was a star-studded group. Secretary of the Air Force Robert Seamans, Chief of Staff of the Air Force John McConnell, and General Moymer of the Tactical Air Command led the list. A number of under secretaries, civilian advisers and consultants rounded out the inquisition.

In these pre–Power Point days, I plowed through the presentation slide after slide that compared each of the three proposals, highlighting their strengths and weaknesses. It was more of an overview than the detailed reports our experts had generated in the source selection process or the one that I had already given to Al Flax. Over an hour later, I was finally finished and McDonnell Douglas emerged as the clear winner. The discussion that followed was brief and informal.

The secretary of the Air Force is the source selection authority for the Air Force. After hearing the presentation and some quiet comments among the generals, he agreed with us.

"Excellent presentation, colonel. Very thorough," Secretary Seamans said. Chief of Staff General McConnell said, "That's it."

General McConnell pointed a finger at the men in the room and said, "When you leave this room, keep your mouths shut! Not one word!"

This was not an idle warning. These meetings were held on Friday in the afternoon. The reason was simple. By meeting then, no final decision was likely until the stock market closed for the weekend. When multi-millions of dollars worth of business are up for grabs, the winning manufacturer's stock would be affected by the decision. Getting the contract meant not only building the aircraft, but at least ten years of parts and service for millions more in business.

"White, you're part of this. Come over here and sit down," General McConnell said to me. "The rest of you are dismissed."

I took my seat as a legion of assistant secretaries of the Air Force and Defense and a legion of high-powered staff officers and civilians filed out of the room. Selfishly, I loved it. Most of them seemed relieved to go. I only caught one or two scowls as they left.

My old friend General Momyer of the Tactical Air Command, Secretary of the Air Force Seamans, and General McConnell were the only ones left in the room besides me. These men would make the final decision.

Finally, Secretary Seamans said, "Okay."

General McConnell said to General Momyer, "Spike, not one more ounce of weight will be added to that aircraft so it can carry bombs."

It was over. The F-15 was under development. I called the base to give the guys the good news. Somehow they knew, because I could barely hear over the noise of the champagne corks popping in the background. They would celebrate, but they would abide by the same secrecy command those of us in the room had been given.

"Sorry you can't be at the party, boss," my engine man told me.

Some weeks later, I had to brief Deputy Secretary of Defense David Packard. I met with Secretary Packard, General Ferguson, the four-star general who commanded the Air Force Systems Command, and General Ryan, chief of staff of the Air Force. The briefing to Mr. Packard was a courtesy briefing so he would be aware of what was going on. I repeated an abbreviated version of the presentation I had given to the larger group earlier, and when I finished, I was asked to wait outside.

General Ferguson came out a bit later and we walked down the hall.

"Bob, the program is going forward. This is really big stuff. We have to have a general officer out front. Nothing against you. You've done a great job, but Brigadier General Ben Bellis will be taking over as the system program officer for the F-15.

To say I was overjoyed by the news would be less than truthful. To say I was relieved to be out of the pressure cooker would be more accurate. But I really did understand the situation. General Bellis had a great reputation for his involvement with the U-2 and SR-71 projects. I had no problem working for him, and with him now in charge, I was one layer more insulated from any problems that might spring up as development proceeded.

My reward was playing a leading role in bringing a premier, world-class fighter aircraft, the F-15, into the Air Force arsenal. After more than thirty years, it is still in service and ranks as one of the greatest fighter planes in Air Force history.

I worked with the F-15 from April of 1968 to July of 1970. It was a singular experience, and I enjoyed every minute of it. When the next promotion list came out, my name was on it. I would soon be a brigadier general. The family and I had another reason to celebrate.

With it came my next duty assignment. I was going back to the desert;

back to Edwards Air Force Base, this time as commanding officer of the Air Force Flight Test Center.

As this period of my career came to a close, I recalled a conversation I had had with Bob Rushworth, one of my fellow X-15 pilots, when we were both in Vietnam.

"What do you want from your military career, Bob?" he asked me.

A book written by President Dwight D. Eisenhower came to my mind. In it he said, "My expectation before World War II was to have a successful career and retire as a major general."

"I hope to have a successful career and retire as at least a major general," I had replied.

"Wow, really?" Bob replied as if I had just said I wanted to follow the general into the White House.

As I left Wright Patterson Air Force Base, I could dream that one day I might get a second star and to me, that would be a successful career.

Chapter 15

Home Again

It was with considerable anticipation that in the fall of 1970 I returned to the Air Force Test Center at Edwards Air Force Base as its commanding officer for the next two years. It was a place that held many special memories. Besides, I had worked so hard to get there the first time, this was a singular honor for me.

Things began at Edwards on a high note. Shortly after I arrived, my first star was confirmed. It was pinned on me by my wife, Doris, and that was a proud day in my life. One more star to go and I'd reach my goal. I was looking up as usual, something I'd been doing since I was ten.

Edwards was the second largest facility in the Air Force system. Only Eglin Air Force Base in Florida was larger. It was a busy base, with a number of aircraft being tested in each of the four divisions: fighters, bombers, cargo and helicopters. We had no research project like the X-15 at that time. The command also included the Parachute Test Center near the Mexican border. We were testing planes from as small as the A-10, a ground attack fighter, to huge bombers.

Later, the F-15 came in for testing. It was a real delight for me since this plane was "my baby." It was an awesome aircraft, according to the pilots who flew it. It was all I could do to stay out of the cockpit, but that was not part of my job description. I never had an opportunity to fly it until late in my career. Although this was one of the few commands where a general officer could still fly, it didn't include flying test aircraft. Had I been able to fly it, I could have appreciated the F-15 as only a test pilot can.

However, during my next command, I did get an opportunity fly the F-15 when it had completed the testing phase and was an official part of the arsenal of the Air Force. It was another unforgettable day in a career full of them. I was in the back seat, because it was only a familiarization ride and my lead pilot was up front.

It was a beautiful sunny day as I eagerly sat on the runway in the aircraft impatiently awaiting an opportunity to fly "my baby." Next to us was a

McDonnell F-4 Phantom II that would serve as our target in the radar and close maneuvering portion of the flight.

At the controls of the F-4 was an experienced pilot with over 1,000 hours in the aircraft. He nodded, which was the signal for us to launch in a formation takeoff. The thrust generated by the F-15 was exhilarating, and in the blink of an eye we were at 10,000 feet and climbing. I looked over my shoulder to check the position of the F-4. To my amazement, it was just clearing the end of the 15,000 foot runway.

After a few minutes of flying to allow me to familiarize myself with the handling characteristics of the aircraft in flight, we went into dogfight mode. Flying as if he was in real combat, the F-4 pilot went through every bank, roll and loop he knew how to do, and to my amazement, he never got out of my gun sight for a second! And all his maneuvering was done with full afterburners on. I never had to light my afterburner to keep him in my gun sight. It wasn't entirely my skill. Part of it was the performance of this magnificent machine.

Back on the ground, I said to the F-4 pilot, "With all that seat time in the F-4 and me only in the F-15 for an hour, would you go up against me with hot guns?"

"No way, sir. No way," was his answer. "I wouldn't stand a chance."

Much later during Operation Desert Storm, the first two French aircraft that were flown by the Iraqi Air Force were downed by an F-15 flown by a Saudi Air Force pilot. Even today, decades later, it's a formidable aircraft, and I'm quite proud of that.

Aerodynamically, the F-15 was a great plane, but the most important advancement for the time was the thrust-to-weight ratio. It supplied enormous power and speed to the air superiority fighter. By comparison, today's F-22 Raptor stealth fighter can go up to one-and-one-half times the speed of sound without using afterburner! In planned combat exercises, the F-22 beats the F-15 nearly every time, showing that the air superiority torch has been passed to a new generation of airplanes. And engine technology has not reached its zenith yet either.

Physically, the base was relatively unchanged since I was there as a test pilot. My chief technical adviser was a civilian who had matriculated from engineering. He was a competent man, and when we inspected the base facilities, it was obvious to both of us that some of the systems needed attention. Time and the advancement of technology dictated major overhauls for our radar and photographic systems, among others.

I had nothing against my technical advisor, but I felt the task could be better accomplished by someone who had been a pilot and who had the necessary technical expertise. And I had such a man in mind, Colonel Dick

Lathrop. He had previously been the commanding officer of the Test Pilot School and had a masters and Ph.D. in electrical engineering.

Because he was from the military, I had to explain my choice to replace the civilian advisor with Colonel Lathrop. It was a politically sensitive issue due to the civilian/military dichotomy involved. Professional politicians get very sensitive about losing one of their appointees. My rationale was that the appointment would be temporary until the refitting of the various systems was completed.

Being commander of a flight test facility is not all happiness and light. One of the unpleasant aspects was notifying the next of kin of anyone killed in the line of duty. Unfortunately, there was a spate of accidents while I was the commanding officer at Edwards. They seem to go in cycles, and I got a bad one. I never got used to that.

I made it a point not to visit the new widow with the bad news until I had a complete condolence team that included, for obvious reasons, a chaplain and a physician. It hadn't gotten any easier than when I was a summary court officer when I was here the last time. The only difference is that I didn't have the same personal relationship with these men that I did when I was a pilot. It was still an awful job.

One of the accidents was particularly senseless. Testing airplanes and pushing them to their limits, and sometimes beyond, carries certain inherent risks. When you lose someone who is not in an aircraft, it's particularly troublesome, especially since following simple safety rules could have prevented the entire accident.

An Air Force captain was working in a cherry picker with the arm extended thirty feet above the ground. He was well aware of the safety rules, but chose to ignore them and did not use the safety belt in the cherry picker tub. While changing position, the tub bumped something that

My official portrait as commander of the U.S. Air Force Flight Test Center at Edwards Air Force Base, California (U.S. Air Force).

caused it to stop suddenly. The man was catapulted over the side to his death on the ground thirty feet away. It didn't have to happen. I see the same senseless thing in automobiles. Snapping a safety belt can save your life. It would have saved his.

The only positive from the accident aspect of the job was that none of the accidents involved the F-15. For that, I was thankful.

Early one morning, as I slept soundly in my bed, I was jerked awake by the jangling of the telephone. My grumbled, grouchy hello turned to rapt attention when the caller identified himself as Major General Grossick from headquarters. I was immediately awake.

There had been a ground accident involving a C-5 aircraft at Warner Robbins Air Force Base in Georgia. A small T-39 passenger jet would pick me up at 0800 for the flight to Georgia where I would head the accident investigation team. It would be my first time for this duty, although it was not uncommon for commanding officers to serve in other roles such as promotion or accident boards, as in this case.

The C-5 is one of the largest aircraft in the world. It can carry outsized and oversized cargo intercontinental ranges and can take off or land in relatively short distances. Ground crews can load and off load the C-5 simultaneously at the front and rear cargo openings. It stands over six stories high and is similar in appearance to the C-141 Starlifter, but the C-5 is considerably larger. It can carry 135 tons of cargo and weighs 420 tons fully loaded. The massive aircraft had been virtually destroyed in a fatal explosion.

Since I had little experience with aircraft of that size, I was allowed to bring anyone along I wished to as technical advisors. I took two full colonels from my command who were familiar with the C-5 aircraft. Once on the ground in Georgia, we'd have all of the military and civilian consultants we would likely need for assistance from various Air Force agencies. If I needed more, I could call them in.

Two workmen had been inside one of the aircraft's massive fuel cells. A spark had caused an explosion, killing the Lockheed employees. That was the primary tragedy. On the economic side, a multimillion dollar aircraft was in shambles.

Our investigation revealed that the workmen had not been following published safety procedures and a spark had ignited the highly flammable JP-4 jet fuel fumes, causing the resultant explosion. It was another senseless accident that could have been prevented. The end result of my inquiry was to see if anything else could be done to prevent such tragedies in the future.

One of our primary recommendations was to shift from the dangerous JP-4 fuel to the less explosive JP-8 fuel. Although there would still be a danger of explosion, the odds would be greatly reduced. It took some time, but the Air Force finally did switch over. There were stockpiles of the JP-4 that had to be depleted and new contracts for more of the JP-8 had to be negotiated.

An interesting sidelight of the investigation involved moving the remnants of the monstrous aircraft from the hanger. Even though there had been a horrible explosion that had blown part of it to pieces, its size was still a problem. It became a major engineering feat to decide what could be stripped from the airplane to reduce it to a moveable size. If such an aircraft were heavily damaged on an airfield with limited runway capacity, it would be problematic until the hulk could be removed. As a result of this accident the engineers developed a specific protocol on what to remove and in what order so a C-5 could be moved expeditiously if the situation arose. The plan was a benefit I never thought of, but having such a procedure in place could be useful in the future.

One evening during the investigation, my two colonels and I were at the base officer's club for dinner. At a nearby table were two Lockheed employees who were also there for the investigation. One of them was a former Air Force colonel. They sent a bottle of wine to our table.

We thanked them and enjoyed the wine. When it was time to leave, I found out from the waiter how much the wine cost and collected one-third of it from each of my two colonels and added my own third to it. The next day I went into the office of the ex–Air Force officer.

When I gave him the money for the wine he was very surprised. I explained that we appreciated the gesture, but he worked for the vendor in this situation and we couldn't accept it. He understood and was obviously embarrassed about the situation. His intention had been above board. It hadn't been an attempted bribe by any stretch of the imagination. Besides, if he thought that the three of us could be bought with a single bottle of wine, then we would have been insulted. Still, I could not allow even the hint of impropriety to cloud the investigation.

Since the Lockheed employees had caused the problem, the company not only had to compensate the families of the dead workers, but they were fiscally responsible for the destroyed aircraft as well. Simple human error had been responsible for not only deaths, but also had a significant fiscal impact on a reputable company.

One of the test centers under my command was the joint Navy–Air Force Parachute Development and Test Center, located near the Mexican border about thirty-five minutes flying time from Edwards Air Force Base and fairly close to the Salton Sea, a large inland sea in Southern California. It was a small base that did research, testing and development on all types of parachutes; personal, cargo and specialty.

The complement of personnel there was small as well. Many of them were master parachutists from both the Navy and the Air Force. As part of my duty, I visited the base for a routine inspection visit.

"Have you ever jumped, sir?" asked a Navy chief master jumper.

"Only once," I answered, and told him of my World War II jump from my crippled airplane.

"Would you like to go through qualification and get your jump badge?" he offered.

I said, "Thanks, guys. I'd really love to do it, but I have a general officer's dream assignment. I can still fly here. All I need to do is break a leg and screw the whole thing up. I'll have to decline."

"We have the Salton Sea just over there," he replied, jerking his chin in the direction of his left shoulder. "We can drop you into the water. No broken bones."

After a moment of contemplation, I said, "Why not?"

I had wanted to qualify while I was in Bitburg, but a two-star general died during a jump, and they shut down the qualification school right after that. As with all the years of flying, it had happened to someone else. I wouldn't happen to me.

For the next hour or two they put me through the ground drills, teaching me how to land and roll and guide the parachute. We went over safety precautions and emergency procedures.

Two weeks later I returned to the base and found myself in a helicopter 9,000 feet over the Salton Sea. I jumped and landed safely in the water. Soaking wet, it was back in the helicopter four more times. When I had completed the five jumps, I was qualified for my military parachutist badge.

My fifth jump was a success as well, and the boat was very close to where I landed. It came right up to me. When I looked into the boat I laughed so hard I nearly choked on the salty water.

My executive officer was a witty young man named Captain Mike Harley who had been attached to the Parachute Test Center in the past. He was in the pick-up boat standing in the bow with a World War II German helmet on.

"Achtung! Achtung! Hände hoch!" he screamed. I had told him about my capture by the Germans, and he was having a little fun with me.

Did I really need to qualify as a military parachutist? Of course I didn't. Was I proud of it? You bet.

For the majority of my time at Edwards, I enjoyed not only the job, but the people. However, I had one encounter with an Air Force hero that I found unsettling, and it occurred as part of a standard military procedure. The inspector general from Norton Air Force Base in California routinely sent inspectors to bases to ensure quality performance. When I heard Edwards was to be inspected, I looked forward to it as an opportunity to improve my command. When you are immersed in the activities of running the base on a day-to-day basis, sometimes you can't see the forest for the trees.

When I found that the inspector was to be Brigadier General Robin Olds, I figured there would be a fair, impartial and insightful look at my command. He was a hell of a pilot and a World War II ace. In Vietnam, he had commanded a combat fighter wing. I thought we had a reasonable relationship, as Robin had flown with me on the raid to the infamous Hanoi bridge and saw bombs hit the bridge.

Robin is a product of a military family. His father, Major General Archie Olds, was an early proponent of air power, and was a respected officer with an impeccable record. Robin, however, was more than a bit of a maverick, so he could be unpredictable.

In Vietnam, General Jack Ryan, commander of the Pacific Air Force, wasn't happy with the bomb hits we were delivering. The newly installed bomb cameras showed we were not the precise bombers we thought we were. He ordered all of us under his command to design a way to remedy this problem.

My wing commander, Colonel John Girado, asked me to come up with a scheme to screen and evaluate the film from our strike cameras to see what bombs came from what aircraft. I had a skull session with a few other pilots, and we came up with charts and files for storage of the data. It was a difficult task since it was sometimes nearly impossible to assign bomb hits on the film to a certain aircraft, particularly when there are a dozen airplanes all diverging on a single target at the same time.

When General Ryan came for his inspection, I showed him my plan. Even though I didn't have much information in the drawer, General Ryan was satisfied. There were three wings that flew the strikes into North Vietnam and the Hanoi area, our wing the 355th; the 8th, Robin Olds' wing; and the 366th wing. Robin was the only wing commander who had done nothing.

While in Bitburg, Robin and all the other pilots stationed in England and Germany went to the bombing range in Libya. Once, when he was there practicing skip bombing, he had a problem of coming in too low, which was dangerous. There was a single control tower on the bombing range, manned by another pilot. If you came in too low or too high, it was considered a foul, and you were fouled off the course. Robin made two passes and was fouled off the course both times.

Frustrated, Robin circled the field and came back at high speed directly toward the tower. He buzzed it with enough force to rattle the windows and scare the young captain out of his wits. Anyone else would have been reprimanded and disciplined. As far as I know, nothing was ever done.

After the inspection, I took Robin out to the flight line to have a look at the F-15. He seemed excited about it. When the inspection report came in, the discrepancies he had pointed out were both reasonable and helpful. The discrepancies were all minor and not overly abundant in number. We began immediately to correct the discrepancies. For example, I walked into one of our shops where a sergeant had a copy of the report pinned to the wall with the discrepancies in his shop underlined.

"See, General, I have the report right here, and I've already fixed all these problems. I'm leaving that up there as a reminder to never let it happen again," the sergeant said.

"Good work, Sergeant," I said. "Keep it up."

This was the attitude that permeated the base. And I'm certain that we were the better for it. There was nothing on the inspection report that was unjustified, and we fixed every one of them.

I never gave it another thought until 2006 when I was inducted into the National Aerospace Hall of Fame. It occurred on Friday night, the day before the induction, when after dinner they gave the microphone to various previous enshrines in a section called "hanger talk."

During hanger talk, pilots entertained the audience with anecdotes from the past, with humor and pathos. When Robin came to the microphone, he asked if I was in the audience. Of course he knew I was there, and I identified myself. I expected some humorous anecdote from Vietnam. Did I get a surprise. Without recognizing me he continued. "I went down there to inspect his base one time and it was really a mess," he said. "I don't know if he ever got it straightened out or not." After a couple more derogatory comments, he went on to do his hanger talk. His comments took me totally by surprise. I have no idea why he chose to try to spoil a really special day in my life. It was supposed to be a night of fun to honor the induction class of 2006, but Robin apparently had his own agenda. I still don't understand why he did it. The only explanation I can think of is that we were contemporaries and I got my second star and he didn't. If that's the case, he has no one to blame but himself. I never did anything to hinder Robin's career, and, he was the one who buzzed the tower in Libya, not me. Unfortunately, I will never be able to ask him about his motivation. Robin passed away in 2007.

I must say, to highlight an inspection that occurred over thirty-five years before is really strange unless it has a good punch line. The inspection that time had Edwards Air Fore Base in a good light. The Flight Test Center had dramatically improved year-by-year as a jewel of flight testing and a showplace for technologic advancement in aviation. Comparing the Edwards AFB of 1946 to the Edwards AFB I commanded is like comparing a Model A Ford to a Lexus sedan today that can park itself.

The overall experience at Edwards could not have been more rewarding, but in two short years it was over. My next stop would be Maxwell Air Force Base in Alabama where I would assume command of the Air Force ROTC program.

Chapter 16

Back to School

I left Edwards Air Force Base in 1972 for Maxwell Air Force Base in Montgomery, Alabama, home of the Air University. There were a number of schools in that command including the Air War College and the Air Force Reserve Officer Training Corps, better known as the ROTC. That was my destination. I was assigned to the ROTC headquarters as the commandant.

Maxwell was a good duty station. The facilities were first rate, and the base housing was excellent. It was a comfortable place for families to live and a comfortable place for officers and enlisted men to work.

On the other hand, my new job was not in that same category. I was more than a bit disappointed that I had not been reassigned within the Systems Command, but I had no control over that. As the rumor mill said when it heard of my new assignment, "Old Bob's in the bull pen now. I guess that's the last we'll hear of White." The assignment was considered a dead-end job for career enhancement. No one had ever been given a second star while serving as ROTC commandant. But it was the job the Air Force had given me to do, and I was determined to bring to it the same energy and enthusiasm I had when I was in my beloved fighters or at the controls of the X-15.

This was my second visit to Maxwell. The first was as a brand new aviation cadet prior to entering flight training during World War II. At that time, I enjoyed any number of good meals and lively discussions in the pleasant mess hall. To my surprise and delight, the ROTC headquarters building was situated in the renovated and reconfigured mess hall! I felt right at home.

The first few weeks at Maxwell were politically tricky for me. Although I was the new commandant of the ROTC, my predecessor, though relieved of command, was still around for a time. In my opinion, that does not make for a healthy environment and made my job unnecessarily difficult for me at first. Nothing untoward happened between us, but it made me feel as if I were being second guessed a time or two, particularly by his old staff.

Shortly after my arrival, while I was still settling in, I met my eager young charges for the first time at their annual conclave. Once a year, cadets from various ROTC programs around the country met to exchange ideas, discuss problems and attend meetings concerning their opportunities for careers in the Air Force. As the new ROTC commandant, I was asked to speak at that conclave.

As I sat on the rostrum with my predecessor and the other civil and military dignitaries, watching a film being shown to the cadets, a T-38 jet trainer flashed across the screen. In an excited whisper, one young cadet within earshot said, "I can hardly wait!" I knew exactly how he felt. I had been there once myself.

The audience was not totally male. There were Angel Flights in attendance as well. These were groups of young women interested in flying and in the Air Force who participated in these female auxiliary detachments. We had not yet reached the season of equality when they could all serve in the same detachment.

A number of luminaries, including my predecessor, preceded me at the microphone. Each gave the expected sterile remarks that would have put the crowd to sleep had they been in a lecture hall. When it was my turn, I decided to liven up the joint.

I began my address with some perfunctory remarks about ROTC in general, service and patriotism. Then, I told them a true story about an ROTC graduate who was a combat pilot. I described his last combat mission with the enemy in graphic detail that would have made Hollywood proud. I made certain to include the bursting flak and the explosion of his bomb load on the target.

Then I told them how he was shot down, again embellishing the details using my own World War II experience as a model, although this young man's plight was much worse than mine. I explained his hardships as a prisoner of war. He was freed from the prison camp and repatriated. I told them how he arrived at my office to be reunited with his wife and of my invitation for him to come and speak to them about his experience.

"I invited him to share the podium with me, but unfortunately he could not. He's still involved in debriefing and medical examinations by the Air Force. But he did send you a message. Tell them I'm sorry that I can't come, and tell them that I love them. I told him that would be easy, because I love you, too," I concluded with a flourish and left the podium to return to my seat.

After a heartbeat of stunned silence, the audience erupted into thunderous applause, cheers and whistles. I had hoped to pump them up a bit, and it seemed to work. There response thrilled me. As we were leaving the dais after the program, my aide said to me, "General, you got 'em!"

Since the command was so different from any of my other assignments, at my first meeting with my deputy commander and a few other selected officers I said, "Just keep doing what you're doing so I can understand what's going on and get a feel for the operation. When I feel comfortable, then I'll begin to inject my own management style."

I found the first thing I needed to change immediately. My staff consisted of nine full colonels, each supervising a geographic section of the United States and the ROTC detachments located at various colleges and universities in those regions. They met weekly, along with the headquarters' staff, to discuss things that had arisen in the various regions; to brainstorm; to problem solve. To my surprise, the meeting was never conducted by my predecessor, but by his deputy.

When I said, "Beginning next week, I will conduct the staff meetings," there were smiles and nods around the table and a sigh of relief from the deputy commander. They felt they had been operating in a vacuum, and relished my presence.

I had not been there very long when word came down that the deputy chief of the Air Force for personnel, Lieutenant General Robert Dixon, requested that I stop in and see him at his office in the Pentagon the next time I was in the D.C. area. Since a request from a three-star general is the equivalent of an order when it is made to a one-star general, I made it a point to schedule a visit to the D.C. area and made my way to his office.

"Bob, I want you to know that it took a fair amount of persuasion, but I persevered. I specifically wanted you for the ROTC job. Your boss at Systems Command didn't want to let you go, but I told him that I had a special assignment for you, and he reluctantly let you go," General Dixon said.

"I know you haven't been there long enough yet to get a real feel for the place, but when you do, I think you'll agree with me that it's a real mess. I need someone to straighten it out and get that program functional again. That's why I picked you. You are young enough, you're aggressive enough, and you've got enough medals on your chest to command respect," he continued, pointing to the rows of service ribbons on my uniform. "Find out what's wrong and fix it!" he concluded.

I felt honored that he had hand-picked me for the assignment, but I was even more relieved to discover that I had not been let go by Systems Command. I had been commandeered for another job. It made me feel a lot better about being in what others considered a dead-end job. It also energized me for the task at hand. I had noticed some things that I felt could be better, now I had a mandate to change them if I thought it would help.

When I got back to Maxwell, I looked at each phase of the operation with a more critical eye. There were 140 different ROTC detachments at different colleges and universities around the country. I had a large map on my office wall and tagged each one of those detachments with a red pin. When I visited a school, I changed the pin to blue.

The war in Vietnam had taken its toll on ROTC programs around the country, and the spirit of patriotism was only now beginning to resurface. It would be my task to tap into that emotion whenever I had the chance. To do that, and to get a true picture of what was going on out there, I would need to personally visit as many of those detachments as possible. By the time I finished at Maxwell, there were 120 blue pins on that map. No prejudice against the other twenty, I just ran out of time.

When I began to visit the various colleges, I arranged to visit them in groups, setting up meetings at a half dozen or so schools in the same geographic area. It seemed like an efficient way to do things. A perk of some of the trips was that I could fly myself to them. Perhaps not in the equipment I was used to, but to me an airplane was an airplane.

There was a flying club at Maxwell, and it had a well equipped single-engine four-passenger airplane. I confined my use of the craft to visits to states close by. For trips farther away, I used larger military or civilian aircraft. With the instruments, I could fly it at night or in mildly inclement weather. Even with my experience, I felt it foolish to challenge the severe weather when there was no pressing need to do so. After all, it gave me a chance to fly, and I was not about to abuse that privilege.

One of my first visits was to the detachment at the University of Miami in Florida. As part of each visit, I met with the detachment commander, either a colonel or a lieutenant colonel, who took me on a tour of the facilities, briefed me on the status of the unit and its operational plans followed by a discussion of the strengths and weaknesses of the program.

When the briefing was over, I paid my respects to the most senior civilian officer at the school, usually the president or provost of the institution. I wanted to give them an opportunity to tell me anything they wanted to, good or bad, about their detachment and how it interfaced with the rest of the school. When we had finished the briefing, I indicated that we should go to the president's office.

Getting nervously to his feet, the detachment commander said, "Do you want to go right now? It's class change time, and there will be students everywhere."

I was thunderstruck. I could tell by his tone that he was worried about going across the campus when there were students there. It was difficult for me to fathom that a colonel in the United States Air Force would be reluctant to walk across an American university campus with a brigadier general because he was afraid to interact with the students. That, I suppose, was the Vietnam War Syndrome.

"Let's go now!" I said, leaving no room for further discussion.

As we walked to the president's office, my detachment commander was amazed at the smiles, courteous nods and waves from the students we passed along the way.

"Hi, General!" an enthusiastic young man said.

"How's it going, guys?" another called out.

"Good to see you guys. Great job. Keep it up," a smiling young woman said.

I had a pleasant visit with the president of the university. On the way back to the detachment there were more rewarding student encounters. It had a profound effect on the colonel. I'm sure the students' reaction to us had astounded him.

As I left his office I said to the colonel, "I think the backlash from Vietnam is settling down. There's a rebirth of national pride and patriotism surfacing. Be a part of it. Get out there and wear that uniform with pride. Show the colors."

"Yes sir, I will," he replied with a crisp salute, and he lived up to his promise.

On a visit to the University of Massachussetts I encountered a similar scenario. I was under a time constraint to catch a commercial airplane, and it was nearing time to leave. The university had at one time been at the center of heated antiwar protests. There were protestors on campus that day, but the war and the military were not their targets. I had no problem with them during my visit. As we walked back across campus, the detachment commander pointed toward the empty flagpole in front of the ROTC building.

"Since the antiwar riots, we don't put the flag up anymore," the detachment commander said sadly.

Flushing with outrage I said, "You get your men together, in uniform, and raise that flag first thing in the morning. Do you understand?"

Reluctantly, he agreed to comply with the order.

Sometime later, I received a phone message from the colonel. In it, he relayed to me the numerous positive comments he had received from both students and faculty about the flag-raising ceremony each morning. The entire campus was happy to see Old Glory flapping in the New England breeze once again. Object lesson: Don't sell Americans short on America.

Considering the tragedy that had occurred on the Kent State campus in Ohio that led to the death of four young people, there was considerable apprehension about my visit to that school. I was flown onto campus by a nearby Army Reserve unit in a helicopter that landed on the university football field. It was a quiet, routine visit without a hint of conflict. And I was treated to typical Midwest hospitality.

At Wichita State University, I got an unusual request from the university president.

"Sir, would it be possible to have an African American officer assigned to this detachment?" the president asked me.

It was during the time of affirmative action, and his request wasn't that unusual. But career black officers were a scarce commodity in the Air Force at that time.

"I'm sympathetic with your request, but we have don't have anyone to send," I answered honestly.

I didn't have one. But I confess I had an unkind thought pass through my mind. I suspected he was hoping I could help solve his affirmative action problem without diluting any of his core classes with African American faculty. If that were true, he'd have to solve the problem within the academic community itself. If many of them thought the way he did, that would be problematic.

The majority of my trips were great. I met a host of wonderful educators who really cared about the students at their university. A special visit was my visit to Grambling, one of the original all-black universities. When I got to the president's office, the legendary Eddie Robinson was there with him.

Eddie Gay Robinson (not short for Edward) spent 56 years as the head college football coach at Grambling State University in Grambling, Louisiana, from 1942 through 1997. He was affectionately known simply as "Coach" throughout college football. During his tenure, Robinson established himself as the winningest coach in college football history, becoming the first coach to record 400 wins. During the era of segregation, Robinson's talent was praised by many white coaches, especially Bear Bryant at Alabama.

The president brought out refreshments, and we talked for over an hour. We discussed the detachment, but the conversation soon deteriorated into a wonderful bull session filled with stories and anecdotes about education and football. Each time I tried to leave, they implored me to stay.

"No, stay a little longer. Have another cup of coffee," they beseeched me.

I stayed a lot longer than I should have, and I enjoyed every minute of it. I will never forget that visit.

On the subject of football, I must admit that my visits to the various campuses resulted in the development of some prejudices. I couldn't help it. I'm human after all.

When I visited the Ohio State University, I was greeted with warmth, enthusiasm and hospitality. The University of Michigan gave me the cold shoulder. When the two play their annual grudge match, I bring out my scarlet and grey sweater.

At the University of Southern Californina, the president welcomed me with a pot of coffee and some Danish as well as a warm handshake and an hour-long conversation. At crosstown UCLA, they didn't have time for me to speak with their very busy president. Guess what? Go Trojans!

When I visited Notre Dame, as well as a number of other schools, I was invited to come back for a football game. Despite my affinity for the Irish, I declined that invitation and all the others, save one.

At Texas A&M University, the corps of cadets routinely marched at every home football game. They marched around the perimeter of the field and passed in review for an invited flag rank officer from one of the services. When I got that invitaton, I accepted. In no way could this invitation be construed as a gratuity. It was my duty as a flag rank officer repesenting the Air Force. It was a great day, and they treated me as if I were a rock star.

The first time Notre Dame played Alabama, my boss, Lt. General Felix Rogers, was invited to the game. Like me, Felix was a certified member of the Notre Dame subway alumni. He was rooting for the Fighting Irish. But he would need to be careful. Alabama was hosting the visit.

I was talking to my secretary about the game, and she found out I was a Notre Dame fan. I could admit to being a fan even if Felix couldn't.

In her delightful southern accent she said earnestly, "General, I just can't believe you aren't rooting for Alabama," she said.

On a trip to the West Coast, I was flying in a T-39, a small passenger-style trainer. A young man in the detachment I was visiting had a medical emergency. His mother was critically ill in the Dallas, Texas, area. I told the young man I would take him to Texas.

"Sir, I'm not ready. It will take me some time to get my things together," he said.

"No problem. I'll wait," I said

My pilot had filed a flight plan to re-fuel in Oklahoma City. When we were in the air, we would refile a flight plan for Carswell Air Force Base in the Dallas/Fort Worth area. I told the young man to have his family meet him at Carswell, and explained what they would need to do to get onto the base.

It was a satisfying feeling to be in a position to do a good turn for the young man. All it cost me was a couple of hours of waiting and a bit of a diversion on the way home. The calls, letters and adulation of a grateful family was more than enough reward.

These were the entertaining parts of my job. The challenging part had been given to me by General Dixon. I still had a mess to clean up. After a long period of study and introspection about our operation, some things became clear.

I had nine full colonels sitting in comfortable offices at a plush base in the Southern United States. Their jobs were spread out all over the country. They had no idea about what actually went on within their regions. They could have an alcoholic commandant, or one that could hardly walk and they were clueless to the situation. That made no sense to me.

The next thing was the region that each of them had to supervise. Although they made a semblence of geographic sense, some of the territories divided states or had irregular geographic boundaries. Two campuses, only a few miles apart, might be in different geopgraphic areas under two different area commanders.

Some of the schools interacted with Junior ROTC programs in high schools. This dictated another level of interaction with city and county governments. Sometimes, more than one area commander had to deal with this in the same state. Again, this was not a sensible way to handle things.

Area commanders visited their detachments twice a year. Most of the time, they were in Alabama forming a close bond with each other. They had blurred the line between command and staff. The pervasive attitude was that ideas should be passed by them for their input before any action was taken. That allowed for a lot of spin-doctoring and turf-protecting.

I called my two sharpest lieutenant colonels in for a conference about the situation. "Gentlemen, I have nine colonels sitting around this office who should be out in the field where their charges are. I want you to divide the United States into seven regions from the current nine. I want no states cut up. Put whole states in each region."

"Next, I want you to look for a military base we can use as their headquarters. Try for something as close to the center of each geographic region as you can get. It would of course have to be an Air Force base. See if we can get office space for an area commandant, his secretary and deputy and a few enlisted men for support. When you have it all together, let's go over it in detail," I concluded.

I had nine colonels but only needed seven. Simple math dictated that two of them under the new plan them would have to go. I knew which two they would be. The fellow who had no idea an alcoholic was running one of his detachments was first on that list. The second was a man with a law degree. When I first met him, he came into the office to talk with me about something. He talked on for fifteen or twenty minutes, and when he left, I had no idea what he was talking about. And I consider myself a pretty good listener.

When the plan was complete, I went over it with my guys. They had done a good job. On paper, it looked like a sound idea. It was ready to be presented to the boss, Lieutentant General Al Gillem.

He listened thoughtfully to my presentation and asked a few insightful questions for which I had the answers.

"Approved," he said simply.

Although I don't think it's an appropriate response to your superior officer, and had not done it before or since, I said, "God bless you."

And I meant it. I had poured my heart into the plan, and I felt certain that it was the right thing to do. The two extra colonels decided to retire, and the others were farmed out to their new duty stations.

Not long after this, I learned from my deputy that the Air University staff, who were all colonels as well, had a friend or two among the seven men in my charge who were reassigned. The word on the street was that General White should have passed the proposal through them for their input before it went to General Gillem.

My one-word comment was "Crap!"

There is no reason for a general officer to pass his ideas to a staff of colonels, unless he feels their input could be useful. Since most of them had no idea what we were doing in the ROTC command, I didn't see how they could help me. It was easy for me to see where the ROTC staff got its idea of staff command relations. Given half a chance they would have manipulated a way for their friends to stay in their comfortable offices at Maxwell instead of going out into the field.

Once in the field, the feedback from the seven men was universally positive. To keep a personal hand on things, we had two meetings a year when the seven men flew to Maxwell for a staff meeting where they summarized their activites, brain-stormed and problem solved. They were usually spirited sessions with lots of give and take.

It didn't take long for the new plan to prove its worth. I received a call from the Southwest area commander. He had a problem at Brigham Young University in Provo, Utah.

A traveling brigadier general had stopped to spend the night with the detachment. This was not unusual at detachments where spare quarters were available. While cleaning the room the next morning, a maid found two empty miniature whisky bottles, in a wastebasket. They were the little one-shot bottles from a commercial airplane. She reported this at once to the university officials. Since drinking was forbidden at the Mormon school, it became a critical situation for the area commander.

Located only a couple of hours from Provo, instead of clear across the United States, the area commander was there before the dust settled. He explained that the detachment had nothing to do with the alcohol. They did not supply it. They did not condone its use and were completely unaware that the general had any alcohol in his posession. He assured the university officials that each new transient who stopped for the hospitality of the detachment would be reminded that there was to be no drinking in the rooms. The university accepted his explanation and approved of the education for future visitors. In a matter of hours, the situation was diffused, and it was business as usual.

This was only one of a number of similar occurrences that reinforced the wisdom of the changes we had made in the ROTC command. I felt like a happy parent who sees one of his children do well.

During the implementation of my plan, General Gillem retired and Lieutenant General Felix Rogers took his place. He was a very bright man and a good leader for the Air University. He would subsequently go to the Air Force Logistics Command and retired with his fourth star. General Rogers got to watch my new plan unfurl.

When the next list for promotions came forward, I was pleased to see my name on the list for a second star. I got that star, and it was the first time an ROTC command brigadier had gotten a star while serving this command. The fact that I was purposely chosen to come here to solve a problem, rather than being put out to pasture helped. Still, I'm positive it was my plan to overhaul the supervisory structure of the command that earned me that star.

When the second star actually came through, an impromptu celebration broke out at my house. General Rogers, who was just returning from a trip, stopped by the house to congratulate me. I thanked him for his support.

"No, Bob, it wasn't just me. It was a panel of officers who made that decision," he said.

I knew that was the truth. When it came to promotion to the general ranks, each command in the Air Force met and compiled a list of names to be sent along to the next round of the selection process until all brigadier vacancies were filled. That was the standard operation proceedure.

I found out later that the general threw his significant weight behind my nomination. When the list went out from the Air University, my name was at the top of the sheet. General Rogers comment was, "Bob White is the number one candidate from the Air University. He is my man without question."

As I look back on my time at the Air University with the ROTC command, I am pleased with what I had been able to accomplish. I had left the command in better shape than when I received it. I had laid the foundation of a plan that would keep things running smoothly for a long time. More importantly, I had indirectly helped those like my young friend at the conclave who said, "I just can't wait," to realize their dreams.

As I had told my friend so many years ago, if I could retire a major general, I would consider my military career a huge success. My career was a success. I had my second star, and with it, a new duty station.

Chapter 17

The Last Stop

In 1975, I received what would be my last assignment for the United States Air Force. I was assigned to the 4th Allied Tactical Air Force in Ramstein, Germany. In those days, the cold war was raging, and Allied forces had to be ready for all-out conflict with the Soviet Union.

SHAPE, the Supreme Headquarters Allied Powers Europe, controlled all the land, sea and air forces in Europe. If that sounds vaguely familiar, it should. It is the modern-day equivalent of the World War II SHAFE, Supreme Headquarters Allied Forces Europe. A fellow named Eisenhower was the boss there in the 1940's. SHAPE is now part of a multinational force that included the North Atlantic Treaty Organization; better know by the initials NATO. An attack on any member country would be considered an attack against all of them. The sole purpose was to create a barrier force between the Soviet Union and Western Europe. In today's world, that might not seem so important, but when I went to Ramstein, it was the world's hope to avoid World War III.

Beneath the umbrella of SHAPE, in central Europe, an area consisting of primarily Germany and the Low Countries, there was an Air Force headquarters called Allied Air Forces Central Europe. AAFCE (I told you the Air Force loved acronyms) had command and control of two tactical Air Forces, The 2 ATAF in the north of Germany, and the 4 ATAF, my unit, in the south.

My specific unit, 4 ATAF, was a combination of American, German and Canadian forces whose charge was the southern half of Germany. The British, Dutch and Germans, 2 ATAF, had the northern half of Germany and the Low Countries.

Complicating factors in the equation were the local air forces. Each of the countries involved had its own air force. The German, Canadian and American forces were three separate air forces all stationed at different bases. To put them all in one place would have been too prime a target. Each had its own contingency of aircraft, spare parts, supplies and personnel. In many cases, most of the support equipment was specific to the national unit and could not be shared.

On the opposite end of the spectrum, the 4th Tactical Air Force had no aircraft, spare parts or supplies, and the only personnel we had were the headquarters' staff and communications networks. In the event of hostilities, these air forces were "chopped" into the command of the 4th Tactical Air Force. It sounds unwieldy, and it was. But, it was a political contingency necessary to satisfy the needs of the individual countries whose air forces had their own idiosyncrasies and would be yielding their individuality to the multinational force. I doubt it would have succeeded any other way. It worked pretty well in the exercises we conducted. Fortunately, we never actually had to go to war. Three wars during a career is enough.

It was a compromise on the command side as well. SHAPE had subunits of control. The commanding officer of the United States Air Force Europe, who was a member of the SHAPE staff, wore two hats. His first task was to control the wings, men material and supplies of the United States Air Force units stationed in all of Europe.

When the multinational NATO forces were activated, he put on his second hat as commanding officer of Allied Air Forces Central Europe, AACFE. As you read on be sure you keep your acronyms straight.

My commanding officer at the 4th Tactical Air Force was Lieutenant General Karl Heinz Grieve, pronounced Grāve-ah, of the German Air Force. A World War II bomber pilot with the German Luftwaffe, he ended the war as a major when the German Air Force was demobilized. When the German Air Force was reorganized and reinstituted, he came out of retirement and went back to active duty. I was to be his chief of staff, and vice commander of the 4th Allied Tactical Air Force.

Before the reorganization that created AAFCE, the American general's second hat would have been command of the 4th Tactical Air Force that would act as a separate command for the duration of hostilities. That happened shortly before I arrived at Ramstein. Now, we were part of AAFCE.

As with my last assignment, my predecessor was still at Ramstein when I arrived. Once a week, he had regularly attended the United States Air Force General staff meeting at USAFE headquarters also at Ramstein Air Force Base. Mimicking corporate America, the military has its share of bureaucracy, endless meetings and corporate conclaves.

Following in my predecessor's footsteps, I attended a couple of those staff meetings. During this time, I had a chance to size up General Grieve, and I got the distinct feeling that my three-star boss wasn't pleased with these arrangements. I analyzed my own thoughts and came to a decision. My job was to be the General's chief of staff. If going to those meeting made him feel insecure, or if he felt he was being spied upon, then I had no business going to them.

The day following the last meeting I attended, I said to him, "General Grieve, I fully understand my position in this unit. I am here to serve you as your chief of staff. I won't be going to any more of the American Air Force General staff meetings. My job is here, and I have enough to do."

I could tell by the hint of a smile that creased the corners of his usual no-nonsense countenance that the decision pleased him, and it was the beginning of a truly rewarding friendship. That was best reflected by a Friday afternoon episode at the office.

The command was divided into a number of branches. There were branches for air defense, logistics, intelligence and the like. A special subunit, not ordinarily found in an air wing was the exercise branch. No, they didn't have a gym and organize morning calisthenics. Their job was to create drills, war games and alerts to keep the wing combat ready.

Unlike in the States, where we worked right up till five on most Fridays, in Europe the headquarters command shut down in the early afternoon, and each of the subunits of the command had their own little after-shutdown "social hour." I think cocktail hour would have fit the description better, because unlike the alcohol-free bases in the States, that wonderful German beer flowed freely.

Our section included General Grieve, me, his driver and clerical personnel from both the German and American staffs. Over a mug and some pretzels each Friday, we discussed everything imaginable, but inevitably, the general and I ended up telling war stories or "hanger stories" as they might be called today. As we held court, the enthralled faces and wide-eyed looks of the enlisted men told us we had a receptive audience.

One day, perhaps after one stein more than usual, in the midst of a World War II reflection I said, "I only made one big mistake in World War II."

With a smile, General Grieve asked, "And, what was that?"

Pointing my finger at my boss I said, "I didn't shoot you down!"

After a moment of hesitation, the general howled with laughter and whacked me on the shoulder in good-natured fashion. The shocked look on the faces of the enlisted men was priceless. But the episode truly reflected the friendship we had developed.

Once General Grieve was walking through the area and saw a copy of *Playboy* magazine that one of the enlisted men had in his possession. As was his custom, when something didn't translate for him, he made up his own word or phrase to fit the situation. And, he was never inhibited from speaking his mind on any subject. After that, *Playboy* was known as the "Naked Eye Book."

On another occasion, I accompanied him on a visit to an air wing at Zweibruken. On the way back, we stopped at the city of Saarbruchen to visit an old friend of the general's who was mayor of the town. As the two men rattled on in German, I tried to follow the conversation as best I could. Not long into their reunion, the mayor produced a bottle of rye whiskey from his desk drawer, and we had a round or three of drinks. Drinking and driving was not an issue. The staff car and driver were waiting patiently, and soberly, outside.

On the way back in the car, General Grieve said, "You know General White, when you drink, your German gets better!"

My boss was also a major league diabetic. If he were in the Unites States Air Force, it may have been enough to get him an early retirement. Certainly it would have grounded him. On a visit to his doctor for his annual flight physical, his flamboyant nature surfaced in spades.

"General, you know with your blood sugar as it is, you shouldn't be flying," the doctor said.

Although he didn't fly a great deal, the general flew an F-104 on weekends to his home in Bavaria so he could spend time with his family who lived there. He was not about to stop.

Reaching into his ever-present briefcase, General Grieve laid a pistol on the doctor's desk.

"I will keep flying, *yes!*" he said, and it was not a question.

"Yes, sir!" the doctor replied and signed the physical fit for flying.

How could anyone not love working for a guy like that?

The peacetime headquarters, as well as our personal quarters at Ramstein were quite comfortable. Today, as it was then, Ramstein is part of the Kaiserslautern Military Community and serves as headquarters for USAFE and is also a NATO installation. The base is near the town of Ramstein, in the rural district of Kaiserslautern, Germany. Besides Americans, the installation's population is comprised of Canadian, German, British, French, Belgian, Polish, Czech, Norwegian, Danish and Dutch forces.

Our wartime headquarters were another matter. An old German World War II ammunition storage facility built into a small mountain was to be used if hostilities erupted. It was the assessment of our engineers, with whom I heartily agreed, that a well-placed, modern conventional bomb would bring down the roof of this non-reinforced space. It was so fragile we didn't even bother to mention a hit with a nuclear weapon. High on our priority list was a new war headquarters.

Part of our job was particularly frustrating. Most of them centered around not owning anything. We had no actual hardware, aside from our communications network, and the only troops we commanded in peace-time were members of the headquarters staff.

Still, it was our main task to prepare the command for war. Using the "chopped" forces at our disposal in the time of war, we had to be ready for anything from a conventional ground attack to an all-out nuclear strike. That's where the exercises came into play, pun intended.

War games are as old as military history. The game of chess was designed to teach military strategy. The Japanese strikes on both Pearl Harbor and Midway in World War II were played out on the deck of a carrier for Admiral Yamamoto's commanders before the actual strikes took place. We used an updated electronic version that was designed to do the same thing. And I loved the games. It was the closest thing to combat we could get. More importantly, all the casualty reports were only on paper.

The drills were of different varieties. The simplest was the scramble drill. An alert would be called, and we would be timed as to how fast could assemble for action. Usually they went off without incident.

One night, my good friend Colonel George Dornberger, chief of our exercise branch, and I were out to dinner when an alert came. We went straight to the headquarters from the restaurant dressed in our civilian clothes. We were criticized by one of the German officers, who was on duty when the alert came, for not being in uniform. I didn't respond to him, because I didn't want to create a ruckus in the middle of a drill, but I took it up later with General Grieve.

"We didn't know this wasn't the real thing. There might have been Soviet tanks rolling through the mountain passes while we're at home changing clothes," I told him.

He made no comment, but he nodded, and I knew he agreed with me. During another exercise, a German Army four-star came into the headquarters in his combat camouflage uniform and took us to task because we were dressed only in our standard work uniform. We had on uniform shirts and ties with rank insignia on the shoulders. Our jackets were nearby but on hangers.

"Why are you not dressed in combat camouflage?" the four-star demanded.

Pointing a finger at his boss, General Grieve said, "I can die in this uniform just as easily as you can in that one!"

Two or three times a year, we had general combat exercises. They were a lot of fun. I remember one of those in particular. We were being attacked by the Soviets, and General Grieve was in charge of the defenders. I had the Soviet order of battle and played the attacker. The exercise allowed maximum time for strategizing and looking for unique ways to respond to the various situations.

I wrote a message that detailed a massing of Soviet fighter wings on a

Czech air base as a prelude to a huge air strike on NATO's communications, command and control centers in the west. The message was a dummy. There was nothing at the Czech base. Then, I told George Dornberger, the exercise commander, to release the message in a fashion that was sure to be intercepted by the aggressors. He followed my instructions, and my ploy worked.

As a result, General Grieve executed a massive raid on the base only to find it empty. At the same time, I launched anti-air missiles across all of southern Germany and included attacks on airfields that might render them unusable for at least twenty-four hours. I quickly followed up on my advantage. After forty-eight hours, my side controlled the sky over South Central Europe. I had completely neutralized my boss's entire air force! The referees decided to stop the exercise there, and re-set it because without an air arm, my opponent had no chance to win. A game certainly, but it gave staffs an opportunity to work on tactics, think in real time and to be better prepared when and if the real thing came.

At the after-exercise briefing, General Grieve said, "After this, our headquarters command cannot be on two different sides in the same exercise. We must be one. We must be one against the enemy as it would be if it were not an exercise. It is too difficult to do it this way." Looking directly at me, he added, "Particularly when you have a smart American general running the other side."

The general was a good man, but he handed out very few kudos. This was as close to a compliment as one could ever get. The fact that he did it in the presence of the entire staff made me feel particularly honored.

Usually once a year, we had a General staff meeting with SHAPE in Casteau, Belgium, near Brussels. There was an opportunity to interact with officers from all the NATO countries. They were professionally and socially rewarding.

At that time, General Alexander Haig was the NATO commander. At one of these meetings, I was standing in a chow line, and General Haig fell into line behind me.

"General, why don't you go ahead up to the front of the line?" I asked.

"No, that's okay. I'll wait here," he said, and we proceeded to have an affable conversation.

I know he had a little trouble with his next job at the White House, but I thought he was a good person and a capable leader of NATO when I served under him.

Professionally, the time at Ramstein was rewarding, particularly my relationship with the other general officers in the command. I've already characterized my boss, General Grieve. The brigadier in the command was quite different.

The brigadier was a Canadian named McNickel. A good officer, he had an outrageous personality to boot. He had an abiding fondness for bagpipe music that he relished in playing at ear-splitting levels after a pint or two of German beer. And he was the life of any party.

We were a good staff. Each of us had markedly different personalities and demeanors. That allowed us to bring to the table our own strengths and to cancel out each other's weaknesses. I thoroughly enjoyed my time with them. Unfortunately, things didn't go as well in my private life. Not long after my mother died, my father came to Germany to live with us. His eyesight was almost gone, and it was an additional burden on Doris that caused some friction between us. Military life is stress enough. A good example was when Doris was delivering a child for the fourth time in her life, just short of age forty-three while I was off flying combat missions in Southeast Asia. I'm afraid that the accumulation of things finally got to Doris.

After we had been in Germany for two years, Doris announced that she had had enough of Europe and wanted to go home to the United States. Our oldest daughter, Pamela, graduated from high school in Ramstein, and was off to college at the University of Florida. Greg, our oldest, had left home to enlist in the U.S. Coast Guard. Maureen, our younger daughter, had graduated from high school in Ramstein and had a job in the Base Exchange in one of the back rooms handling money. She must have enjoyed it, because she is now an executive in the corporate offices of Regents Bank in Alabama. She, too, was ready to go back to the States. Dennis, who was only ten at the time, would have to live with what we decided. In the meantime, I think my father sensed that the atmosphere in the house was cool and tense.

While having lunch with me in town one day, Dad said, "I'm getting homesick, and I'd like to go home." Subsequently, I took him to Frankfurt for a flight to New York. My brother met him there and took him to his nice home just north of New York City where Dad would live with him. It was the last time I would see my father before I flew home for his funeral.

I arranged for Doris's departure. I had my car shipped to New York. I flew to New York, picked up the car, and drove to Charleston, South Carolina, where I met Doris and the children as they arrived from Germany. We drove to Fort Walton Beach, Florida. I purchased a house in Shalimar for them, left the car and returned to Germany. We concluded that our life together was essentially over, and agreed formally to a divorce that was filed in 1977 and became reality in 1980.

The breakup of a marriage may imply it must be accompanied by vitriol and enmity. That is not necessarily so. Much to her credit, Doris has actually pursued maintaining strong family ties with the children and with family reunions. Upon my return to the United States with my second wife Chris, we were able to participate in several of my family reunions.

Once, at Christmas time, we had a reunion at my oldest son Greg's home in Orlando, Florida. Greg had invited Doris, and she and Chris chatted amiably in an exemplary example of civility. On another occasion, Pamela invited Maureen, Doris, Chris and me to dinner at her house. The discourse was animated, much of it centered on children. There was no rancor anywhere.

I have always provided materially for Doris without reservation. When Chris and I decided to marry, I explained to Chris that I had a financial obligation to Doris and the children. I'll never forget her response.

"Of course, if you did not assume and continue that obligation, I would lose the respect I have for you," she said.

Once again the forces that guide my life had looked favorably upon me. Doris, as my first wife and the mother of our children, will always have that special place in my heart. And, each day I spent with Chris was a joy. Their interaction with each other speaks more about the quality of the two women in my life than anything else I could say.

Fortunately, both Doris and I have a good relationship with all our children. As I mentioned, Gregory had left for the Coast Guard and Pam for the University of Florida. Unfortunately, I think our divorce may have been more difficult for Maureen and Dennis who were still at home. Despite that, they have both grown to be fine adults.

I returned to the United States, as I often did, to visit my children and my friends. On one occasion I was with Dennis, who had graduated from high school and was doing odd jobs. I convinced him that he needed to continue his education. He agreed and finished a junior college program and went on to graduate from the University of Northern Florida.

Maureen, on the other hand, was not a bit interested in schooling and came at it the hard way. She worked through the banking system from the ground up until finally reaching an executive position at the largest bank in Alabama.

After college, Greg joined the Coast Guard with an eye on a sea-going military career. Unfortunately, he proved to have an anatomic inner ear problem that left him prone to violent and intractable motion sickness. Every time he went to sea, he was incapacitated by the nausea and vertigo. This was obviously incompatible with a career in the Coast Guard. He was transferred to New York where he worked on a new traffic control system for New York Harbor. His performance was exemplary, and his commanding officer was impressed with him, but he also advised Greg of the obvious. His motion sickness would be the death knell of a career in a sea-going service.

About that same time, my father passed away, and I returned to New York for his funeral service. Of course, Greg was there, too. After the funeral, he approached me very hesitantly and asked, "What would you think if I left the Coast Guard to go to college?"

"Of course, considering your motion sickness problem, it makes perfect sense to me," I replied. Since I was a career military officer, he was afraid that I might insist on a military career for him. Nothing was further from the truth. What was good for me certainly did not have to be good for my children. Greg was tremendously relieved by my answer.

During my three years at Ramstein, I met with the four-star general in command of USAFE to discuss my future. I only had a couple of years left after this assignment, and I wanted to finish my career in Ramstein.

It is a part of military life. Progression through two stars is accomplished through the selection board process. After that, it becomes a designation process. The closer you get to the top of the pyramid, the less room there is. The jobs that carry with them that third star are hand-picked from the much larger two-star pool. Since I was obviously not in the hand-picked group, I wanted to stay in a job I liked until the end.

When I made my request, the general said, "You've done a good job here, and your boss likes you. I see no reason why you can't stay."

Career Management 101 strikes again.

At this same time, the construction of the new war headquarters was well underway near the German town of Ruppertsweiler. Due to its proximity to Heidelberg, it made logistical sense to move our peacetime headquarters to that venue. I never conducted any exercises in the new facility, because it wasn't completed until after I had retired, and the Soviet Union was disintegrating.

My time in Heidelberg was delightful. A beautiful town along a picturesque river, it is dominated by an ancient fortress and is home to an historic university. Mark Twain spent a great deal of time in the city and agreed with my assessment of it.

The routine there was the same as it had been in Ramstein. We occupied ourselves with intelligence assessments and preparedness drills. Military service has been described as ninety percent tedium and boredom and ten percent sheer terror. Fortunately, on my watch, we never experienced that ten percent that we constantly prepared for.

While in Heidelberg, I became better acquainted with Chris Kasper, the secretary for United States Army General Erick Shinseki, who was involved in the administrative changes that saw the emergence of AIRCENT, the acronym for Air Forces Central Europe, the new entity into which the 4th Tactical Air Force was folded. LANDCENT, for Land Forces Central

Europe, was formed at the same time. General Shinseki was the boss of the latter. Chris and I began to date on a regular basis.

Later, after surviving in Bosnia, General Shinseki was the chief of staff of the Army when the decision to invade Iraq was made. He strongly suggested a bigger force, and made his opinion clear. It proved detrimental to his career when his decision became an unpopular one.

I had been having trouble with a torn meniscus in my right knee, and it finally reached the point where something had to be done. Minimally invasive arthroscopic surgery was still years away, so I had it repaired the old-fashioned way—they opened me up. I was told I would be out of commission for some time, but vowed to make that time as short as possible.

The rehabilitation was considerably more difficult than I had anticipated. I was on crutches or a cane for three full months before I could walk unaided. One day, after completing 1,048 leg lifts with a weight tied to my ankle—yes, I actually counted as I did repetitions of twenty each—I was finally able to walk across the room without a cane. It literally bought tears to my eyes.

In mid-1980, my divorce from Doris was finalized, and in December, Chris and I were married. I had arranged for us to go to Berlin for our honeymoon. Chris had never been there before. We would take a duty train that had to pass through East Germany.

The duty train stopped at Potsdam, site of the famous post–World War II conference, and a Russian officer inspected all passports that had been collected for that purpose. Chris was particularly nervous; because of her job, she had a top-secret military clearance. So did I, but she had a German passport. Nothing adverse happened, and we arrived safely at the central railroad station in Berlin.

A staff car was waiting, and we were soon on the outskirts of Berlin. Despite her entreaties, I wouldn't tell her where we were headed. In a short time we were in the picturesque and historic Wansee District.

Turning into a long driveway, we came to a gate where two German soldiers stood guard. After verifying my identification, the gates swung open. The car started down another sweeping drive. We came to a stop in front of a palatial mansion. The driver opened the door, and we got out.

"Is this it?" she asked, and I nodded.

"What is it, a hotel?" she asked again.

"No, it's a private residence, not a hotel," I replied as her jaw went slack with surprise.

It was actually the official guest house of the commandant of West Berlin and sat on the shore of Lake Wansee. The beautiful lake is infamous as the site of the Final Solution House, where the 3rd Reich high command met to plot the destruction of the Jews, but I had no idea how close we were to that historic site.

"Who all will be here?" she asked.

"No one, just us and the staff," I said.

The mansion was usually reserved for guests of the United States ambassador or other high-ranking government officials in West Berlin. The guest book read like a who's who of the military and political world. Since it was the New Year's holiday, the house was empty except for a cook and a butler.

It was a great spot for a honeymoon, and we stayed there for three nights. We had the car and driver, and toured West Berlin during the day. The cook was a good one and we ate most of our meals at the mansion.

The real surprise to both of us came at check-out time. I knew our food and drinks came from common military stores, and I knew it would be a reasonable bill. But with three days and nights at the equivalent of a world class resort and spa, our tab was a whopping thirty dollars! Even in 1980 dollars that's a bargain.

From right, Lieutenant General Karl Heinz Grieve, Chris Kasper-White, me, and the commander of U.S. Air Forces Europe in Ramstein, Germany, for the presentation of my Distinguished Service Medal. The medal is for service and is the highest non-combat award available to a uniformed serviceman.

In 1981, when it came time for me to leave the military, there was an important decision to make. Chris was still working and although she was willing to resign and go back to the United States with me, I didn't view that as a good decision. In a few more years, she could retire with a pension and full medical benefits. Besides, I had always been intrigued at the opportunity of living in Europe as an expatriate. We decided to stay in Heidelberg and allow Chris to continue to work.

My retirement was rather simple. It began a few days before my actual retirement date when the commander of U.S. Air Forces Europe pinned the Distinguished Service Medal on me. The medal is for service and is the highest non-combat award available to a uniformed serviceman.

At the same time, thanks to the efforts of my old friend, General Grieve, the commander of the 4th ATAF hung the German's Knight's Cross for service around my neck. It was an award that could be given to a non–German. It was a proud day for me.

On the day of my retirement, I walked out of my office. The entire staff had turned out and lined the walls of the hallway. I went down the stairs where the walls were again lined with well-wishers. Outside at street level, I stood with the Canadian general who was our deputy of operations as a bugler blew taps and the American flag came down the flagpole. The Canadian general and I shook hands. I got into my staff car and was driven home for the last time.

I was glad that it was a simple send-off from the people at 4th ATAF. I felt very good. I made it through thirty-two and one-half years of military service, three wars, and I was still in one piece. How could I not be pleased and completely satisfied about what I'd done with my career? I could drive away and never look back

Since we had decided to stay in Europe, it didn't take me long to acclimate. It was a wonderful experience. We used every opportunity to travel: Spain, North Africa, Italy, France and the Slavic States. We didn't venture too far north, but we went everywhere else. In 1997, Chris was ready to retire, and in all honesty, I was ready to head back to the States to begin the next chapter in this wonderful thing we call life.

Chapter 18

Going Home

Staying in Europe for an extended time after my retirement wasn't burdensome to me. Many years before, when I was still a major, I told a colleague who had never been to Europe how much I liked being there.

"After I retire, I wouldn't mind spending some time there as an expatriate," I told him. I did, and I loved it.

Many people look toward retirement with trepidation. Some can't let go of the job, either out of real love for the job, or an over-inflated opinion of their value to the workplace. Others simply can't imagine what they will do with all the free time now at their disposal. I suppose it's a control issue as much as anything. I never had any such issues. When the time came, I was ready. "Been there, done that, got the T-shirt," as the popular expression goes today.

All my life, I have dealt with the decisions and difficulties of life as nothing more than problems that needed to be solved, or jobs that needed to be done. There are any number of plans and solutions that can handle specific jobs and solve individual problems. I just had to figure out which one worked for each situation.

I have also never been one to look backwards or have regrets. Oh, if there was something that happened last week, I might say, "Gee I'm sorry I didn't do this or that," or "I wish I had done that another way." Then, it's a lesson learned. Get over it and get on with things. To go back and moan about what might have been or could or should have been is counterproductive to say the least.

I also have to say that I felt extremely satisfied with my military career. It had been everything and more than I could have hoped for. The dreams of that ten-year-old boy on the steps in New York had gotten up there ... way up there!

Serving my country in three great conflicts gave me an intense sense of pride in a job well done. I had been fortunate enough to be part of aviation history with the X-15, and to shape the future of military combat aircraft with the F-15. I had helped to restructure the ROTC program to better serve the next generation of officers and pilots. I had even achieved my "impossible dream," that second star! What more could I ask for?

Being career military had another distinct advantage when it came to retirement. At each step along the career path, I bumped up against the possible end of my career as I either was selected for advancement or passed over, which would have severed my ties with the military. A sudden return to civilian life was the next promotion away for those of us in the military. When I was not in the hand-picked group for the third star, I saw the end of my military career at least two years before the actual retirement date came. I can't think of anything I would have changed or done differently. I could be proud of what I've done. But it was time to move on, and I did it without regret.

Was it totally without emotion? Of course it wasn't. I had many friends and colleagues that I was close to, but I knew those ties would loosen and dissolve with the passage of time. I would miss them. And since I had spent most of my adult life in the military, there would be some necessary adjustments when I transferred to civilian life. My orders might not be so eagerly obeyed, and people might actually tell me that they disagreed with me.

My emotions were best summarized by the Canadian general who was standing beside me on that last day. I had walked outside, and we were standing at attention saluting the flag as it crawled down the staff lowering the colors for the day, but also for the last time in my military career. After piping down the colors, the bugler added one more poignant chorus.

As the last plaintive note of the bugle echoed into silence, the Canadian general turned to me and asked, "How do you keep a dry eye?"

It was a question for which I didn't have a good answer at the time. Mostly, I suppose, I'm not an outwardly emotional person. I just never look back, and I was anticipating my retirement. That's the best answer I could come up with in retrospect.

I enjoyed retirement, and I loved the little village of Sandhausen, Germany, where we lived. Chris was approaching her own retirement, and we downsized into a small apartment in anticipation of moving back to the United States. The scenario was eased immensely by Chris's positive attitude. She couldn't wait to get to America. I have to admit as we approached that final year, I had the itch to return to the good old USA as well.

While we were living in Germany, each year we came back to St. Petersburg, Florida to stay in a condo for a month. I had enjoyed the city and the sunny weather when I'd been stationed there in the 1940s, and thought I'd like to live there after retirement. Having my old friend and fellow fighter pilot George Dornberger in the area was a plus. I always enjoyed spending time with him.

Each time Chris and I visited, we scoured the area for potential home sites. It was a pleasant task since there were a plethora of attractive neighborhoods to choose from.

One area we visited, south of Tampa, near the tomato farming community of Ruskin, was called Sun City Center. Brainchild of the entrepreneur Del Web, it was a community for senior citizens. At least one member of the couple had to be fifty-five years old to purchase property there.

Chris and I enjoyed playing golf, and as part of a promotional package, we received a free round of golf at the excellent golf course in Kings Point, the gated community that is a subdivision of Sun City Center. We loved the course, and the people we came into contact with were very friendly.

The rest of the community was pleasant; the amenities bountiful and the bang for the buck was exactly what we were looking for. There was only one drawback as far as Chris was concerned.

"It is really very nice, but there are a lot of old people there," she said in her honest, matter-of-fact way.

I didn't think it prudent to point out that very shortly we would be two of those "old people" and would fit right in. Despite that impression, we eventually decided on a condo in Sun City Center. Since I had been in the military or in some foreign country much of my life, I had little in the way of a credit history in the States. To begin to build that history, we took out a small mortgage of $35,000 on the condominium which would be built over the next six months or so while we were still in Germany. As soon as the home was finished, and everything was as it should be, we would pay off that mortgage in the next year and a half and cement our credit rating. I hoped it wouldn't be another Dayton home building experience. Fortunately, it wasn't.

A secondary reason for choosing Sun City Center was its proximity to MacDill Air Force Base with its medical facilities and commissary. We joined the MacDill credit union as well. That was all well and good, but the thought of escaping the long, drab, cold winters of Central Europe was an equally strong incentive. We headed back to Germany to finish out Chris's employment and get packed to come home.

Actually, there was little packing to do, and the time passed quickly. We prepared one small shipment of dining room furniture and personal belongings. Other than that, it was our suitcases and the clothes on our backs.

Multiple moves are a part of military life that is inescapable. Although it is impossible not to collect a certain amount of "things," each time a move is made, the closets are cleaned, the cupboards bared and excess "things" jettisoned. Many of the more permanent pieces of furniture and the mementoes of our years in the military had gone to the States with Doris. Chris and I lived quite simply though very comfortably. And with our vagabond attitude about life and travel, we hadn't collected a great deal of our own "things."

Although she had lived her entire life in Germany, Chris was anxious to go America to live. It meant leaving her two adult children Judith and Sven behind, but she was ready to go. She would still be able to call and visit with them often.

We went to the United States Embassy in Frankfurt, Germany, and waded through the necessary paperwork to apply for Chris's green card. Aside from the tedious lines and the seemingly endless forms, the process went smoothly enough. When we had run the gauntlet, we were given a sealed envelope by the Embassy clerk.

"When you get to the airport in Atlanta, just give this to the customs agent there. It should only take a few minutes, and you'll be just fine," she said with a smile.

It seemed too easy, but it wasn't.

After an uneventful flight from Germany, we arrived in Atlanta, Georgia, a bit jetlagged but filled with anticipation. I had allowed a three-hour layover so we would have plenty of time to make our connecting flight to Florida. When we reached the immigration and naturalization station, Chris handed over the envelope she had been given in Frankfurt to the agent behind the counter.

"You'll have to come with me," said the curt young man with the insignia of a major on his INS uniform jacket.

"I'll handle checking us in with the connecting flight and meet you at the gate," I said.

"No problem. That will be fine," Chris answered with a nervous smile and followed the agent out.

I believed that living in Europe, and being a German in a divided country where immigration was taken seriously and border crossings could get contentious were the reasons for her apprehension.

After an hour's wait at the gate, I began to get concerned. After another thirty minutes, I went in search of my wife. She was still with the INS officer, and no one seemed to know how long it would be. The time came and went for our Tampa departure. Finally after an intolerable wait and the impatient question "How long, Bob?" my angry spouse joined me, and we tried to arrange another flight to Tampa.

Apparently, Chris had been ushered into a room that had a window that looked into the major's office. The man sat at his desk, sipping coffee, shuffling papers, and once or twice he left the room for a few minutes only to return to his desk. He also spent a great deal of time talking to another woman who was in his office. Once she had missed the flight, the agent brought her a form to sign, took her thumb print, and told her she could go.

Chris was upset and angry, and when she told me what had transpired, I was livid. It was all I could do not to return to the office and give the man a piece of my mind. But I did not want to compound the problem so I kept my mouth shut as we left the immigration area past a big sign that said WELCOME TO THE UNITED STATES. Welcome indeed! We finally got to St. Petersburg at twelve-thirty in the morning.

I later learned that there was absolutely no reason for the delay. All the INS needed to do was a brief interview, take the papers from Chris, take her thumbprint and send us on our way. That information did not make me feel any happier about the situation.

Next, we went to the United States consulate in Tampa to begin Chris's trek to citizenship. Of course there were more forms to fill out. We were informed that she normally would need to be living in the United States for five years before she could apply, but since we had been married long term, that wouldn't be necessary and the waiting time was shortened to just three years.

The most onerous portion of the process was the travel record. If someone travels outside the United States for more than six months, a detailed explanation is required. They also wanted specific details on all trips made by the individual for the past five years. To say the least, after living in Europe and traveling abroad, as well as coming back to the United States to St. Petersburg, this was a monumental task. In time, we got it done, complete with detailed whys and wherefores for each one.

Next, Chris had an interview with a female INS agent. She felt that the interview had gone well, although the woman seemed to be a bit curt.

"When will the citizenship ceremony take place?" Chris asked at the end of the interview.

"Don't worry about it. You'll be informed," the agent replied impatiently.

Then we simply had to wait for the bureaucratic wheels to grind. And grind they did, finally spitting out the application form stamped unapproved.

Chris was devastated, and I was hot under the collar. This was impossible! There was not a thing in that application that should have raised a red flag or derailed the process. There had to be another cause. I suspected it was INS incompetence.

Once the temperature under my collar approached normalcy, I composed a diplomatic letter to the INS. We mailed it off and waited ... and waited ... and waited. We never got a response.

So I wrote a second letter with a bit more edge to it. The result was the same. We got no response! In desperation I wrote a third letter to my congressman.

The congressman's reply was timely and simple. Instructions had been relayed to the INS, and Chris was to reapply. Although it meant filling out another batch of forms we were more than eager to do it.

This time, at the end of the paperwork, Chris had a second interview with a male agent. She told him the story beginning with the Atlanta airport. His answer was our vindication.

"It's a tragedy. That's all I can say about it. There is nothing in this application or your background that should have caused this," he said.

They had a great chat; she answered his questions; he complimented her on her command of English, and told her she had been well-prepared.

At the end of the interview he said, "Welcome to the United States of America. You'll make a good citizen."

In retrospect, I'm still at a loss to explain what happened. Maybe the Atlanta INS agent got up on the wrong side of the bed. Maybe he didn't like Germans, or German women, or women in general. Perhaps Chris somehow struck a wrong chord with her first interviewer. I'll never be certain.

The only thing I could even remotely speculate as the reason for the difficulty Chris encountered could perhaps have been related to her father's unfortunate circumstance. He had been a German Air Force officer and spent seven and one half years as prisoner of the Russians.

No one I have ever known was any more patriotic than Chris. She kept up with current events and politics. She closely followed the proceedings of state and federal House and Senate sessions. She studied the candidates and was an informed voter. And it all came shining through at the Tampa Convention Center during the citizenship ceremony.

Hundreds of new Americans gathered for the ceremony. Every continent in the world save Antarctica was represented.

"When your name is called, come up and get your citizenship document. Before you leave the hall, check it carefully. If there is any error, no matter how insignificant, take it to room 227 for corrections. This is very important. Read and check your documents thoroughly and carefully," the man at the podium said.

When they called her name, Chris floated to the flag-decked stage as if her legs were wings and with tears in her eyes accepted her document. When the song, "Proud to Be an American" by Bruce Springsteen poured from the loudspeakers as each new citizen waved a little American flag they had been given with their citizenship document. Chris waved hers so hard I was afraid her arm might fall off.

That love of America never wavered. Several years later in a telephone conversation with her daughter Judith in Germany, Chris surprised Judith with her answer to one of Judith's assumptions.

"I suppose when Bob is gone, you will come back to Germany to live," Judith said.

"No, this is where I live. I'm an American citizen, and this is where I'll stay," Chris responded.

Chris was born in Germany, and she never tried to conceal that fact or dishonor her German lineage. But I don't think I can ever remember her referring to herself as a German-American. When she acquired her American citizenship, she *became* an American.

Before we left the auditorium, we dutifully opened the citizenship folder and read the document. I threw up my hands in surrender to the bureaucracy.

White is a simple, Anglo-Saxon name of Irish derivation. It is the same name as a primary color. On the document in bold letters was the name Chris Whtie. I realize it was probably a typo, but after all we'd been through in this process, it was the last straw.

In room 227 the agent shook his head and said, "You can take this to the INS building across the street, and they will make the change, or I can make the change and send it to you."

"Just send it," I said. "I'll be happy if I never have to set foot in an INS building again."

Considering my prior dealings with the INS it might have been wiser to seek an immediate change, but I was in no mood to have further dealings with them in person.

We arrived at Sun City Center in January of 1998. We decided to keep our small apartment in Germany to use as a summer refuge from the July and August heat of Central Florida. So our condo was quite bare.

At first we stayed in a motel until we bought a bed, a small television and the basic necessities of day-to-day living. Gradually, we furnished our new home a few pieces at a time. This required nearly daily shopping trips. They got to be our private joke. After a day of extended shopping, I would check today's receipts and say, "Gee, this is a great day. We only spent $925 today.

Our major recreation in those early days was golf. As I mentioned, the courses at Kings Point were available to us, and we played often. One day, the starter asked us that if we would mind if another couple joined us. We readily agreed, and they introduced themselves to us.

Jack and Maureen Johnsonbaugh turned out to be delightful. We had a great time sparked by a hint of humor. During the course of the round, Jack asked me what I had done for living, and I told him that I had made my career in the Air Force. Jack related that he, too, was in the military. Then he asked me my rank. I told him I was a retired major general.

Leaping from his golf cart, Jack snapped me a crisp salute and said, "General, I was only an enlisted man. Pleased to meet you, sir," he said with a smile, and that was the beginning of what has been an enduring friendship.

Over a beer in the clubhouse, Jack told me about a new golf group that was being formed from some men who had split off from a group that was getting too large. He asked me if I might be interested in joining them, and I said I was. He nominated me for membership in the new group that called itself, Dilligas, and I was accepted for membership.

The new group had thirty-six players, enough to fill nine of the twenty-seven holes at the golf club. We played twice a week and had a monthly golf scramble that included wives, sweethearts and significant others. The scramble was followed by a dinner party. It was a a great way to make friends and for Chris to meet some of the other women. I still play with the group regularly.

I needn't have worried about Chris being lonesome. She had no problem developing a circle of her own friends, and we soon felt right at home in Sun City Center. It was indeed the right choice for us.

Our summer trips to Germany consisted of two months the first year, nearly two the second year, and one month the third year. We found that, except for family, our circle of friends there had disappeared. Going back to Sandhausen recalled the old Tom Wolfe statement, "You can't go home again."

Chris had family there, and it was always nice to visit with them. They were gregarious, spirited and welcomed me as family. I remember one relative who lived on a very large farm. I have fond memories of climbing into his plum tree to pick the ripe fruit and eating it while gazing across a lush German countryside of crops as far as the eye could see.

We also continued to do some traveling. Although we had traveled extensively, we had never been to Rome. Chris was not a Catholic, but she eagerly accompanied me on an inspirational journey to the seat of Catholicism. Because of my heritage, I wanted to see Ireland, and we went there as well. I admit to some genetic bias, but short of the Australians, the Irish are the friendliest people in the world.

Despite that, I was becoming weary of long plane trips, and we mutually agreed there was little reason to keep our German apartment. Chris was free to visit her kids whenever she wanted to, so we gave up the apartment and ceased to be long-distance "snowbirds."

Chris did make several trips to see her children, but once while she was away, a hurricane descended on our community. All she got on the European news channels was the horror stories cable news networks are so fond of propagating. She was beside herself until I reported the storm had passed with minimal impact.

When she got home, Chris put her feelings for me into words when she said, "I will never leave you again."

Settling into retirement, I had time to reflect on a satisfying career through requests from people around the world for information and autographs. In the beginning, when I was actively flying the X-15 with all its attendant publicity, there were times when we pilots felt like rock stars. Whenever I made a public appearance, autograph seekers were in abundance. We were constantly bombarded with requests for autographs or signed pictures of the X-15. When the history of the experimental plane was written, a whole new generation seemed interested in those pioneering years. Although the number of requests has diminished, I still get ten to fifteen pieces of mail per month from young and old alike.

I never considered myself a star of any kind for that matter. I was simply a man who made the most of his opportunities, did every job I was given to the best of my ability, and tried to treat everyone with whom I came into contact with respect and dignity. If that somehow is inspirational to others, so be it. If my example allows one dreamy-eyed boy or girl on steps somewhere in the United States, Poland or Czechoslovakia, to get "up there" and follow their dreams, that makes me as proud as anything else I have accomplished in my life.

Chapter 19

Reflections

My years of retirement in Sun City Center have been fulfilling. Unlike in the military, where rank is always there and a certain "pecking order" is essential to smooth operations, retirement is the great equalizer. Although most of my friends know that I was an Air Force general and that I flew the X-15, to everyone here I'm just Bob, one of the guys. You know, I like it that way.

Fame came to me in the course of doing my job. I never sought it. I never relished it. To say that rubbing elbows with presidents and being photographed with movie stars isn't exciting would be less than truthful. But it was just part of the job. I realized that it was all fleeting, and when I drove home after one of those events, I usually felt a sense of relief at being back in my element; back where I belonged.

One aspect of the notoriety that never ceases to amaze me is the fan mail. When I started in the X-15 program as a captain, literally cargo bags of mail poured in from aviation enthusiasts all over the planet. That was clearly not surprising. We were doing cutting-edge flight research, using the most modern technology available. The avalanche of letters was certainly to be expected.

As individuals, answering that much fan mail would have been an insurmountable task for any of us. Thank heaven for the Air Force Public Information Office. They did the lion's share of the trench work, and the rest of us did what we could to help.

I have never resented one moment of the time and energy devoted to fan mail. Again, I considered it part of the job, and part of my responsibility for the privilege of being involved in the X-15 project. I just wish I had a nickel, or perhaps with inflation I should say a quarter, for every picture I have signed over the years.

The amazing aspect of the fan mail is that it has never stopped! To be sure, the avalanche of letters slowed, at first to a torrent. Then it became a flow and at last a trickle as the years since 1962 have flown by. But that trickle has never stopped! Despite the fact that it's been more than four decades since the X-15's mighty engines fell silent for the last time, it is a rare week that passes without one or two pieces of mail, many from people who hadn't yet been born when I flew the X-15.

Ever since the mail has been reduced to a doable number of pieces a week, I have personally responded to each of them. I never allow them to pile up on the corner of the desk for fear I will procrastinate until the pile reaches a daunting height. I never let it get more than two high before I answer. I consider it an honor.

A number of the requests are for signed photographs. Thanks to the professional website at www.bobwhitex15.net, instigated by my friend Al Hallonquist and put together by Kevin Taylor, a web site professional, I ask those requesting pictures to download them from the site, or any other site, and I'll gladly sign them promptly. And requests still comes in from all around the world.

I don't consider myself a hero. I was just doing a job. But if what I have been able to accomplish by being at the right place at the right time has inspired one young dreamer to "go for it," my life has been meaningful. In that vein, many of my fellow retirees have asked me if I ever get the urge to climb into an airplane and get back up there. I can honestly say I do not.

What would I do if I couldn't fly anymore? That's the same question the factory worker, office worker, doctor, lawyer and Indian chief ask themselves. What will I do if I don't go to the plant or the office? What will my patients or clients do without me? Who will lead the braves on the warpath? If I could no longer fly, I'd find something else to do. Fortunately for me, I had time to prepare for a life without flying.

Throughout my entire career, including when I was a brigadier general at Edwards, I was able to fly. When the second star came along, I knew it was over. That gave me a splendid opportunity to reconcile myself with the fact that when I got into an airplane again, someone else will likely be at the controls.

Reflecting on my career assisted in the reconciliation. In my lifetime I had the opportunity to fly nearly everything in the Air Force arsenal, from my old P-51 to bombers, nearly every significant jet fighter of the time, vertical takeoff and landing craft, helicopters and even a commercial 747. And I was privileged to be one of the twelve special men who strapped themselves into the cockpit of the X-15. To top it off, I was instrumental in the development of the F-15 Eagle, the dominant fighter plane of its era. I had been more than fortunate. Aviation had been good to me, and that was enough. The job of flying today's jet aircraft belongs to a young man or woman, and I proudly pass the torch to them.

I am still occasionally called upon for a speech or a public appearance. I admit that I decline most of them these days. Travel for me is not as easy as it once was. I do, however, respond to them from time to time. One of them that I did accept reunited me with the X-15.

Some renovation had been planned for the National Air and Space Museum in Washington, D.C. At the completion of the project in 2005 a celebration was planned.

They invited a number of people who had some connection to the relics in the museum to return and represent their piece of history. I was chosen to represent the X-15. So Chris and I packed our bags and headed for Washington. It was a first-class, black-tie affair that occupied an entire weekend. As I walked into the building, surrounded by tangible evidence of aviation history that had been used by the real pioneers of my profession, it was difficult for me to conceptualize that I was one of them.

When I walked into the gallery and looked up, she was there! Suspended from the ceiling was the 35,000 pound monster that I had ridden into space. The thunder of the powerful engine sounded again in my ears. My pulse quickened a beat at the thrill of a launch replayed in my memory. And a wave of nostalgia mixed with sadness tugged at me as the image of the other men who had been there with me, some now gone to their place in history, crowded in on me. How I wished they all could have been there with me to pose for one more group photo. I remain grateful to those at the Smithsonian who chose me to represent so many wonderful people.

In December, I received another honor I will cherish. On Friday, December 16, the Florida Aviation Historical Society, in conjunction with the Florida Air Museum at the Lakeland Airport in Lakeland, Florida, and with Sun 'n' Fun Fly In and the Sun 'n' Fun Fly In Committee held a luncheon to honor the year's inductees into the Florida Aviation Hall of Fame. The attendees were welcomed by the VP of Sun 'n' Fun Fly In, Inc., and museum director Greg Harbaugh. Greg, a former space shuttle astronaut, acted at the master of ceremonies throughout the day.

The president of the Florida Aviation Historical Society, Dr. Michael Bishara, introduced the honorees. Each inductee then was introduced by either the person who nominated them, or someone familiar with them. Of the four inductees, Bell's X-1 test pilot Chalmers H. "Slick" Goodlin and the legendary John Riddle were deceased. Gen. Paul Tibbets, pilot of the B-29 that dropped the world's first nuclear weapon which brought World War II to an end in the Pacific, was unable to attend. Fortunately, I was still living *and* able to attend.

After being introduced by my good friend Al Hallonquist, I spoke about duties and personal aspirations and the state of the country. I surprised the audience by making an announcement that filled me with pride. I would be inducted into the National Aviation Hall of Fame in July of 2006. I had been waiting for this since I was nominated for the hall in 1998. And I was so pleased to do it in the presence of Al Hallonquist, the man who did so much to get me in there. It was worth it all to see the smiles of joy and the pride in the eyes of my wife Chris, sons Greg and Dennis, grandson Greg Junior as well as two colleagues from my test flight days at Edwards, Al Crews and Bud Evans, who were there to support me.

Before I was off to my induction into the Hall of Fame, there was one more stop on the Honor's Trail. It was the Gathering of Eagles at Maxwell Air Force Base, home of the Air University. The university has several divisions, such as the Squadrons Officers School for captains; the Air Command and Staff College for majors; and the Air War College for lieutenant colonels and colonels. When it had been my turn to go there as a major, I was in the Edwards Test Pilot Program. So as not to interrupt that duty, the Air Force allowed me to complete the Command and Staff College by correspondence. I went there this time near the end of the school year in June 2006 for a week with fifteen other members of the Gathering of Eagles Class of 2006.

The Gathering of Eagles is an air and space event that traces its origin back to 1980, when the Air Command and Staff College (ACSC) invited retired Brigadier General Paul Tibbets to visit Maxwell AFB, Alabama, to share some of his experiences with the students. The first official GOE occurred in 1982 when the ACSC leadership energized the faculty to develop an aviation heritage program for the graduating class. The faculty designed a program that encouraged the study of aviation history and emphasized the contributions of aviation pioneers.

It's been a long and rewarding journey from the days when Bob's son Greg (left) sat atop the nose cone of his Dad's F-104 Starfighter at Edwards AFB as a young lad. Here, a beaming father and son celebrate Bob's induction into the National Aviation Hall Of Fame in Dayton, Ohio in July 2006 (Jack Summers personal collection.)

The team, which included four students, selected 15 distinguished aviators and invited them to share their unique personal experiences through a series of teaching interviews and social events with members of the class.

They were a diverse group and included military and civilian aviators who had served in the Air Force, Navy, Marines, Army, and National Aeronautics and Space Administration. The ACSC commandant endorsed their efforts and enthusiastically presented it to the Air University commander who concurred. Their joint support laid the foundation for the current GOE program.

During the initial planning process in 1982, the program became known as "Great Moments in Aviation History." The first "Eagles," as they would later be called, spanned aviation history from World War II to the Space Age. George Vaughn became an ace in the Royal Air Force and then joined the U.S. air service and added more victories. Leigh Wade flew around the world in 1924, only 20 years after the Wright brothers made the first controlled powered flight at Kitty Hawk, North Carolina. Jimmy Doolittle pioneered instrument flying and was a famed air racer. Curtis LeMay helped prove the importance of the Boeing B-17 Flying Fortress. George Gay, Joe Foss, John Mitchell, and Chuck Yeager all earned honors during combat in World War II. Gail Halvorsen demonstrated the "heart" of America during the Berlin Airlift. Paul Tibbets helped test the Boeing B-47 Stratojet, which helped to defend the free world during the Cold War. Gabby Gabreski commanded North American F-86 Sabres through Korea's "MiG Alley." Robin Olds led McDonnell F-4 Phantom raids over the Red River Valley in North Vietnam while Mike Novosel flew Bell UH-1 Hueys in South Vietnam to rescue over 5,500 wounded soldiers and earn the Medal of Honor. Pete Knight went to the edge of space in the North American Rockwell X-15, then Neil Armstrong went "where no man had gone before" and left his footprints on the moon!

The 1982 ACSC graduation dinner began with an opening monologue by Bob Hope. It was a history-making event that spawned the continuation of GOE for 25 years. Others who have been honored include George H. W. Bush; Pappy Boyington; Benjamin O. Davis, Jr.; Jeana Yeager; John Glenn, Jr.; Robbie Risner; Alan Shepard; Steve Ritchie; and Bud Day—just to name a few. You can imagine my feeling at even being mentioned in the same breath as these other men and women.

My class was equally impressive. One of my prize possessions is a wonderful picture showing each of us in our prime as well as our airplane. They were:

F. G. "Hal" Moore	Bell UH-ID Huey
Kevin A. "Mike" Gilroy	Republic F-105F Thunderchief
Barbara Erickson	London Lockheed P-38 Lightning
Paul W. Airey	Consolidated B-24 Liberator
George E. "Bud" Day	North American F-100F Super Saber
Eugene F. "Gene" Kranz	Apollo CSM/LM
Susan J. Helms	Space Shuttle Discovery
Lee A. "Buddy" Archer, Jr.	North American P-51 Mustang
Spiro N. "Steve" Pisanos	Supermarine Spitfire
Kermit A. Weeks	Weeks Solution
Robert M. White	North American X-15 of course
Robert "Rosie" Rosenthal	Boeing B-17 Flying Fortress
Stanley L. Wood	Sikorsky MH-60L Black Hawk
Joseph W. Kittinger, Jr.	McDonnell Douglas F-4D Phantom II
Frederick C. "Boots" Blesse	North American F-86E Sabre

There are 700 students at the Air University, and many of them are members of the air forces of other countries. Each day, three inductees are individually interviewed in front of the entire student body. It was fascinating to hear the life stories of the heroic men and women in this class and to listen to the description of their accomplishments.

I enjoyed my time on the hot seat. The questions were thoughtful, the interview professional, and the entire experience memorable. Benjamin Franklin was dramatically opposed to having the eagle as our national bird. But he never had a chance to meet these eagles, and I was glad to be among them that week.

On July 16, 2006, I received an honor I shall always cherish. I was enshrined into the National Aviation Hall of Fame at Wright Patterson Air Force Base in Dayton, Ohio. When I received the news of my election it was overwhelming. As with any hall of fame, the National Aviation Hall of Fame is a who's who of aviation and space pioneers. From Orville and Wilbur Wright, to the Mercury and Apollo astronauts, and beyond, it's a litany of the history of aviation and space. To think that my name would be there alongside theirs was a singular honor.

The three other people who would join me in the class of 2006 were Bessie Coleman, David Lee "Tex" Hill and Oscar-winning actor Cliff Robertson. As is customary in such ceremonies, we would be presented in alphabetical order, so White would be at the end of the line ... again.

Bessie Coleman was America's first African-American pilot, and woman to boot. She had to go to France to learn how to fly and get a pilot's license because she couldn't get anyone in the United States to teach her.

"Tex" Hill, a fellow Florida Hall of Fame inductee, was one of the original Flying Tigers when he downed twelve of the 297 Japanese planes destroyed by the Tigers. He later came back in a P-51 Mustang instead of his old P-40 and scratched another six Japanese aircraft ranking him among the top American fighter aces. Cliff Robertson is a famous actor who won an Emmy for his leading role in *The Game*, and an Oscar for best actor in *Charlie*. He played President John Fitzgerald Kennedy in *PT 109* as well as appearing in a total of seventy-seven motion pictures. A lifelong aviation enthusiast and pilot, he had long been an ardent supporter of both civil and military aviation. His work in the organization of relief flights to Biafra and Ethiopia, and his work with the EAA's Young Eagles program were among his accomplishments. He also holds a Nevada state distance soaring record.

All weekend long I felt like a movie star. I had my own personal guide for the weekend, a wonderful young Air Force officer. He played "Mother-Hen" for Chris and me the entire weekend. There were briefings, rehearsals, photo shoots, and press interviews. He was our guide, our chauffer and our alarm clock, making sure we were where we were supposed to be on time. Still, we had a lot of time on our own.

More importantly, I had an entourage of family and well-wishers on hand to celebrate the weekend with me. My four children, Greg, Dennis, Pam and Maureen, Chris and her two children, Judith and Sven, and my friends from Florida, Carl and Suzanne Metoff, Jack and Pat Summers, Ted and Dolly Bogel, and Dindy Chandler, Al Hallonquist and George Dornberger came to Dayton to give me more support.

The public activities began with a cocktail party and reception followed by the annual president's dinner on Friday evening. It was an opportunity to see old acquaintances and renew old friendships. Flyers tend to be gregarious people by nature, and this cadre of overachievers was certainly no exception.

The dinner was wonderful, and after dinner came the hangar talks. Selected members of the hall of fame were chosen to present rambling discourses and tell tall tales concerning their colorful and action-packed lives. It was indeed entertaining, and gave a different perspective to the evening.

Saturday evening we came back for the formal enshrinement ceremony, a gala black tie dinner and program. The red carpet was literally out. It ran down the center of the auditorium toward the dais and was flanked by round tables immaculately set for dinner. The entire front of the auditorium was a computer-generated view through the windshield of a large aircraft. It was complete with controls and accompanied by air-to-ground dialogue. Flanking it on each side were replicas of the Hall of Fame medal and electronically generated American flags. The festivities began when the cockpit view came to life and our "flight" took off for the evening.

Tony Bill, the Academy award–winning producer, actor and director, was the master of ceremonies for the evening. Each of us was introduced with a formal presentation by someone who knew us well. This was followed by a video summation of our lives and accomplishments. After the video, each of us took center stage for our acceptance speech.

When my turn came, my heart beat a bit faster, and I blushed with pride at the speech given by my oldest child, Greg, who presented me. His kind words were filled with love and respect for a father who was often absent as my duty took me away from home. After my video, I walked across the stage and Greg invested me with a hug and my Hall of Fame medal. I will be eternally grateful for that moment.

We had each been told repeatedly that our acceptance speeches should be time specific. After an experience with long-winded presenter, I understood the wisdom of this maneuver. I stepped up to the podium, and said:

"Good evening. I'm well aware that there are many both within and outside the hallowed Hall of Fame who have contributed to my selection. I may know some of those and not know many others, but I do want to thank Ron Kaplan and his wonderful and most helpful staff for all their help—and special thanks to my friend Al Hallonquist for his selfless efforts on my behalf.

"Of course to be able to share this evening with my children and my wife Chris' children is particularly rewarding. My children: Gregory whom you've met, my son Dennis, my daughters Pam and Maureen and my stepchildren, coming all the way from Germany, Judith and Sven. Thank you kids, I love you all.

"In an isolated monastery in northern Italy, there is a map of the world drawn by monks in the 15th century. Beyond the great ocean, in the newly discovered area of the Americas, are written these words, "there be giants here." How prophetic those words. Each of the immigrant families, including mine from Ireland, who helped to forge this great nation, brought with them their hopes, their dreams and their ideas. On December 17, 1903, from atop the aptly named Kill Devil Hill at Kitty Hawk, North Carolina, two of those young giants named Orville and Wilber saw their dream come true, and launched generations of giant offspring whose dreams reached for the sky. To name just a few more, Charles Lindbergh, Jimmy Doolittle, and Jacqueline Cochran.

"I feel unworthy to stand beside these giants, but am privileged to stand humbly in their shadows. I can be content in those shadows knowing that, although my contribution to aviation might pale in the light of theirs, my dream, like theirs, reached for the sky.

"I am proud to live in a country where the dreams of a young boy from

New York City could take wings. I am proud to have served my country in World War II. My great nation was in peril then, and the country was united against the enemy in an outpouring of patriotism unparalleled in our history. But that was easy. I knew who the enemy was. I knew the color of their uniforms. Today, I fear our nation is in equal peril, but this time many of its citizens sleep. The uniforms are the indistinct garb of the merchant, the taxi driver, the student. Their weapons are intimidation, car bombs and terror. It is my fervent prayer that those of us who sleep wake from their slumber before the world is once again ablaze with the flames of war.

"I am sad that in these modern times the words 'God and Country' must be muttered apologetically lest they offend someone. At times in my life, alone in the cockpit of an airplane, I have come face-to-face with my own mortality. That reality has been shared by many sons of liberty, be they in a fighter plane, a foxhole or the pitching deck of a destroyer. In those times I knew I was never completely alone. A Greater Pilot's hands covered mine on the controls. As I approach the twilight years of my life, the principles I knew were important as a youth, God, Family and Country, are as real and ring as true as they did nearly four score years ago.

"When I look at my life, and the things for which you honor me today, I am humbled that you consider them worthy of notice. In each instance, I saw only a challenge, a job to be done, and I did each of those jobs to the best of my ability. As a youngster, my heroes were Tex Hill, Jimmy Doolittle and—yes—perhaps even John Wayne.

"I yearned to emulate them, and in some small measure I have succeeded. If my life's work is worthy of notice, then I pray it will prove inspirational to this new generation of young men and women whose dreams reach not only to the sky, but into outer space and beyond. Thank you very much."

After the ceremony, I was engulfed by a wave of well-wishers and autograph seekers. There were men and women, boys and girls of all ages. They came with programs, downloaded photographs, and models of the X-15. It was gratifying and overwhelming. Needless to say, it is an evening I will never forget. And, if that wasn't enough, July 15, 2006, was proclaimed Robert M. White Day by the mayor of Dayton, Ohio!

Life at times can be unfair. At a time in my life when I was resting upon my laurels, receiving these honors and enjoying life to the fullest, a dark shadow crept over the sunshine that enveloped me. My wife Chris began to experience symptoms of fatigue and chronic respiratory difficulties. She consulted her physician for a battery of tests and x-rays. The news was ominous. I remember the hollow feeling I felt as the doctor told us, "There is a mass in your lung, Chris. I'm afraid it's cancer. I'm going to have you see a surgeon." Chris wasn't surprised with the diagnosis as she had been a smoker at one point in her life. She vowed to fight the disease and do what was necessary.

I have been in tense situations in my life, but none more stressful than the time between visiting the surgeon and the actual surgery itself. It was almost a relief when we went to the hospital for her operation. When the surgery was over, we were told that the tumor appeared to be confined to the lung and that they had removed the tumor along with part of her left lower lung. The pathology report showed no positive lymph nodes, but an aggressive tumor cell type. When she recovered from surgery, they felt that she should see an oncologist for additional therapy.

Her recovery was relatively uncomplicated but difficult. The surgery had taken a lot out of her, and it took her longer than we had expected for her to get back on her feet. When she felt strong enough, we went back to the oncologist for her therapy. She seemed to tolerate the first dose of chemotherapy well. But a few days later, she became weak, fatigued and rapidly went downhill. She was hospitalized and more tests were done. I was told by the doctors that her white blood count was falling rapidly and that she was in critical condition. As she had done with everything else in her life, Chris faced this adversity bravely.

Unfortunately, her condition continued to worsen, and I was told there was little else the doctors could do for her. On January 9, 2007, I went home from the hospital after my daily vigil. When the telephone rang later that evening my heart skipped a beat. The nurse at the hospital told me I should come back immediately.

Leaping into my car, I broke every speed law

Chris and I stand beside my induction plaque at the 2006 induction of National Aviation Hall of Fame in Dayton, Ohio (Jack Summers personal collection.)

on the book as I raced toward the hospital with my heart in my throat. I prayed like a madman that my worst fears would not be realized. As a man of faith, I believe every prayer is answered. To my dismay, this time the answer was no. When I arrived in the hospital's intensive care unit, my darling wife was gone.

I had a memorial service for her in Sun City Center and was strengthened by the outpouring of love and support from our friends. Unfortunately her children, who were devastated, could not make it to that ceremony. After the usual delay that always accompanies such things, she was laid to rest in the Arlington National Cemetery where one day I will rest next to her. Life has been generally good to me. This was one of the exceptions. I am basically a self-reliant person. I'm still adjusting, but I know life goes on. After my divorce from Doris, I stopped attending Catholic Mass because I understood the structure of the church and its position on divorce. One day, many years later, I discussed my feelings with a priest friend of mine named Brian Sweeny. He recognized my earnest desire to be reunited with my faith and advised me that reconciliation was possible and guided me through the process. I will be eternally grateful to him for bringing me home. My faith was a great comfort to me when Chris passed away. I feel that my prayers were heard and that Chris rests with our Lord in Paradise.

As I reflect upon my life, the places I have gone, the people I have met, the things I have been able to do; I can honestly say that I have no regrets. God has been good to me. I have worked hard to manage to be in the right place at the right time. I have no idea what else life has in store for me. But, each time I look up into the sky, I still see part of it through the eyes of a seven-year-old boy sitting on a concrete step and yearning to be "up there."

Epilogue

On March 17, 2010, Major General Robert M. White took his final flight. Bob was eighty-five years old when he died peacefully in his sleep after a long struggle with failing health. Surrounded by family, Bob knew the end was near and faced it with the same courage he faced all of life's adversities. It was simply another problem to be solved. No time for panic. Be sure all bases were covered and get on with it.

His old friend Al Hallonquist and his grandson Blake visited Bob very shortly before his death. As they left Bob for the last time, he pointed a finger at them and rasped, "Arlington." His compass was set; he was on course and knew his final destination.

Arlington National Cemetery is unfortunately a busy place. The day of Bob's interment there were twelve funerals. As he did in life, Bob waited patiently for his turn.

The morning of June 24 dawned clear and steamy in the midst of an early heat wave that pressed the mercury toward a hundred degrees. The friends and family were greeted in Parlor B of the administration building by Mrs. Campbell, the cemetery representative, and Major General Davis, representing the Air Force.

At nine A.M., we walked to a flat meadow nearby. Waiting there was a hearse, a horse-drawn caisson, honor guard and a band. Eight airmen removed the flag-draped coffin from the hearse with military precision and placed it reverently on the caisson as a flyover by a pair of T-6 Texan II's roared overhead. Following the caisson with riderless horse and the honor guard, we walked toward the gravesite a quarter of a mile away.

The mood was quiet, respectful but not somber. Hushed conversations centered on a life well lived, professional accomplishments of epic proportions and a family man who loved his wife and children. Echoes of those sentiments were mirrored in the short service by the white robed priest at the graveside. Twenty-one rifle shots echoed from a surrounding elevation followed by the plaintive strains of Taps.

An old soldier is laid to rest at Arlington Cemetery June 24, 2010 (Jack Summers).

Major General Davis received the folded flag from the honor guard and presented it to the White family. Following the benediction and condolences to the family, we filed quietly from the gravesite leaving the old soldier to rest with his beloved Chris who had been waiting for him since January 9, 2007.

The following day, the family and a few close friends gathered at the Army Navy Country Club in Arlington for a "Final Flight Luncheon." These aging test pilots and war heroes are each legends in their own right and deserving of their own biographies. Our hosts were Gene Deatrick and Rear Admiral Whitey Feightner.

Gene is a retired Air Force colonel and was a member of the first class of test pilots at the historic Edwards Air Force Base. He had an exemplary military career distinguishing himself in Viet Nam. He may be best known for his role in the rescue of United States Navy Lieutenant Dieter Dengler during the Vietnam War. The rescue was recounted in the Werner Herzog films *Little Dieter Needs to Fly* and *Rescue Dawn*.

Rear Admiral Edward "Whitey" Feightner was commissioned as a naval aviator in early 1942. During World War II he shot down nine Japanese aircraft while operating from a carrier and then Henderson Field on Guadalcanal. A member of the Blue Angels Demonstration Flying Team, his post–World War II aviation experience as one of the first graduates of

Bob White's friends and colleagues, Col. Kenneth O. ("Ko") Chilstrom, Rear Admiral Whitey Feightner and Al Hallonquist, wish Bob a fond farewell (Jack Summers).

the Navy's new Test Pilot School was followed by extensive duty at the test center in Patuxent River, Maryland, where he was involved in projects that made very significant contributions to national security, with emphasis on naval aviation.

And these were but two of the heroes who came to say good-bye to one of their own. Kind words were spoken in memory of Bob, many of which would have embarrassed the quiet man who was our friend. When the luncheon was over, we all parted that day with fond memories of a true American hero that we will cherish until it is our turn for a "final flight."

Index